Brit,
You ar positive

BILLY'S
NEVER-ENDING
BATTLE

of all the power,
we can harness!
There are No limits!

All the best,
Billy

William G Brett

BILLY'S
NEVER-ENDING
BATTLE

CREATING A WONDERFUL LIFE
WITH IMAGINATION AND PURPOSE

William G. Brett

Fourth Lloyd Productions, LLC
Burgess, VA

For permission to reproduce selections of this book
please contact:
FOURTH LLOYD PRODUCTIONS
512 Old Glebe Point Road
Burgess, VA 22432
e-mail: stodart@kaballero.com
www.FourthLloydProductions.com

Printed in the USA
ISBN: 978-0-971-78069-9 Paperback
Library of Congress Control Number: 2011922326

Book and cover design by Richard Stodart

Cover photo of Billy Brett, Summer 1986.

For my wife, Jackie, and our daughters, Emily and Sarah—
the three most beautiful reasons why I will never give up
the "Never-ending Battle". You are the source of all my
powers!

For my mother, Eileen M. Brett, whose unwavering strength in
the face of adversity will forever be the example I draw upon.

For my late father, John J. "Buddy" Brett (May 16, 1934 –
July 21, 2010), who taught me that there are no accidents in
this life—"Everything happens for a reason."

The Face Of God

My eyes have been opened,
My ears finally hear.
I find to my amazement,
I had nothing to fear.

When I give I get back
More than I gave,
And I've lost that longing
That caused me to crave.

This has happened to us,
Not to me alone.
And it comes as a gift from God.

Not a God that sits on a throne
But a God who walks amongst us,
Whether Christian, Muslim, or Jew.
The funny part is, he looks like you,
And you, and all of you.

—John J. "Buddy" Brett

CONTENTS

Acknowledgments

I wish to thank my brothers and sisters in law-enforcement, especially members of the Fairfax County Police Motor Squad, whose patience and friendship have been a constant source of inspiration for me. I am truly honored to be able to count myself among them.

I wish to express my special appreciation for Second Lieutenant Mark Payton, who left us too soon.

I would also like to express gratitude for my friends, both old and new, for their indispensable support at crucial times in my life, even making it possible for me to believe that a man could really fly!

Among family members who have always looked out for me and protected me when others called me Billy "BRAT," were aunts, uncles, and cousins—especially Peggy Haslach, Mary Beth Powers, and Anne Marie Harold. I will never forget their love and generosity and will always aspire to their kindness.

I would also like to mention my mother-in-law, Geri, whose love and support matches that of my own family.

Finally, I would like to thank my family—John, Regina, Mark, Rose, Eileen, Chris, Rob, Megan, Jimmy, Ansley, Ryan, Christopher, and Deirdre—for their enduring love and patience.

*"There is one thing I do know, son,
and that is you are here for a reason!"*

—Glen Ford in *Superman*

*"They're a great people, Kal-El. They wish to be.
They merely lack the light to show the way.
It is for this reason, above all —their capacity for
good, that I have sent them you, my only son."*

—-Marlon Brando in *Superman*

1 Black Cloud

How? Why?

How does this happen, and why does this seem to keep happening to me?

My failure is all I can think about. This time, however, it has really hit a nerve. Despite my optimistic outlook, my life feels as if it could be summed up as great potential with no real results. Here I am standing over my Harley Davidson police motorcycle that is lying on its side with orange traffic cones strewn about the road. I've successfully maneuvered this course in practice, but I've gone down once again in competition! I'm convinced that there must be some great black cloud that over-shadows my life and prevents me from realizing my full potential. Deep down, I've always felt this. And the crazy thing is there's absolutely no logical reason for it! I mean, it's not as if I've had a tragic life. In fact, the opposite is more true. So how the hell is it that I can never get things right, and why can't I change what's happening to me?

WHERE DO I BEGIN TO FIND ANSWERS TO THESE QUESTIONS? I MEAN, THERE'S so much to talk about. How does one choose where to begin? For someone who is wired like me—who has trouble making a decision and sticking with it—the very beginning seems a good place to start.

ON SEPTEMBER 11, 1965, EILEEN AND BUDDY BRETT WELCOMED ME, William G. Brett, their fifth child, into the world. I was named after my grandfather, William R. Sheerin, and we were both called "Billy." Having four older siblings and a live-in grandfather, I could not have been born into a more loving family. Even after the arrival of my younger brother, Robert Emmet, my mother came to refer to me as her "heart child."

My father was the fifth child of John and Winnie Brett, two Irish immigrants from Sligo, Ireland. My father was named not only for his father but also for an older brother who had died tragically from pneumonia at the age of two.

My mother was the middle of five children born to Rosemary and Bill Sheerin, also of Irish-American decent.

Both my parents were baptized and raised as typical Irish-Catholics in Brooklyn, New York. They met and fell in love attending Brooklyn Prep Elementary School. Both attended Fordham University in the Bronx.

After graduating from Fordham, Mom and Dad married and settled in Brooklyn. My father worked for an electrical fittings corporation, and my mother was a stay-at-home mom at first. They soon started our family in somewhat rapid succession. First, my brother, John, was born and then my sister, Rosemary, came along. Shortly after Rose's birth my parents moved to a house on Eldeberry Road in Syosset out on Long Island, just off the Long Island Expressway. Although the house lacked a great deal of square footage, it did have five bedrooms and a nice-sized backyard. Not long after moving in, my sister, Eileen, was born. Just eleven months apart, she and Rosemary were typical "Irish twins." My brother, Jude Christopher, followed—then me and Robert Emmet. What a crowd!

Grandpa Sheerin came to live with us after the death of my grandmother. "Gramps" had a big sales position with Schaefer Beer, the number one beer of the time in the New York area. Two of my mother's sisters also lived in Syosset with their families, and all of my father's sisters lived in nearby towns on Long Island.

MY FAMILY TELLS ME THAT IT WAS ONLY WHEN MY BROTHER, ROB, WAS BORN that my "gifts" began to emerge. Being just two years apart, Rob and I were both in diapers at the same time and were on the same sleep schedule.

One afternoon, my mother put us both down for a nap in our bedroom and closed the door. Sometime later I got up, made my way over to Rob's crib and removed one of the safety pins from his diaper. Remember when they used real cloth diapers and safety pins? I then used the pin to jimmy-open the bedroom door and make good my escape. It wasn't until my parents spotted me playing in the backyard that they realized I was not in my crib. When they brought me back to the bedroom and saw that Rob's diaper was missing, they realized how I had opened the door—an unusual mind finding an unusual solution to a task. Needless to say, I was never again allowed within reach of Rob during nap time.

The next few years went by with the usual milestones; walking, talking, my first taste of beer. Thanks to Gramps there was always plenty of Schaefer Beer in the house. Gramps would give us a sip at dinner time if we asked. Maybe that's why in my teen years I would not be tempted by beer. Besides, it couldn't compete with the taste of Nestlé Quik.

We had a great bunch of neighbors, with kids of all ages always running around. While Halloween was one of my favorite times of the year, Christmas really made me shine! For as long as I can remember, the sights, the sounds—everything about the entire season—always struck an inner chord with me. The fact that a wonderful saintly old man brought us toys on Christmas Eve didn't hurt either! I became so enthralled with Christmas that my parents would have to wait until well into January before they could even think of taking down the tree, and even then they'd have to wait until I was asleep for fear of upsetting me! (My wife will say that still holds true today!) All in all, I was a happy kid.

My biggest concerns were where Mommy was going to take me to play, or when Popeye, Speed Racer, and Superman were going to be on the TV. Not until I started school did my real issues begin to surface. I couldn't understand why I now had to leave my mother and go to school during the day. "Why do I have to go to school? "I just want to stay with you, Mommy!" was all I could think.

My only real memory of kindergarten was being left on the bus one morning and being found across the parking lot at the elementary school entrance. I had missed my stop! I vividly remember the feeling of being so alone and out of place. Luckily for me the bus driver had the wherewithal to know where I belonged, and he quickly returned me to South Grove kindergarten. I never forgot that isolated feeling. Little did I know that this feeling would be a familiar one throughout my entire scholastic career.

My advancement to the first grade did not improve my outlook, especially in such a structured environment as St. Edward the Confessor Catholic School! I couldn't stand the strict rules. I would constantly break the tips off my pencils in a feeble attempt to escape the work assignments.

The only thing this accomplished was a visit to the principal's office. If this ploy were not enough of a headache for my family, every day after school when I'd get off the bus I'd conveniently drop my books right there on the sidewalk and just walk away. It became my older brothers' and sisters' routine to follow me and collect my "chum-line" of scholastic waste. I figured that once I was free of the bonds of the school bus, it didn't matter what I did with the books. I was home safe and sound.

One afternoon, however, this sense of security was shattered. For some reason I found myself alone when I got home. Upon walking through the front entrance to our house, I discovered to my horror that no one was home! I began screaming and crying, frantically searching the house for my family members! I can remember that feeling again... "I'm alone!" I thought, "How could they just leave me alone???"

This was also the first time in my life that I can remember lashing out in frustration or anger. In my panic I ran into the dining room and grabbed two of my mother's fine stemware champagne glasses. I then stormed out the front door and in a fit of rage and despair I launched those babies right into the street where they exploded in a fantastic shower of broken glass.

The commotion caught the attention of the neighborhood kids up the street who all came running to see what was going on. As I turned around to go back into the house, Gramps, too, came out to see what all the screaming was about. He had been in the backyard on his lawn chair the whole time and had not heard me come home. Later that evening, he told my parents, "Billy has some temper!" He had no idea...

I cannot describe my relief upon seeing Gramps—after feeling I had been left all alone. I remember my relief to this day, which for me is one of the many reasons why Gramps exemplifies love, security, and positive feedback. His patience and understanding are the standard by which I think all grandfathers should be measured. His skillful patience must have rubbed off on my parents, and I most certainly put it to the test!

Gramps always had something for us when he returned from one of his business trips or from a cigar errand into town He was also very playful. Every morning before he shaved, Gramps would trick us into giving him a kiss. When we tried to do so, he would turn his cheek away from us at the last second, scrape us with his whiskers, and say, "HAHAHA, I gotchya with the barber's itch!"

2 Moving

In August 1972, my father was transferred by his company to their Chicago office in Glen Ellyn, Illinois.

The good people of Glen Ellyn had no idea what they were in for!!!

The only knowledge of flight I had at this point was watching George Reeves as Superman on television, so I had no fear or reservation whatsoever of the event now at hand. I was just so excited that the whole family was moving to Chicago, wherever that was, and that we would all be going together on an airplane. WOW! The one thing I remember most vividly while sitting next to my father and looking out the airplane window was the takeoff. I never knew that something this large could move so fast! I grabbed my father's arm and held on for dear life. My father swore for years afterwards that he no longer had full feeling in that arm! I had never felt anything like this before! My fear slowly turned to exhilaration as we climbed over the New York City skyline and soared into the clouds. "So, this is what it's like," I thought. "Look! Up in the sky! It's a bird! It's a plane! It's..." COOL!

Before I knew it we were on final approach to O'Hare International Airport in Chicago. After landing and collecting our bags, we drove a short distance to the Holiday Inn in Elmhurst, Illinois, which would be our home for the next few weeks until we could move to our permanent home in Glen Ellyn. How my parents stayed sane with six children living in a Holiday Inn, I'll never know. My father at least could leave for eight to ten hours a day to go to his new office, but Mom was stuck with the brood 24-7!

Of course, Rob and I thought this was the greatest thing ever! We had the time of our lives! From hallway relay races to bouncing from bed to bed in the rooms, we thought everything was so cool! If we never moved into our house Rob and I would've been just fine! For our siblings, and more so for our parents, things could not be worse! My older brothers and sisters had to deal with the trauma of leaving all their friends behind to start over again in a new high school. My parents had to juggle two mortgages because our house in Syosset still had not been sold. Through it all, however, they managed to maintain a healthy, happy family atmosphere for all of us.

We finally moved out of the hotel and into our home at 377 Marion Avenue in Glen Ellyn and quickly settled in. The house was a cozy Cape Cod style but deceivingly large inside. It had four bedrooms, two full bathrooms, and a bonus room, off the finished basement family room, which became a fifth bedroom. We had an awesome backyard with a huge wooden shed that Rob and I quickly claimed as our fort for the many adventures yet to come! The neighborhood, the entire town of Glen Ellyn for that matter, had a "Norman Rockwell feel" to it! With picturesque tree-lined streets, it was a perfect setting to raise children. Main Street in the middle of town looked like a movie set, complete with a nineteenth century horse trough right in the center of town.

The biggest events in this town were the Glenbard West High School football and basketball games. Throwing a parade was also a top event, and the town would throw one for pretty much any occasion. The entire town would turn out to participate in a huge home-coming parade and bonfire. The Fourth of July celebration, however, took the cake! It's only rival would be the Macy's Thanksgiving Day Parade in New York City.

A Glen Ellyn parade would start at the beginning of Main Street, go all the way through town, work its way through the adjacent neighborhoods and end up at Lake Ellyn. Again, as one might imagine, Lake Ellyn is as picturesque as the rest of the town. Huge trees surrounded the three or four acre lake located directly next to Glenbard West High School's football field. The high school looked more like an Ivy League college, sitting majestically on top of a huge hill just behind the football field. The hill was perfect for sled and toboggan races during the legendary mid-western winters.

The Brett family always attended these events. The Fourth of July started at the home of my parent's friends, Pat and Ethel Lynch. Their house was on the parade route, only half a block from the lake. The parade would run through the morning, and there'd be an all-day picnic at the lake afterward. There'd be the usual fare of live music, food, and games. There was even a good old-fashioned handle-bar mustache contest that my father always entered and sometimes even won! The day would always conclude with the entire town converging at the lake for a huge fireworks display. There was never a bad Fourth of July in Glen Ellyn!

Every Halloween there were hundreds of kids out in costume, trick-or-treating door to door without care, knowing they were safe to do so. There was even a tour of "Capt. Danby's Haunted House," sponsored and put on by the local chapter of the Jaycees. The volunteers would take over an old abandoned warehouse next to the railroad tracks that ran right through town and turn it into, in my opinion, the scariest place on earth! To this day, I cannot go into a "haunted house" because of Capt. Danby's!

With this kind of a setting it would be hard to imagine that anyone, especially a seven-year-old boy, would have any problems. Well, everything was perfect until my first day of school.

As a kid and throughout my entire adult life I've always had an over-abundance of outward physical energy. Despite this, I was pretty shy around new people and situations. When my parents enrolled me at St. Petronelle Catholic School, they hoped and prayed that this new school in a new town would have a positive effect on me. It didn't.

From the very first moment I walked into the building I felt uneasy and different. As if this initial feeling weren't bad enough, I arrived late and was escorted to my second grade classroom only to find that everyone had already been seated! Talk about all eyes on the new kid!

It gets worse.

After finally finding a seat in the rear of the classroom, a lady from the front office came in and pulled me out of the class. "Now what?" I thought. I was really scared. Already I hated this place! The woman walked me down the hallway to another classroom where, once again, all the kids had already been seated. I was directed to an empty seat and took it. I don't know when it hit me, but suddenly I realized I had not been moved to another second grade classroom. "This is a first grade classroom!!! They're making me repeat the first grade!" I exclaimed to myself. I couldn't understand why I was "left back". All the negative thoughts that a seven-year-old could come up with were racing through my mind!

"I don't want to be here!" was all I could think about.

St. "Pet's" was more progressive than St. Edward's School was back in Syosset. First of all, there were no uniforms that the students had to wear. Instead, a casual but neat dress code was the norm. This was just fine by me, but I still didn't want to be there. Despite my feelings about the school, however, I began to make friends after I settled in. With all my fears and anxiety about school, I found myself concentrated on one aspect I enjoyed... recess!

Even as a child I possessed better than average size, speed, and strength, of which I was unaware. These physical gifts coupled with my over-abundant energy made me a force to be reckoned with in the playground! I became pretty good at dodge ball but even better at mawl-ball, which was like rugby, just not as sophisticated...and we played on asphalt. The rules were simple: Whoever had the ball was on their own and subject to gang tackles by the entire male population of the class out on the playground! Looking back, I imagine it looked to the faculty a lot like what the tower guards at Joliet State Penitentiary might see at "yard time". At least the "cons" at Joliet State play on grass!

With recess over, however, that same old feeling of "I don't want to be here!" that I had felt at St. Edward's would come over me. Once I was seated in the classroom I would soon find myself drifting off, my attention being drawn out the second floor windows to the scenery outside. I think this is where my greatest gift of imagination began to emerge. I would imagine what amazing adventures awaited me once I got back outside. "What would it be this time?" I thought, "cowboys and indians, cops and robbers, army? Or would it be my favorite game involving me donning a familiar red cape?"

This is where I was truly powerful! All I had to do was immerse myself in my imagination and I was indestructible! It's ironic then that my super-senses couldn't hear the teacher ahead of time, "BILLY BRETT! Stop staring out that window and pay attention!!!"

Back to reality. I thought, "I don't want to be here!"

3 TESTING

It didn't take the faculty long to realize what my family already knew: "Something was very different about this Billy Brett."

Despite my energy and zeal for recess, as well as my interest in drawing during art class, I could not stay tuned in for anything else. And with the usual threats and punishments for inattention, I would just retreat further.

That's not to say I was an unhappy kid. In fact, I was just the opposite! I thrived in Glen Ellyn outside the structured environment of school! To this day some of my fondest childhood memories are from my years living there and of the friends I made! Glen Ellyn was a shining place for me with my first team sports experiences, especially baseball! Some of my close teammates were also in my class, including my best friends, Pat and Bart. They helped make my hours at school seem a little less dreadful. It didn't bother them one bit that I never seemed to do well in class or that I never did my assignments. They just liked me for who I was. And the fact that I was bigger than most kids and could hit the ball a country mile made it good for me to be on their side!

In spite of my fear of the teachers calling on me, knowing full well that I wasn't paying attention, I could never bring the same enthusiasm I had for play to the classroom. Although the teachers hoped that my fear would keep me focused, I would eventually drift off again. I would be too scared then to raise my hand to ask a question and look stupid in front of the rest of my classmates. So, a wall inside me just got higher and higher.

I had no idea how much this situation was laying the groundwork for the rest of my life!

Clearly, something different was needed. At the suggestion of the faculty, my parents took me to numerous doctors and specialists in the field of behavioral science, who did a series of tests to try to understand why I couldn't focus. Some of these "experts" suggested that my issues were diet related. They believed that eliminating sugar and any foods with artificial flavorings was the solution. Can you believe that??? Telling a little kid that he can't have a can of Coke or a bag of M&M's anymore! After all, I didn't have diabetes!

I have to admit, though, that one of my favorite daily meals was eating powdered Nestlé Quik by the spoonful right out of the container! That could not have been helpful to my diet. To this day the idea still causes my older brother, Chris, to cringe!

Some of these specialists were very nice, in particular a doctor more than an hour's drive from home. His office was very warm and inviting and not the least bit threatening, as I imagined it. In fact, I always looked forward to going there since he kept the biggest collection of toy cars that I had ever seen, and he would let me play with them for as long as I liked! Once I started playing, however, I would zone out from the doctor's questions.

My parents then took me to a specialist whose uninviting Chicago hospital office looked more like a large examination/classroom. It had a large chalkboard, and since I did not enjoy just sitting around waiting, I made quick work of it. At first my mother wasn't too thrilled with the idea, but she let me draw anyway. Only when the doctor came into the room did she say, "Okay Billy, put down the chalk and come over here and sit down." He then said to my mother, "Why did you tell him to stop?" and then to me, "Billy if you feel like drawing, you go ahead and keep drawing." He told my parents that there was nothing wrong or abnormal about a little boy wanting to draw on a chalkboard. "I really like this guy!" I thought.

After several more doctor visits and numerous tests and questions, even the nice doctors were becoming boring to me! If I had to look at those stupid ink blotch Rorschach flash cards again and tell them what I saw, I was going to scream! I mean, come on! Everyone knows the first one's a bat wearing a cowboy hat, the second one is two eagles playing poker!

The specialists and doctors had listened to my parents and sometimes even my teachers describe my behavior and my inability to focus in the classroom environment. They had also heard the stories of my seemingly limitless physical energy. They became concerned, however, when they heard that I had a very bad temper. I was always humiliated and, more often than not, I would cry when reprimanded by an adult authority figure. If, however, I were provoked to anger by one of the neighborhood kids or my siblings it could be potentially dangerous! For example, if the teacher yelled at me in class for not paying attention and a classmate in turn called me stupid, I'd become withdrawn and depressed. If later that day, however, one of my siblings hit the wrong button, I'd fly off in a fit of rage smashing anything in my path.

My brother, Chris, knew this and was especially gifted at getting me fired up as a kid. Something about seeing me fly into a rage and smash inanimate objects gave him a sense of pleasure, especially if he survived the encounter! He also knew that I had never, ever, taken out my frustration or rage on anyone. The victims were always my mother's flatware or various other household items.

One day, however, Chris thought it would be a good idea to lock me out of our house. As he did so, he tormented me by pressing his face up against the small diamond-shaped window in our huge front door. As I pounded on the door, my frustration boiled over into rage. I grabbed a rock out of the flower bed and launched it at the door. The rock left my hand with the speed and precision of a Cy Young award winner and hit the window just as Chris was starting a second barrage of taunts. The window shattered and my brother fell backward and started screaming! Rage ebbed and fear overtook me, for I thought I had killed my brother! (I can feel the fear now as though it just happened.) I began crying because I knew I was finished. It was one thing to throw school books away or smash my mother's good crystal, but to kill my older brother... I was dead! As though on cue, my mother pulled into the driveway and saw what had happened. She walked toward the house without saying a word to me. To my astonishment, at that moment Chris opened the door without even a scratch on his face! To this day I can only cite divine intervention on both our behalf.

What also caught the doctors' attention was the way my family described my unusual display of physical strength during these fits of rage. They all reported separate incidents of watching me grab large heavy objects and launch them across a room. These were usually objects that ordinarily I, or any adult for that matter, could not budge!

All the experts my parents spoke to agreed that "Billy has an over-abundance of physical energy coupled with an inability to focus in a structured environment. This inability to focus causes frustration, which in turn, triggers rage issues."

They called it "Hyperactive". Although the condition and the research into it were all relatively new, they prescribed an equally new medication called "Ritalin". My family hoped and prayed that it would finally help me focus. It did... sort of.

At first, the Ritalin appeared to be exactly what I needed. I was calmer and was on my best behavior without so much as a hint of disagreement. My parents and my teachers, however, noticed something else was now very different. My playfulness ceased, and I showed a marked loss of appetite. My teachers reported that my usual "spark" and artistic creativity had disappeared. One of my teachers finally told my mother, "This isn't the Billy Brett I know! Get him off that Ritalin, now!" Some of my parents' friends made similar comments.

From what they understood at the time about Ritalin, only a very small percentage of people would not benefit from it. Now, guess who was in that small percentage!

So, after about ten months my parents, doctors, and teachers agreed to stopping the Ritalin. I honestly can't say how Ritalin made me feel. I can remember having to take the medication daily, but I have no recollection of its effects. All I knew was that I didn't have to take those pills anymore!

It didn't take long before I was back to "normal," bouncing off walls and moving faster than a speeding bullet! My creativity really began to surface in unusual ways as well.

One evening, on Valentine's Day in fact, my parents had gone out for a nice romantic dinner. My older brothers and sisters had gone to visit their respective friends while Rob and I were left in the care of Gramps. When my parents got home that night, Gramps handed my mother a drawing that I had made in their absence saying, "That Billy is some artist!" My mother was amazed at the drawing's incredible detail... almost too much detail. "He must've traced this," she thought. It wasn't until she saw the family room television that she realized where my "detail" had come from. I had taken a set of magic markers, the permanent kind that bleed through paper and stain whatever they touch, and drawn all over our 20" color TV! Now remember, in 1973 a 20" RCA color TV was like a 60" SONY LED is today!

My parents' reaction was less favorable than Gramps'! That was the last time that easy going Gramps or "Mr. Strict" was left in charge of us!

Although not a disciplinarian, Gramps always knew how to make things right. The following summer he accidently ran over my bike and crushed it. Before I even knew about it, he had gone to the store and bought me a brand new one! This is how I remember him best. He would always do whatever it took to make us happy, no matter what. Little did I know then that my time with Gramps was running out.

The following January I would have one of the worst experiences of my childhood. I remember being awakened early in the morning by my mother. It was a school day, but this was way earlier than normal. It was still very dark outside. My parents were scrambling around the house trying to get something organized with my older brothers and sisters trying to help them. Gramps had not been feeling well lately, and my father was going to take him to the hospital. I went into Gramps' room and saw him having trouble getting up. I went over and helped him get his boots on. I can see his face now, and I will never forget how blank his expression looked.

"Are you okay, Gramps?" I asked.

He did not respond because he was having trouble breathing. I had a feeling something wasn't right, but at the time I had no idea what that feeling was.

It wasn't until four days later that I found out why I was feeling so uneasy. My parents had come home late from the hospital without Gramps. Both of them were visibly upset when they called my older brothers and sisters into the living room and told Rob and me to wait in our bedroom. Shortly thereafter my father came into our room and told us "Gramps had to go to heaven." It was one of the few times I ever saw my father cry, as he tried to comfort Rob and me.

"I don't want Gramps to go away!" I yelled into my pillow, crying harder than I had ever cried in my life. I can still feel my father's tears on the back of my head as he leaned over me and tried to comfort me through his own grief. My father and grandfather were as close, if not closer, than any in-laws could ever be. It seems that Gramps had the same effect on everyone he touched! All I knew, though, was that I wasn't ready for Gramps to go!

The following days were a blur. We flew back to New York to bury

Gramps in Brooklyn next to my grandmother. During the flight—I was a seasoned pro now, so I wasn't scared—my thoughts were how heaven might look. Was it just like the clouds that were outside the plane's windows, I wondered? Was Gramps now sitting in a big cloud easy-chair smoking his cigars? Was he now watching me as I looked out into heaven?

Then a thought hit me, "So now you know how to fly, too, huh Gramps?"

My grandfather's funeral was attended by countless family and cousins and numerous friends from the beer business where he had worked. The last time I'd seen Gramps was when he left for the hospital that terrible morning. I'll never forget when I first saw Gramps laid out in the biggest room at Beney Funeral Home in Syosset. It was the first time that I'd ever seen a dead person. For me as a eight-year-old, the sight was not as bad as one might think. I'll always remember the way Gramps looked in his casket, as if he were grinning! He looked in death the same way I'll always remember him in life! Fitting, considering the man he was.

Even though Gramps was now gone, his spirit never left! To this day I catch a glimpse of him whenever I trick my daughters into kissing me before I shave and say what he used to say to us, "HAHAHAHA, I got ya with the barber's itch!"

Of all the gifts my grandfather gave us, this is the one for which I am most grateful.

4 IMAGINATION

As my childhood years progressed, the greatest of my "gifts" was my ability to pretend to be anything or anyone! Like my favorite super-hero being exposed to a yellow sun, I grew more powerful whenever I used my imagination!

Ironically, with all of my behavior issues, whenever my mother punished me and sent me to my room, I became calm. I was content to play by myself with no concept of time or place. They could never get me to come out of my room once my "time out" was over! I'd lose myself in the various adventures with the dozens of action figures I had stockpiled in my room. More often than not, my adventures involved my donning the familiar red cape!

When I was here, nothing could hurt me! No fear of teachers yelling at me for not doing my homework. No classmates calling me stupid for being "The kid that got left back." No, not here! Here I was made of steel!

"More powerful than a locomotive, able to bend steel in my bare hands!" And, since I was wearing "his" cape, I could defy gravity!

I'm sure every healthy American boy has played this game at least once in his life. I am also pretty sure that they all understood and obeyed the laws of basic physics… namely, gravity! But those laws didn't apply to me! Not here! Not in my imagination!

On one particular morning, I was battling evil-doers inside my sisters bedroom, which had a window that overlooked our sunken driveway. My mother had just returned from nine o'clock mass with one of her dear friends, Marg Rielly, and they were just sitting and chatting in Mrs. Rielly's car. My mother loves to tell this part of the story! They were parked with my mother's back toward the house. She was in the middle of saying something when

Mrs. Rielly's face went as white as a ghost, "Oh my god, what the hell is Billy doing?" My mother turned around just in time to see me in my cape do my best "George Reeves" right out that second story window! Without missing a beat, my mother says, "Oh that's just Billy playing again," and turned around to face Mrs. Rielly. Mrs. Rielly was even further astonished when she saw me bound off the roof of our car unhurt and run into the backyard to continue my "never-ending battle". At the time I never gave a second thought to these "super-feats" killing me! This was just the way I played.

My younger brother, Rob, and I turned the wonderful old shed in our backyard into the coolest fort any kid could imagine! We had every single conceivable toy gun, from every era since the firearm was invented! Growing up with shows on TV such as *Starsky & Hutch*, *The Rookies*, and *SWAT*, we'd recreate the shows the very next day after we watched them. Those were the times I didn't have to imagine as much. Those were the times we'd see how far or how high we could jump our bicycles off home-made ramps, once again not paying any attention to the laws of physics! I remember actually trying to convince my father to let me build a ramp so I could jump my bike over our driveway which was one floor below ground. Of course, my father did not allow it. For whatever reason, call it "divine intervention," this was one of the few times I listened to my father without question. Looking back on it now I thank God for that one moment of clarity!

Whenever I was with my friends, I tended to be more mischievous, playing the usual after-dark games like Ding-Dong-Ditch, flashlight tag, and manhunt. During the day I played stunt man and accomplished the usual tasks, such as jumping off the roof of our neighbor's garage.

One beautiful day, Rob and I were hanging out in the front yard near the driveway. My mother was in the back yard with Mrs. Rielly having coffee. I was bored and thought it would be cool to see if I could hit Mrs. Rielly's car with a small pebble I had found on the walkway. Poor Mrs. Rielly always seemed to be around when I got bored! I had to have been thirty yards away from her car when I threw the pebble, and on a high arc at that! I discovered then what hitting the exact stress point of a rear windshield made of safety glass sounds like! The window exploded as though I had shot it with a bazooka!

"Oh, you did it this time, Billy!" my brother screamed as he ran off.

For some reason I just stood there. There was no use running from this one, I thought. So, I did something then that I can't explain. I went into the backyard and told my mother and Mrs. Rielly what I had done! After the initial expression of shock on my mother's face transformed into rage, Mrs. Rielly, saint that she is, told my mother, "Take it easy, Eileen! He did come right back here and tell us what he did!" Needless to say, I received a lot of time-out for that one!

Of all my childhood antics, there was one fascination that in 20/20 hindsight makes me shudder to think how absolutely blessed I am! I know a lot of my friends went through a "burning" stage during their childhood, but for me it lasted a little longer than average.

As human beings we are, by nature, drawn to fire. It warms us, cooks our food, and is relaxing and almost hypnotic to watch—the original "caveman TV". For me as a kid it was even more so.

I never set fire to any buildings or houses or anything. No, usually I just burned leaves, sticks, newspapers, or cardboard boxes. When I got bored with that, I would see how some of my toys reacted to fire. IMPORTANT SAFETY TIP HERE! Never combine a book of matches and a can of gasoline with a bored ten-year-old hyperactive kid! I'm still amazed at the amount of smoke and flame that a plastic "Tonka" truck doused in gasoline produces. The fact that I never burned down the old wooden shed in our backyard is nothing short of miraculous!

Like most of my "little" experiments, it didn't take long for me to get caught by my parents. When confronted, I would do the one thing that I was NEVER good at... I'd lie about it! That just made matters worse. Still, never in my entire childhood was I or any one of my brothers and sisters ever beaten as a form of discipline. We might once in a while get a well deserved kick in the ass and be sent to our rooms for the rest of the day. This was one of those times. "Back to my fortress!" I thought. Thankfully, I lost my fascination with fire before something tragic occurred!

I also lied to my teachers or classmates even when I had no reason to. I would make up outlandish stories that I owned a pet chimpanzee or that I was independently wealthy! Anything that I thought might show me off in an unusual or positive light. I thought that by doing this I could draw attention away from the fact that I never had the answers to any of the questions being asked in class. "Maybe they won't think I'm so stupid," I thought.

As my academic studies floundered, I was able to keep focused on only two things—Christmas and summer vacations! My parents and teachers always noticed how much I would perk up prior to these breaks. As soon as the realization that I had to return to school began to loom on the horizon I would fall into a slump.

My vacations were fantastic! During the summer of '76, right after I saw the movie *JAWS*, we went back to New York for a two week stay. Every day when we went to the beach I was surprised to see that no one was afraid to go in the water, despite what I had seen in that movie!

One day the lifeguards suddenly started whistling wildly for everyone to get out of the water and everyone rapidly complied. It was an amazing sight to see one of the lifeguards jump into a lifeboat and paddle out into the surf! As we beach-goers watched from the safety of the shoreline, we were shocked to see the lifeguard dive into the water and swim back to shore! Shortly after he reached the shoreline, as though on cue, a large whale breached the surface of the waves and made a spectacular splash! As anyone would expect, the typical New York crowd cheered for the whale! "Man, that was the coolest thing I've ever seen!" I thought, and still do. The whale had been injured and was trying to beach itself, but it eventually swam on. What a great trip that was! School was just around the corner though, and I would be starting the fifth grade in a few weeks. "God," I thought, "how I hate school!"

I was barely able to move from grade to grade, and by the time I started the fifth grade I had become extremely phobic of the classroom setting. So much so that I was willing to do anything, no matter how crazy it seemed, to get out of it! For a ten-year-old kid, however, the thought of "escaping" from a four-story catholic school was virtually impossible. I doubt if even the most hardened criminals would have been as intimidated climbing the fence at Alcatraz!

But one day I again found myself upset and wanting nothing more than to leave. So, after taking a long, deep breath, I raised my hand and asked to go to the bathroom. I then walked out into the hallway with my heart racing at the thought of what I was about to do! "No kid's ever walked out of St. Pet's before! You'll never make it!" I thought, as I started walking towards the boy's room. Since I had to pass the doorways of several other classrooms on the way I thought that surely one of the teachers would spot me and know what I was planning! (Kids are convinced that all adults have

ESP and can see their thoughts!) But no one did. My heart really pounded now as I passed the door to the bathroom and kept walking! There they were, the doors to the stairwell and the gateway to my freedom. As I walked through the doors, I stood there for a moment alone in the stairwell to collect myself. "No turning back now!" I thought. My excitement mounted. Not smart enough to be afraid, I felt like Steve McQueen in the movie, *The Great Escape*, as I descended the final flights of stairs to the playground doors and... freedom! "I made it!" Not quite. I still had to get from the doors to the edge of the playground one hundred yards away, all of which was in full view of every single classroom at the rear of the school! "Well? Too late to turn back now," I thought. "Okay, three, two, one, GO!" I ran faster than I had ever run in my life! I didn't even turn around to look until I had cleared the north wall of the parking lot. I carefully scanned the entire side of the school for any sign that I had been detected. Nothing. Not even so much as a single kid staring out the window like I did. "I don't believe it... I made it!"

I walked home not even thinking about the consequences of my actions. I didn't care. I had done the unthinkable! They were going to write songs about me! This thought lasted until my mother came home and found me sitting in front of the TV eating Oreo cookies!

"Billy! What are you doing home already?"

"Uhh, I didn't feel good, so they sent me home."

My talent for lying didn't save me this time either. It was clear to my parents, doctors, and teachers that something needed to change.

St. Pet's now had a new fifth grade teacher named Jim Brabbits with whom all of the kids seemed to have a great rapport, and everyone hoped that he could connect with me. Of all my previous teachers at St. Pet's—Mrs. Snedden, Mrs. Wiemer, Ms. Kepple, Ms. Griefenkamp, Mrs. McCloughlin, Mrs. Russell, Mr. Palarski, and Mrs. Lopano—none of them had more of an impact on me than Jim Brabbits.

From my first day in Jim Brabbit's classroom, I knew he was different. He was young, athletic, and had bright red hair and mustache. It was a new experience for me since, apart from Mr. Palarski, I had only been taught by middle-aged women. Mr. Brabbits also treated me differently, more like a little brother than a student. He would always speak TO me, rather than DOWN AT me. I found out quickly, however, that he wouldn't take any crap from me!

We definitely clicked, and something funny happened. I started to like going to school! Sort of. I liked Mr. Brabbits so much that my parents had a tee-shirt printed up with the word "Superteach" on the back. You can guess what superhero insignia was printed on the front! I still had my issues, but Mr. Brabbits took the time each day to make sure "I got it" before moving on to the next lesson. He would make the classroom environment fun as well. There was almost a party atmosphere. He would turn his lesson plans into games with prizes for correct answers. This guy was a pioneer, and I don't know if he knew it at the time! His class was exactly the kind of learning environment that I needed! But as with all the other teachers, I soon began to lose interest. I would do sporadically well for a while but then begin to drift off.

My father then teamed up with Mr. Brabbits to coach my basketball team. Even so, the basketball court began to feel too structured for me as well. Nothing was working now. I wasn't doing any of my homework. I was drifting off during class more than ever, so much so that I wouldn't even hear my name when I was called on to answer a question! Even Mr. Brabbits became frustrated and sometimes angry with me. I just knew that I was miserable and that all I could think about was not wanting to be there.

At the suggestion of my doctor my parents decided to switch me to public school the following year. So, after a total of six years in the Catholic School system, I began the sixth grade at Churchill Elementary School.

"Here we go again!"

5 Transition

September 1977. *Star Wars* was the blockbuster movie of the summer, and Elvis had just died in August. Change is inevitable, I guess.

From the very first day I could feel the difference in this school. The most obvious: NO DRESS CODE! A kid could wear virtually anything here! Jeans, tee shirts, sneakers, whatever. "How cool is this?" The classrooms were laid out differently too. There were no desks per se, but octagonal tables at which six students faced one another. The rules here were very liberal with a principal who was even more so. Mr. Hill was one of the nicest people I remember from my childhood, and a principal no less!

At this school I met a teacher who, like Mr. Brabbits, would have a positive influence on me. The first and most obvious impression one had of Ms. Prelozny was her imposing size! Not a fat woman, to be sure! But very tall, and very strong like a power-lifter from the Czechoslovakian women's Olympic team! She, like Mr. Brabbits, had a different style of teaching. Like Mr. Brabbits, she and I hit it off right from the start. She apparently had been briefed about me and had seen all of the files containing my academic history. She was not the least bit intimidated or doubtful—not that even a speeding Mack truck could intimidate her! She was going to get me to pay attention and learn! She was right!

Although I'd still have my down and drifting days, the majority of the time I thrived in this atmosphere! I actually liked this place! Learning actually was fun! Who would have dreamed this! This new experience wasn't without its setbacks, however. I still hit some serious bumps in the road in the first few weeks.

Like I said, I was doing great! I liked school and I was making new friends. I was even planning a birthday sleep over for my twelfth birthday, which makes what happen next so unexplainable! I guess I was having a bad day, or it may have been a careless comment from a classmate. Whatever the reason, I decided that I didn't want to be there. I couldn't explain it. This feeling just came over me and I knew it was time to leave. So, without a word or fuss, and without permission, I just walked out the front doors to freedom! It almost seemed anticlimactic. I mean, after my previous escape from "Stalag 17," I mean St. Pets, and all! The funny thing about public schools is that kids are always coming and going due to their diverse schedules. So an eleven-year-old boy walking out the front doors would not have drawn a second glance. Besides, "No kid would dare to even think of doing such a thing!" Not so with this kid.

This time, however, I did not feel the same thrill of accomplishment I had felt running away from St. Pet's. No, this time I felt something else. As I was walking home, I could feel remorse, as though someone had placed it in a backpack and hung it on my shoulders. "UH-OH!" I thought, "This one's going to cost me!" I kept walking anyway. Even though I knew I was going to get into BIG trouble, the overwhelming feeling of needing to leave that school was far more compelling.

When my parents got home that day, my fears were confirmed. Yet, something was different. Oh, my parents were pissed, make no mistake! But they didn't yell or fly off the handle like one might have expected. No. This one was going to cost me, big-time!

Not only did I get grounded indefinitely, but they did something I never saw coming. They canceled my birthday! No, I don't mean "No-cake for-you-mister," kind of canceled! I mean they canceled the entire day!!! There would be no party, no gifts, no cards, no cake, no nothing! (Looking back, I can't say I blame them!) I had to call each and every one of my friends to tell them why the party was canceled. After I made the final call, I was remanded to the custody of my room until further notice. "The Man of Steel" couldn't help me this time! I had no power strong enough to defeat my guilty conscience. Especially since I overheard my parents talking and worrying about me now more than ever. My mother's crying sealed my guilt. All too familiar thoughts surfaced; I did it again, idiot! I must be a bad kid. All I do is cause trouble. Now, however, a new thought was added to the list: I made my Mom cry because I can't behave like a normal kid! This last thought above all stuck with me. Little did I know that this self-blame would be the beginning of a life-long thought process.

After the initial shock of the incident had cooled off a few days later, things settled down somewhat. True to their word, however, when September eleventh arrived, no one even acknowledged it. Man, I had really messed up this time! I remember that I wasn't overly saddened by it. It was as if I knew I had it coming. That evening Robert Emmet and I were in the car with our parents coming home from the store when my father pulled the car into the parking lot of a bowling alley. Upon parking, my parents turned around to face me.

"Uh oh! They're gonna kill me and dump me behind the bowling alley!" I thought.

Instead they said that even though I was being punished it was still my birthday, and that since I had behaved so well that day and had not caused any problems whatsoever over my party's cancelation, they were taking Rob and me bowling!

Although I've never forgotten the seriousness of what I did, this was one of the many reminders I have of how loving my parents are! I don't think any birthday slumber party could've topped the fun we had that night!

I eventually settled into the Churchill Elementary School routine. The environment there was open and fun compared with all my other school experiences to that point. One of the great things I remember about my time there was a segment of classes held in the afternoons called "Humanities," which exposed students to diverse world cultures. I don't exactly know why I absolutely loved this part of my school day, except perhaps that it involved us moving periodically from various points of the library and adjacent classrooms. The classes were very hands-on, too, with actual displays of artifacts and clothing. We learned of the history and traditions of people I had never known even existed! In addition to ancient history, we also learned about modern pop culture. One of the teachers even brought in an authentic "Creature From The Black Lagoon" costume, and displayed it for us all to see and touch! To a twelve-year old kid like me, this was the coolest thing I'd ever seen in school!

As the weeks went by, Ms. Prelozny and I were getting along great. Although I could not say that I was up for the honor role or anything, and

I'd sometimes have a day or two where I'd drift off, the feeling of dread I often felt was now gone. If I strayed at all, it wouldn't be long before Ms. Prelozny would "reel me back in."

The atmosphere at Churchill Elementary School was always kept exciting, what with us putting on plays and pageants of one kind or another. That Halloween in fact, we were allowed to wear our costumes to school! I was extremely excited since I had just bought the coolest, most authentic looking "Frankenstein" mask ever! Then again, compared to the ultra-flammable plastic mask with matching polyurethane costume dipped in petroleum that came in a cardboard box with the clear plastic window, anything looked authentic! We had a huge party in the afternoon and the entire student body assembled in the gym/auditorium and paraded across the stage to show off the various costumes. Once school let out that day we trick-or-treated our way home! Of all the Halloweens of my childhood this was by far the best ever!

Thanksgiving came and went and my focus was now on one thing—Christmas! I know that for most people Christmas really is "The most wonderful time of the year," but for me it is much more! As I've said before, Christmas always struck an inner chord with me. Living in the Midwest virtually guaranteed us a white Christmas every year, but it went deeper than that with the music, the television specials, and the food. The presents also didn't hurt! Maybe I liked it because when Christmas approached I noticed that everyone began to "act like me" ... I don't know. At school we even put on a play of our own version of "Merry Christmas, Charlie Brown!" What I've always been sure of, however, is that at this time of year I was completely focused!

The next year went by without incident, except that I began experiencing changes. Physical changes. Puberty. "Oh! So that's what they were talking about in health class!" I thought, as I was getting out of bed one morning. If I were a ball of energy before, imagine what raging hormones and a stronger physique will add to the mix! If things weren't chaotic enough before, when I was being distracted by my formidable imagination, now I had my female classmates' changing physiques to contend with as well! In spite of it all, however, I somehow managed to make progress.

As springtime approached, we all talked about how exciting it was going to be next year going to Hadley Junior High School. One afternoon, however, I didn't think I would get out of Churchill alive! You see, I did something very stupid and dangerous, I made Ms. Prelozny angry with me.

I was in the hallway between classes horsing around with Corey, one of my female classmates, who was kind of cute and fun to be around. I soon found out that Corey had a short fuse. For some reason she started throwing things at me. Nothing that would hurt me, and not in a malicious way, but in a "I'll show you" kind of way. So, being the suave guy I was, I took her winter cap and soaked it in the water fountain. Predictably, she went to the classroom and told Ms. Prelozny what had just happened. It got worse. While Ms. Prelozny was in the middle of giving me a stern talking to, for some reason I thought of interrupting her. With all the tough-guy attitude I could muster, I said almost verbatim, "Hey, maybe I just don't like having things thrown at me, okay?!"

As the words left my mouth, I saw the initial look of surprise on Ms. Prelozny's face. Then, this very tall, strong, and very pissed-off woman stood up and roared, "What do you mean, okay???! No, it's not okay!" While she continued to berate me, I braced for what I thought would be the inevitable stomping of her very large foot on my head!

I've heard people describe near-death experiences, and the "moment of clarity" often associated with them. I now knew what they were talking about! Luckily for me, however, the largest part of her anatomy was her heart, so she allowed me to live. Needless to say, I never made that mistake again! Throughout, however, Ms. Prelozny always looked out for me. As I said, she made a very lasting impression!

I soon learned that I would not be attending Hadley Junior High after all. Throughout the years living in Glen Ellyn, my father's career had prospered. With seven U.S. patents for innovations in the electrical fittings industry to his name, he was then the Vice President of his company. As the summer of 1978 approached, my father's superiors were giving serious thought to transferring him back to the New York office. When I first heard the news I was excited. I thought that moving back to New York would be awesome. After all, it's where I was born, and all of our relatives still lived there. Not to mention all the fun I had during those summer vacations! I figured it would be non-stop fun and excitement! Boy, was I wrong!

While all of this was going on, my other grandfather, "Pop" Brett, became very ill. Still living in Brooklyn, he and my grandmother, "Mom," were well into their eighties. Pop's condition got worse, and I'm sure this must have worried my father. As the school year came to an end, the transfer back to New York was all but assured. Pop's condition however, was not getting any better and my father feared for the worst.

This is where my life got a lot more confusing for me. Apparently, my father's company decided to forego the transfer and keep him in Chicago. Obviously, Pop's condition weighed even more heavily on my father. I remember telling my father after I heard the news of his company's decision, "You ought to quit that job, Dad!" You can imagine my surprise when he replied, "You're right. I should!"

I never knew what actually took place between my father and his superiors, but that following August we were back in New York for good.

6 If I Can Make It There...

At the beginning of August 1978, my sister Rose and I came back to Long Island ahead of the rest of our family. She was returning to Northern Illinois University in a couple of weeks, and it was felt that because of my "issues" a change of scenery would do me good. As well, because of Pop's condition, they thought that Rose and I could spend some quality time with him.

Since my father's sisters and their families still lived in the nearby western portion of Nassau County, Rose stayed with Aunt Anne while I stayed with my god-parents, Aunt Marian and Uncle Jimmy. I could not have been happier with the arrangement, since Uncle Jimmy was a retired NYPD cop I idolized, and my cousins Jimmy, Mary, Trish, and John treated me like a brother, which was good since I ended up staying with them for four weeks!

Meanwhile, my father had begun his new job working Monday through Friday in Queens, while also trying to find us a new house in Long Island. Each weekend he would catch a plane out of La Guardia for Chicago to help my mother get the house in Glen Ellyn squared away.

Aunt Marian spoiled me rotten. Anything and everything I wanted to eat or drink was always there for me! If that weren't enough, their house on Bond Avenue in Malverne was right around the corner from an authentic New York Deli! I'd go to "Bob's Deli" every single day and load up on so many Yodels, Devil Dogs, and Yankee Doodles that I'd get sick! I was so excited because you couldn't get Drakes' cakes or Entemenns' products in Chicago!

During the day we usually went to the beach at Point Lookout, and at night we drove the thirty minutes into Brooklyn to see Mom and Pop. I roomed with Cousin Jimmy and Cousin John, who kept the scariest creature I had ever seen! Now, having seen the movie *JAWS* at a fairly young age, you'd think I could handle any marine life that was relatively small and confined to a tank. That was before I met "Oscar."

Oscar was the biggest, meanest, ugliest, and most aggressive fresh water fish I'd ever seen! He looked like a giant piranha on steroids, and he hated me! What's even worse, his tank was right next to the bedroom door, forcing me to walk right next to him to get in or out. Every time I'd pass the tank this behemoth would slam himself against the glass trying to get me! "God, I hate this friggin' fish!"

My fear of Oscar aside, my Cousin Jimmy and I stayed up half the night once talking about sharks. I was only twelve, and Jimmy was seventeen or eighteen. He had spent his entire life on Long island, so as far as I was concerned he was an expert! We covered every single species of man-eaters that one could possibly imagine. Suddenly Oscar wasn't so scary anymore.

I was having a great summer, and I was thrilled that we'd be living here permanently! I had all but forgotten my school phobias! This feeling of euphoria, however, would soon be over-shadowed by great sadness. Looking back now, I'm profoundly thankful I was able to spend the time that I had with Pop that summer, especially on those good days—he was often completely bedridden and unaware of his surroundings—when he'd be sitting up in bed totally alert and able to tell me of the many blessings in his life, none of which were more dear to him than his numerous grandchildren and great grandchildren. This, from an Irish immigrant who came to Brooklyn with little in his pocket, who found the love of his life in my grandmother, and who worked as a motorman for the Brooklyn Transit, spoke a lot about his values.

I vividly remember how Pop looked as he laid in bed the night he passed away. As I write this, I can feel that feeling again as if I just saw him. Somehow, even at that young age I knew it would be his last night. I remember telling Rob, "Pop isn't going to make it through the night." I was right.

As with Gramps' funeral, there were hundreds of mourners, all with their fond memories of my grandfather. I thought of him as a gentle soul with a rich, sweet Irish brogue to match! He was the quintessential "Quiet Man."

To this day, Pop is remembered by his grandchildren whenever a glass is raised with a simple toast that was all his own: "The Best!"

Of my grandfather no truer words have ever been spoken.

EVENTUALLY, OUR SADNESS GAVE WAY TO THE PROSPECT OF MOVING INTO OUR NEW house, which we found in Syosset on the north side of town on Renee Road, only a few blocks from the center of town and the Long Island Rail Road. Easily twice as large as our old house in Glen Ellyn, it had five bedrooms and a huge backyard. No cool fort this time, however! After having to double up most of our lives, it was nice to finally have our own bedrooms, as long as Rose and John were away at school, that is. The kitchen was huge and had a walk-in pantry that led to the staircase and the semi-finished basement.

The first thing I noticed upon entering the house was an unusual, musty smell. Not terribly unpleasant, but a musty smell nonetheless. It was when I looked into the formal living room that the source of it became obvious. The previous owners had installed by far the ugliest deep pile shag carpet that I, or perhaps anyone else for that matter, had ever seen! Not only did this brown and yellow nightmare cover what turned out to be beautiful hardwood floors, but it had never been cleaned since the day it was installed.

The one ingenious item in this house was a duct system for a wall mounted air conditioning unit in the basement stairway. There were two ducts: one that led up to my parents bedroom, and one that led to the formal living room. When the unit was running, both of these rooms were ice cold! Besides being as big and loud as a car engine, it had been manufactured during the Eisenhower Administration, when electrical efficiency was not even a consideration. So, whenever we turned this monster on, the entire neighborhood would go dim! Needless to say, the earth could be hurtling towards the sun with both polar ice caps melting in the ensuing inferno, but if our parents caught us turning that thing on we were dead meat!

Still, even without the air conditioning this house was going to be perfect! I was starting junior high in a week, and I felt that this time things were going to be different. Oh, they were going to be different alright!

A few days after we had moved in, and only two days before the first day of school, my parents took us to dinner at the home of two of their closest friends who lived just on the other side of Syosset. They were such close friends, in fact, that in my entire life I've only known them as Uncle Bob and Aunt Sally!

Well, after we had eaten dinner, I was hanging out with their son, Greg, up in his room. Greg was a few years older and had attended South Woods Jr. High where I would soon start. He began to describe what a routine day at South Woods was like—kids getting worked over in the hallways between classes, rampant drug use in the bathrooms, stabbings, etc. Good old fashioned honor-student stuff! Since he was older than I, I figured that he must know what he was talking about! Well, it was all I needed to hear! If I had school phobias before, imagine what I was thinking now! When my parents heard about it they panicked, and Aunt Sally was ready to kill Greg! Although he told me at once that he had made most of it up, it didn't matter. I was going prepared for the worst.

Strangely, however, nothing happened out of the ordinary on my first day in the seventh grade! It was definitely a new atmosphere for me but nowhere near the "Orwellian" nightmare that Greg had described! On the plus side, all the kids were new. With several elementary schools feeding South Woods, I guess no one really felt at home yet. Still, I felt very uneasy.

Although I was always physically bigger than most people I knew, I have never, and I mean never, been aggressive towards anyone! My self-esteem was now so low that I would avoid confrontations like the plague! It didn't take long for some of the "alpha males" in my school to pick up on this and to exploit it. There would be times when I'd be teased, or even bullied, but I wouldn't respond. I'd just sit there and take it even though I was bigger than any of them. In my mind, I felt that if I lashed out at them I'd be seen as the bully. So, I kept it bottled up. Eventually I was going to need to vent!

My academic life wasn't improving either. I just flat-out would not participate in class. Ironically, I became that which I had wanted to avoid: "That tall, stupid kid who never does his homework!" All I could think about was how I didn't want to be there!

One morning, I decided that I wasn't even going to bother going to school. My parents had gone away for a long weekend, and my sisters were left in charge of the house. When Rose tried to get me to go to the bus stop, I flatly refused and locked myself in the upstairs bathroom. After several failed attempts to scare me into opening the door, Rose called Aunt Sally, who came over and pleaded with me to open the door. When I refused, they even tried to force the door open with a screw driver. When this also failed, I heard the sound of disbelief in Aunt Sally's voice as she said, "I can't believe you're not opening this door! Alright then, I'm going to have to call the police!" was her final salvo as she left the house in total disbelief. Eventually, I came out and went to school, but I could not understand why I had to bother.

Days dragged into weeks. Although I wasn't doing any better in school, I was making new friends, which helped the days go by more easily.

Then I met Mr. Fusco, my favorite teacher of them all.

Tom Fusco was a twenty-four-year-old, first-year Social Studies teacher, who had a reputation with the students as the coolest teacher in the school. Built like a full-back, he wore jeans, sneakers, and rugby jerseys to school. This guy didn't even remotely look like a teacher! When the administrators decided to move me into his class, they had hopes that his teaching style would hold my focus.

From the very first moment I met him, Tom Fusco made it clear that he wasn't going to put up with any bullshit! Oh, this guy was like no other teacher before him! I got a serious big brother vibe from him, but unlike Mr. Brabbitts back in Glen Ellyn, Mr. Fusco gave me the feeling he'd kick the shit out of me if I crossed him! He'd never have to. His classes were sometimes tough, but I enjoyed them more than any other. He genuinely cared, taking the time sometimes after school to make sure I understood something before cutting me loose.

Some of my other teachers, however, were not as caring or supportive. My math teacher, for instance, clearly thought that insults and humiliation were good tools to use on students with self-esteem and attention issues. Her appearance was typical of a thirty-something woman born and raised on Long Island. Easily fifty pounds over-weight, she seemed to apply her makeup with a putty knife and her perfume with a garden hose. A "shaper of young minds," she thought that it was appropriate in front of the entire class to call me lazy for not turning in my homework assignments and stupid for not having the answers during class when she called on me, knowing full well that I was not paying attention!! This just added anger and resentment to the mix of negative emotions I already held about school.

I began to put genuine effort into her class, if for no other reason than to prove to her that I could pay attention and turn in my homework. But even with the help of my sister, Rose, who was going for her teaching degree,

I still struggled to do so. I just could not concentrate or get motivated. Somehow, perhaps because of peer pressure or because I had made some good friends, I was able to slowly make progress.

For the first time, I was becoming profoundly aware of my mind. I began to see that when something held my attention I could learn it fairly easily. I also began to notice "the white noise" in my mind as I raced from thought to thought as if changing television channels without ever stopping to see what was on.

I remember thinking, "I know I'm no angel, but do I really deserve to feel this crappy?"

As Christmas came that year, we had the usual Brett celebration with all the trimmings. One memorable gift I received made this Christmas special—my first weight set. A life-long quest of strength training began. Since none of my siblings or cousins ever showed any interest in strength training it was mine alone. It is the one thing in my entire life, even today, that has held my complete and total focus! It's the only time in my day where "the remote control stops running through the channels." At the time, I had no idea how therapeutic this practice would be—and continues to be to this day! What a game changer!

Another great thing happened that 1978 Christmas. While on school break, the usual Hollywood holiday blockbusters were in the theatres that week—including the motion picture version of my favorite comic book hero, Superman. There was media frenzy about veteran actors Marlon Brando, Gene Hackman, and Christopher Reeve, a total unknown who would be playing the lead. Marlon Brando was being paid gazillions for thirty seconds of work. I didn't care, I was just curious about how they were going to pull off making people believe a man could fly! You see, in the previous two years a certain little boy had become cynical, bitter, and frustrated. He had lost interest in a superhero who was unwaveringly good toward all humanity. Instead, he had begun to relate more to the Incredible Hulk, a lumbering, raging green monster who smashed the things that frustrated and angered him.

As the lights in the theater went dark, my life changed forever.

The first and most obvious thing that struck me was the music. Another in a long line of legendary themes by composer, John Williams, this one was immediately iconic and worthy of respresenting Superman. Then, the most recognizable symbol the world has ever known seemed to fly right off the screen as the music seemed to actually "say" his name!

"WHOA!" I thought. It wouldn't be the only time I'd say so that night!

Marlon Brando was perfect as Jor-El, and so well worth that eighty gazillion bucks, and Gene Hackman set the standard by which all super-villians should be measured! This guy, Christopher Reeve, though, it's as if he flew off the pages of the comic books!

The scene in which Superman's parents debate about choosing earth as his foster planet, while placing their infant son in a rocket, made me feel even more connected to my hero. His mother worried that he would be an outcast, which is how I felt. "He'll be odd, different. He won't be one of them! He'll be isolated, alone." I wasn't the only one after all!

Despite my physical gifts, my low self-esteem made me feel more like Clark Kent than Superman. Watching the movie that night, I remembered the times when I chose to be Superman to escape reality. I had all but forgotten how I used my imagination to become invincible. Here he was now, right up there on the big screen! "I remember how this feels," I thought to myself.

I left the theater feeling "more powerful than a locomotive!" I wondered at how a simple change in feelings and emotions can alter one's entire outlook! At the time I had no clue how profound that sentiment would prove to be!

THE NEXT DAY WAS ANOTHER ROUTINE, HUSTLE-BUSTLE DAY IN THE BIG CITY WITH executives all scurrying to their big power-broker breakfast meetings, unaware of the evil plot that's about to change their lives forever. The noise is deafening. This city has seen its share of twisted criminals hell-bent on world domination, but this explosion is like no other they've ever heard. Within a millisecond, the east wall of the biggest bank in the city is reduced to flying debris and ashes as a plasma bomb explodes on impact. Due to the early hour, there are only four employees in the bank, three of which are now critically injured. The lone survivor, an armed guard, tries in vain to get to his feet. He instinctively unholsters his .38 caliber revolver and tries to point it at the large shape he sees lumbering towards him through the dust and smoke. The large shape is a fully armored battle-suit piloted by a frustrated psychotic weapons-designer who is now pointing the plasma cannon at the guard's head! "You had your chance to run, and you blew it! Now you're gonna die!"

You'd think after all these years these psychos with too much time and money on their hands would know enough to concentrate on what they were doing instead of rambling on and on about why they plan on taking over the world! He might have heard the sound of the high pitch rush of wind, or seen that streak of red and blue that he catches in the corner of his eye... too late.

As I slam into this clown at eight times the speed of sound, he realizes too late that he's wasted too much time running his mouth announcing to the world his evil intentions. His little tin suit just becomes crumpled tin foil. I know it protects him from any permanent injury. With my super-hearing and x-ray vision I can tell his vitals are fine. Thankfully, all of his intended victims, although in serious condition, will survive. Once again, Metropolis is safe! Thanks to Super... "

"Billy! Time for dinner!"

Back to reality. It felt nice to be back in the battle, however! I couldn't help smiling as I carefully placed my action figures back on top of my bedroom dresser right next to the record album of the movie sound track!

This music would serve as a "mood-booster" for the rest of my life!

SOMETHING ELSE BEGAN TO DEVELOP AS WELL. DUE TO A STEADY ROUTINE OF weight training, my physique was becoming more formidable. I guess it was no small coincidence that the "alpha-males" began to keep their distance at this point. Besides, I had made friends with so many new people that I learned to ignore the bully mentality and just walk away from the taunts. They lost interest altogether. I guess they figured that it wasn't worth the risk!

Seventh grade moved on without much improvement, but I was able to make it to the eighth grade. Although I was fully involved with the basketball and baseball teams now, and pretty happy in general, deep down, especially in the classroom environment, I still had that feeling of being too stupid to "get it!" Although I periodically put serious effort into a subject, I felt the most inept then. The more I tried to concentrate on something the more I'd screw it up! "How the hell can that happen?" So I would just let it go and accept the inevitable "D" or "F" grade.

Only because of my family and friends was I able to make slow progress from grade to grade. As my ninth grade year at South Woods began, I was fully integrated into the mainstream of the student body. Although I was passed up for membership on the honor role because of my trademark antics, I was voted "Best Comedian" in the school!

Something else happened. Because I was so relaxed now with friends, I wasn't even thinking about my scholastic shortcomings. As a result, I was showing some improvement. As well, my basketball team finished in first place in our division and went undefeated!

Basketball was always a staple in my family. Rose, Eileen and Chris played in high school and John won a four year scholarship to college for his skills. I was now standing at about 6'3," and crushing the scales at a sidewalk-cracking weight of 175lbs! What I lacked in height compared to my brothers, John and Chris, who both stood at 6'7" and 6'9 respectfully," I more than made up for in vertical leap and speed!

During this time John, a textbook big brother, took Rob and me into Manhattan to see "The David Letterman Show." When we arrived at the NBC studios, we were among the first in line. As the crowd grew, two of the assistant producers started talking to some of the people in line. When they took a look at John they said, "You guys must be basketball players! How would you like to play on Dave's show today? Today's guest is Nancy Lieberman, and she is going to give Dave a few pointers on the game."

Too scared to even form a reply, I just stood there with my mouth open. After all, Nancy Leiberman was the first and only woman ever to be drafted into the National Basketball Association! Thankfully, John was as calm and cool as a big brother could be and said, "Sure." They had us sign some waivers, or something that ensured we couldn't sue Dave in case we got hurt. Then they brought us upstairs into the studio before anyone else! This was by far the coolest experience of my life! The producers told us that the segment would be towards the end of the show, and they'd come and get us when it was time.

Now the butterflies started. All I could do was think about how I was about to be on live national television! I remember watching the show but not really seeing it. Then, it was time. I started to feel panicked. When they came to get us, I told them I had changed my mind and didn't want to do it. All this did was get me the dirtiest look I'd ever seen before or since from one of the producers! John just reassured me and said, "Don't worry, we'll play."

John went first and when Letterman saw him he laughed and said something to the effect, "Are you sure you want to do this, Nancy?" They played typical school yard rules, and Nancy had the ball first. She took an outside jump shot and hit it. The crowd applauded as my brother then took possession. As he was trying to drive towards the inside lane, Nancy struck his hand so hard there was an audible "Slap" sound. With that, Letterman says, "Oh, come on Nancy, we ALL heard that one!!!"

It was only after one more missed jump-shot by my brother that they called me out to try. Suddenly, all sound disappeared. Time began to move in ultra-slow motion. Just as before, Nancy had first possession. She attempted to drive the lane on me but missed. My turn. I took the ball, and before I even knew what I had done the ball was swishing through the net! The crowd went ape-shit! Here I was, some pizza-faced kid from Long Island on national TV, and I had just scored a basket on the best female athlete in the world! As the crowd was cheering, Letterman laughed, and said, "Uh-Oh Nancy, there goes the contract!"

On reflex, Nancy hands me the ball again. This was "Winners" in school-yard ball rules, but Letterman, who was not one to ever miss a trick said, "Come on, give her the ball! This isn't schoolyard ball you know!" She then attempted another jump shot that she had used on John, but this time she threw a "Brick"! "Holy shit!" I thought. "I beat her! I played basketball on national TV against the number one female player in the world and I beat her!" (Yeah, I know! One friggin' hoop in a make-shift NBC studio court! But come on, give a kid his moment, will ya?) That little brush with greatness gave me a little, albeit temporary, celebrity status around Syosset.

I DISCOVERED MY FOOT-SPEED PURELY BY ACCIDENT ONE HALLOWEEN NIGHT while hanging out with a large group of friends in a neighborhood near Harry B. Thompson Junior High on the other side of town. Together with a bunch of upper classmen that we had run into from the high school football team, we started throwing eggs at some kids we didn't know. It was all fun and games until a car came screaming up and screeched to a halt right in front of us! This huge guy got out holding what appeared to be a .44 caliber revolver, only bigger! He then screamed at all of us, "Hey, you @$#*%, what are you doing?!!" Well, we didn't need any more motivation than that to start running!

What I didn't notice, aside from the lack of a gunshot—not that I would have heard anything over the sound of my pounding heart!—was the fact that I was now running way ahead of everyone! When I finally stopped and turned around, I saw my friends and the upper classmen football team all staggering to catch up. When my friend, Brian, caught up to me, a look of astonishment was on his face. Brian was no slouch himself, having ended up getting a four year ride to Harvard for Lacrosse. He gasped, "How the hell did you move that fast?" Apparently, I had ran past perhaps the fastest athlete in the high school as if he were standing still. "I don't know! Did you see the size of that friggin' gun???" It turned out to be a pellet gun wielded by the older brother of one of the other kids. Thank god! Man, what a little adrenaline dump can do for the heart rate!

My teachers and parents were still very concerned about my lack of focus and progress in the classroom. Thus began a new series of tests and interviews with various school social workers and psychologists. "Terrific." I thought.

I first met Dr. Pearson in his office on the second floor of Syosset High School, located directly across the soccer field from South Woods. A large, balding man who wore glasses, Dr. Pearson was the school district psychologist assigned to my case. He told me that he would be conducting some tests over the course of a few weeks and hoped that maybe we could find a way to help me start improving in school. "So far, so good," I thought.

"Okay Bill, I want you to take a look at these pictures, and tell me what you see..."

"Oh great," I thought, "Here we go again!" (Remember the "bat in the hat, and the two eagles playing poker?) Luckily, those weren't the only methods of testing Dr. Pearson had in mind. Over the next couple of weeks we had a series of question and answer sessions about everything, from faith to history to geography. I specifically remember Dr. Pearson asking me if I knew the capitol of Greece. Being nervous and unsure of myself, I always tried to use comedy as a tension breaker in these situations. "John Travolta?" I replied.

Dr. Pearson didn't so much as look up from his legal pad. He just kept taking his notes, no doubt recording every syllable that left my mouth. "Athens," I thought to myself, but now too embarrassed to say it!

The sessions with Dr. Pearson culminated with a standardized I.Q. test. It would take a week to get the results back, so Dr. Pearson told me we'd go over the results then.

I was in the car with my parents, Rob, and Eileen one day that week and they were all talking about something or other while I was going over the week's events in my head. Finally, curiosity took over and I interrupted their conversation… "What's the capitol of Greece?" I asked. Before my voice faded, my sister Eileen shouts, "John Travolta!" and started laughing. My parents tried to cover my sister's *faux pas* by saying, "Athens, maybe." But it was too late. I knew now what I had always suspected. My "issues" and all those tests were public knowledge! "Wow!" I thought. "People really do talk behind my back!" From this point on I started listening to my instincts a little more closely.

A few days later I met with Dr. Pearson who told me my results were "all over the charts." In certain areas, I showed unbelievable comprehension that was way above expected levels. In other areas, however, I was way below average. None of this really mattered to me. I couldn't be bothered anymore.

I had too much on my mind now.

BECAUSE OF MY SKILLS DISPLAYED DURING THE BASKETBALL SEASON, I HAD BEEN noticed by the high school varsity basketball coach. Shooting some hoops in the high school gym one day, coach Lenny Mintz approached me saying, "You keep up that hard effort Brett, and I'll have a spot for you on the varsity team next season."

"Well," I thought, "at least this was one aspect of school that was showing serious promise."

It wouldn't be the only thing.

While all this was going on, someone else was taking notice of me. Not for my athletic ability nor my status as "Rhodes Scholar" (Yeah, right!) but for me. Her name was Michelle. She was cute, a cheerleader, and as sweet as the day was long. And for some odd reason, she liked me and thought I was cute! So, after much encouragement from two of my best friends, Glenn and Alex, I asked her to go out with me. This was definitely one of the high points of my life at South Woods—first, an undefeated basketball championship season and now a cheerleader girlfriend! It couldn't get any better than this!

If I live to be one hundred, I'll never forget the night at a Valentine's Day party when Michelle gave me my first kiss! I could not have felt or acted more awkwardly! Michelle, bless her heart was so sweet that she picked up on this and finally said, "Well, are you going to kiss me or what?" I was no stud in a Speedo rolling around the surf with her like Burt Lancaster in *From Here to Eternity*, but it was a sweet moment, nonetheless. We went out for a couple months, but we were two different people. She actually was an honor student, and I, well... We eventually parted ways, which did not bode well for me at first. That feeling of rejection really sucked! I got over it in time, but it would be a while before I had any girls interested in me again. Michelle and I eventually became friends throughout high school.

As that year came to a close, I was feeling more optimistic than usual. When June finally arrived, my career at South Woods ended without fanfare.

"Who cares? I'm officially a high school student now!"

THE SUMMER WENT BY IN A FLASH WITHOUT INCIDENT. MY FOCUS WAS TOTALLY on basketball now. I'd play every day and lift weights with my friends at night. Things were going pretty well, but I was starting to get anxious about getting my driver's license.

Being impatient, I decided to start practicing my driving skills with one of my best friends, Ricky. My family had a 1974 Chevy Malibu that would just sit in our driveway all day, unused. Well, there was a pretty good reason for that, you see this car was so old and rusted that the rear floor boards were completely rusted through. You could actually see the pavement rushing by if you were unlucky enough to be sitting in the back seat! This didn't bother Ricky or me one bit. As far as we were concerned, this was the coolest ride in town. And we had a set of keys for it!

So, one day we took her out for a spin around the block. No sooner were we out of the driveway than an unmarked Dodge Grand Fury pulled up behind us. The Dodge Grand Fury was the standard issue patrol car used by the Nassau County Police Department. Two plain clothes officers had figured out what Ricky and I were up to! As we pulled back into the driveway, they pulled in behind us. "Oh we're screwed!" I said. When they approached the car, they put us through the third degree! Once they determined it was my family's car, they told me to stay there because they would be returning later to tell my parents what we had done. Then they put Ricky in the back seat of the cruiser and began to drive away! I was really scared now! This was all my parents would need to hear. As I went into the house to ponder my fate, I heard Ricky walk in shortly after me. "Dude, what happened?"

"They let me out up at the corner!" They had tried the "good cop/bad cop" routine and had threatened to take him in but then let him go after getting the desired reaction. They must've had bigger fish to fry that afternoon. "Whew, we dodged a bullet on that one!"

One week later, Ricky and I tried again. This time I had just put the car into reverse when my father pulled into the driveway blocking us in and scaring the shit out of us!. The look on his face said it all. I was dead, and Ricky would be maimed so that others would hear the tale of my fate! Yet, my dad didn't kill me! He didn't even lose his temper. Although I received some serious down time as a result, my father later said that what really amazed him was how anxious I was to start driving.

At this point I had definitely learned my lesson, right? Wrong!

My friend, Steve, who was a year older and in the eleventh grade, already had his driver's license. He would let me take the wheel of his parents' Chevy Malibu station wagon whenever we tooled around town. I was soon very comfortable behind the wheel and felt that I could handle anything. When Steve bought his own car—a 1978 Chevy Camaro—I quickly discovered that it had a slightly more powerful engine than the V6 powered Malibu... slightly.

On one fine autumn afternoon, a bunch of us were hanging out after school shooting hoops in the main gym of the high school. During a break, I noticed that Steve had placed his keys on the bleachers so that he could also play. That's when I had one of my big ideas! Wouldn't it be funny if I took Steve's keys and moved his car to the other side of the school? "He'll freak out!" his brother told me. But that didn't discourage me. This would definitely be hilarious! Besides, I knew how to drive! How much different could this car be from a station wagon, right?

As soon as Steve's attention was drawn away from his keys, I made my move. With the hand speed of a spy in East Berlin making an open air transfer of classified documents, I had those keys out of Steve's coat and in the palm of my hand before anyone knew what had happened! Once outside the gym, I found Steve's Camaro parked smack-dab right in front of the school. The timing could not have been planned better, because the second wave of buses were just about to pull out of the school's front driveway. "Perfect!" I thought. "I'll just blend right in with the traffic and pull the car into the north side parking lot! I'll have his keys back in his pocket before he even realizes they were gone!"

When I started the car I knew that something was very different. The engine was louder and had a serious "rumble" to it. Certainly more so than his mother's station wagon! When I put the car in gear, it felt like it wanted to jump off the curb! "WHOA! This thing's got some serious balls! I better just ride the brake and idle my way out of the parking lot."

As I pulled up to the stop sign at the end of the driveway that let out onto South Woods Road, I waited as long as I possibly could and then gave it some gas when the way seemed clear. I moved my right foot from the brake to the accelerator. I swear I could hear that annoying commercial for Raceway Park in Englishtowne, New Jersey: "AAAAAhahahahaa, Raceway Park! SUNDAY, SUNDAY, SUNDAY! This Sunday, top funny cars and jet-fueled dragsters," except in my mind I now added, "and a special appearence by stunt driver, Billy Brett."

As I pressed down on the gas pedal ever so slightly, the car rocketed from the stop line, leaving behind any semblance of control I had. The car fishtailed right, then left, finally coming to rest around the base of a very large tree directly across the street from the front doors of the school!

Too scared to move and really not too sure as to what just happened, I sat there with a death-grip on the steering wheel. Several people came running over to check on me. Except for two cuts and bruised knees, I was unhurt. "Too bad," I thought, "I am now a dead man!"

Mr. Greenspan, the Dean of Syosset High school, came into the parking lot to see what had happened. Now outside the car, I was subject to the taunts of all the students passing in the school buses. "Hahahaha, nice going Mario Andretti!"

Mr. Greenspan brought me into the nurse's office to get me checked out so I'd be healthy when I faced the firing squad!

"What happened?" the nurse asked.

"He stole a car!!!" barked Mr. Greenspan, while trying to call my parents. They were out of town, however, and weren't due back until that night. He then called my Aunt Sally and Uncle Bob. Poor Aunt Sally. As with Marg Rielly back in Glen Ellyn, Sally and Bob always seemed to be around when I had my big ideas!

On the way home, Uncle Bob finally broke his silence and said to me, "What do you think? Is this enough now? What's it going to take, Billy?" obviously referring to my life-long behavior issues. I had no response. How could I? I knew he was right. I really felt low now. I never meant to do anything wrong, but even I realized now that I had some kind of an impulse problem. In my heart I knew I wasn't a malicious person, I just never thought through any of these antics before setting out on them. As soon as we arrived at my house, I went right up to my room and lay down on my bed. My mind then went into the now all too familiar soul-search for why the hell I kept doing this to myself and my parents. Not finding an answer in the darkness, I eventually fell asleep.

The next few days were a blur. Because both my parents had to work full time now to make ends meet, (Mom worked at Grumman Aerospace) we did not have the money to pay the $3,000 worth of damage I had caused to Steve's car. Interestingly enough, Steve was not mad at all when he called me the next day to see if I was okay. He said he was pissed at first. Then he realized that a car could always be fixed, but that a 6'4" basketball player couldn't be replaced! Looking back now, I realize what an incredibly compassionate outlook Steve had on life, which had a lasting impression on me.

I still had to find a way to pay for the damage I had caused. Because of our family's financial problems, the pastor of St. Edward's, Fr. John P. Martin stepped in to help. Fr. Martin was born and raised in New York and always had a very street-wise sense about him. With piercing blue eyes and a grin that told you, "Don't even think of lying to me! There isn't a thought in your head that I didn't think of first," he could intimidate me with a simple look. He was however, one of the most caring, compassionate people I've ever known. When I went with my father to meet with Fr. Martin, he said, "I don't care about the money. Money is just money. I keep it around for just such emergencies. I'm just not going to let you get away with what you did, is all! You're going to start working off your debt here at the rectory and around the church grounds. I don't care how, when, or if you pay me. I just want you to start taking responsibility for yourself."

True to his word, for the next two and a half years that I worked at St. Edward's, Fr. Martin never said another word about giving me the money. Just one more in a long line of good souls who would bail me out of trouble! He wouldn't be the last. Fortunately it would be a very long time before I put anyone in that predicament again.

The only activities I was allowed to participate in were eating, sleeping, going to school, working at St. Edwards, and playing basketball. Through all of the craziness, I was still permitted to try out for the varsity basketball team. I had no idea at the time how big a deal that was: I was only a sophomore, and I was the only one asked to try out! What did I know? I was just a stupid kid. For whatever reasons, I made the varsity! I never put any thought into it, I just played. It was the one time in my day where I didn't have to think. It felt more like reflex, really. The season went by with few victories. The only memorable game was the night we played St. Dominick.

St. Dom's always had a strong basketball program, and that year was no exception. One of their major assets was a 6'7" behemoth named Tim Kempton. He was their star center and was averaging fifty points a game that year! He was being heavily recruited by a lot of the big schools, one of which had sent their head coach to watch our game that night. Did I mention the school happen to be Notre Dame, and the coach's name was Digger Phelps? Yeah, no pressure! Now, I only stand 6'4" and played forward. We did have a 6'7" center ourselves, but he was assigned to cover St. Dom's other threat, a 6'6," 240 pound power-forward with quick feet and a dangerous jump shot. So guess who I had to cover? Yeah, my thoughts exactly!

We started warming up in the auxiliary gym and getting psyched up. We all figured we were the underdogs with nothing to lose. As we were doing our practice lay up shots, I did something I had never done before. As I approached the hoop, I felt so good I jumped higher than ever. "Hey, why not?" I thought to myself. With that, I slammed the ball through the hoop with both hands—executing a textbook two-handed tomahawk slam dunk! This just added to the already pumped-up feeling we all had! Our center then also started dunking the ball, and everyone was feeling invincible.

At this point reality caught up with us. My friend, Billy Foster, went up for a lay up and grabbed the hoop. Trying to correct his decent, however, he fell awkwardly to the floor, breaking his wrist in the process. Obviously, this changed our focus. Billy was one of our best players and had a very dangerous jump-shot himself. We now had to play without him, not that it really mattered. The outcome was predictable. St. Dom crushed us by sixty points. Since I wasn't worried about the outcome, I just went out there and played. Now, I don't know if it was my defensive skills or just the added pressure of playing in front of the head coach of Notre Dame, but that big center only scored fifteen points that night.

My basketball career, however, just went south from there.

As Christmas approached, I had a "wonderful" experience that I had never had before. The season began the usual way on Thanksgiving night with Rob and me putting on the Christmas records. Like most families, as soon as you heard Johnny Mathis, Andy Williams, Nat King Cole, and The Ray Coniff singers, it was officially Christmas!

One night, while I was flipping channels, I caught the beginning of what was obviously a black and white Christmas movie. Normally, I don't watch black and white films, but for some reason I kept watching this one. The opening credits featured various Christmas cards with winter scenery on them. Having tuned in well into the credits, I did not recognize any of the names. "Directed by Frank Capra. Who's he?" I wondered.

As difficult as this is to believe, I had never seen *It's a Wonderful Life* before. The film stars James Stewart as George Bailey, a man whose imminent suicide on Christmas Eve brings about the intervention of his guardian angel, Clarence Odbody (Henry Travers). Clarence shows George all the lives he has touched and the contributions he has made to his community. Until now, I thought the only Christmas shows that mattered were *The Grinch*, *Rudolph*, *Charlie Brown*, you know, the usual. Well, man, did that ever change! I could not believe how great a movie this was, and still is! I also had no idea how profoundly the movie would affect my life! I especially remember the line, "It's strange, isn't it, how one man's life can touch so many others. When he's gone, it leaves an awful hole, doesn't it? You see George, you really did have a wonderful life!"

Needless to say, it was forever secured in my Christmas vault!

The year went on without further incidents, and the summer was devoted to working out, playing basketball, and finally taking driver's education! "Yeah baby! I'm finally going to be able to drive a car! Legally!!!" Now, despite my previous lack of talent behind the wheel, I was able to complete and pass the drivers' course with flying colors. By the time school restarted in September, I was licensed and ready to conquer the roads of Long Island!

Around the same time, a lot of my friends were starting to experiment with alcohol. Although they mostly drank the cheapest beer they could find, they sometimes stole various bottles of hard liquor from their parents' homes. Perhaps it was because of my early exposure to it and the fact that it was always accessible to me, but I never had any interest in it. That was a perfect arrangement for my friends since that always made me the designated driver.

Not that any of us even had a car yet anyway! The only thing I had limited access to was the old Malibu. (You remember that one, right?) Of the eight cylinders it had when it left the assembly line in Detroit, only two now possibly worked! But as my friends started to drive, some of their parents bought them cars! My friends could party all they wanted, and since I was always the sober one I did all the driving from start to end.

My intentions, however, were not all that noble. You see, while most of my friends would be inside somebody's basement getting wrecked, I'd be taking whatever car I happened to be piloting that night through it's paces.

My favorite neighborhood to do this was in Woodbury. Woodbury is located just east of Syosset and in reality isn't even a town. It started out as a subdivision of high-end houses on the eastern portion of Syosset near the high school. When the subdivision spawned several more subdivisions, some developer with a bagful of money was able to convince someone to give them a zip code of their very own. I digress. This particular neighborhood had winding streets and lots of hills. "Perfect for a test drive!" I thought.

My friend, Jon, had decided to stay in the car with me one night to see how this particular car fared with my skills! The model to be tested that night was a 1982 Ford Escort, leased for a friend by his father. As my road testing would show, this vehicle was a sound investment.

I started out with some basic J-turns and emergency brake tests at a mild speed of sixty miles per hour, both of which this model passed with flying colors. It wasn't until the final tests that the car showed its true metal! I came down one of the hills at a speed I don't care to share with you as I'm not sure if any applicable statute of limitation on liability has elapsed yet. Anyhow, as I came to the bottom of a hill, I hit an upward angle rise in the pavement giving us "lift." Airborne wouldn't be an accurate description of what that car did. No, I think "hang-time" would be a better analysis. When we hit ground, the car immediately responded to my input, and I was able to maintain control throughout. Just to ensure my research was accurate, I repeated this maneuver several more times, and each time the car responded perfectly! Like I said, a very sound investment. I should have worked at *Road and Track Magazine*!

As the year went on, I lost interest in stunt driving. I became distracted by something else. Well, more like someone else. Since junior high, I had all but given up on ever hoping to find another girlfriend. Then I met Angela.

She was a year younger and had a smile that lit up a room. We had been introduced by mutual friends, but as it turned out, our parents had known each other for years through St. Edward's. I'll never forget my father telling me one night, "Now don't do anything to embarrass us, Billy." As he just gave me kind of a "you know what I mean?" look. I guess this was finally our talk about the birds and the bees. Good talk, Dad!

As it turned out, they had nothing to worry about. Although I really felt strongly about Angela, as with Michele we were just too different. Not only did Angela handle her school assignments, but she had a steady job as well. She was very savvy with money and could not understand why I was not. Obviously, she didn't hang around too long. How could I blame her? That old familiar feeling was back. Rejection. "Well, this certainly sucks!" I thought.

This situation didn't help my focus with basketball, either. The more I practiced and worked hard on my game, the worse I became at it! The "worry factor" took over whenever I did anything that I was hoping to do well! So I was beginning to lose interest in basketball as well. I remember how upset my father became when I told him I wanted to quit the basketball team. Fighting back tears, he asked me to keep my chin up, saying that things would eventually get better. At that moment, I began to realize how much I worried my parents. I didn't mean to. I couldn't help how I felt. I was just growing tired of failing all the time—especially now, at the things that interested me! I just didn't want to fail any longer.

With the season almost over, I stayed on the basketball team and drudged through the next few months of school with the help of my friends. Never to stay down too long, I was way too interested in having fun with them than in worrying about anything else!

Jon and I were out and about one day when we went into Selmer's Petland in Huntington looking to buy a puppy for a friend's birthday. Well, as fate would have it, I ended up bonding with a little bundle of energy that was a six week-old female German Shepherd/Mastif mix. Jon wouldn't let me leave the store without the dog, since she had made such an impression on us! So, I called my father and gave him this sob story that if we didn't take this dog the store was going to send her to the shelter and have her put to sleep. Of course, my dad didn't believe this bullshit, but he relented anyway. He immediately fell in love with her as well, just as soon as I brought her into the house. She then christened the place by taking a huge dump right in the front hallway! Funny how you forget what work owning a dog is until you bring them into your house! We kept her anyway.

As junior year was drawing to a close, we were all excited because this was the beginning of the end of high school for all of us! Everyone was in the final preparation for the SAT's (Scholastic Aptitude Test). I kept thinking why I should even bother taking that test since I'd be lucky to even get out of high school, let alone go to college! I remember the Saturday morning we took the SAT's. I walked into the classroom and shortly after sitting down, one of my classmates whispers, "You get fifty extra points just for signing your name!" "Fifty points, huh?" I thought to myself. "Oh well, fifty points is fifty points!" I said, as I filled out the scan tron sheet. I made it perhaps a quarter of the way into the test when I totally lost interest. "I have no idea what they're talking about here!" I thought. "What the hell do they mean by this question?" I started to aimlessly fill in the dots on the sheet, not even bothering to look at the questions. I tried to make them appear as random as I could, not knowing at the time that no other "human" eyes would ever really be looking at this sheet. I didn't care. All I knew was I just wanted to get out of that place! Still nowhere near the honor role, I was managing to scramble to the next level. That, after all, was all I that could hope for with my scholastic aptitude!

My friends were all convinced that I should become an actor. With all of my character impersonations and slap-stick routines, they thought it was all but guaranteed. Who was I to argue? Typically, I never once auditioned for a single school play or show of any kind! I always figured that I'd have plenty of time for that stuff later. Since I felt in my heart that I would be a movie star, I figured why bother with school subjects that I'd never have to use anyway.

DURING THAT SUMMER, I WAS FULLY ENTRENCHED IN BASKETBALL TRAINING TO please my father. My entire basketball team travelled to Boston University to attend a training camp put on by Boston University's head coach, Rick Patino. We had a freaking blast! We doubled up in the dormitory that overlooked the football field. While our camp was going on, so was a football camp. I roomed with my buddy, Rob, who shared my knack for getting into trouble.

On one fine evening the rest of the team opted to break curfew and leave campus to go to a pizza place across Commonwealth Avenue. Rob and I decided not to go. When they returned, they were nice enough to bring us back a ton of pizza. After Rob and I had eaten our fill, we decided to ditch the evidence on the football players coming up to the building after a long hot day of practice. Careful to keep our lights off and our heads down so no one would know where the pizza snipers had fired from, we bombarded the footballers with two large pizzas from twelve stories up! "The perfect crime!" or so we thought.

The next day during breakfast in the cafeteria there were wild rumors about people who had left the campus grounds looking for hookers and one crazy story of a madman who had been throwing food from the roof! "What kind of a place is this?" Rob and I said, faking our shock!

Coach Patino called everyone at the camp into the main gym after breakfast. With several hundred of us assembled in the gym, he began telling us a motivational story of how when he was young he had done something wrong and had lied about it. When his conscience got the better of him he had eventually come clean and had earned the respect of his father, or coach, or something like that.

Then he said, "I want to know who left campus last night and crossed Commonwealth Avenue."

I guess our teammates were moved by the coach's story, because they all stood right up.

"Okay guys, I respect your honesty. You'll be doing thirty minutes of laps every morning for the rest of the week. Thanks for stepping up. Okay, now I want to know who threw the pizza out the window."

Rob and I never even twitched or looked at each other. "Who is this guy kidding?" I thought! "Oh yeah, we'll just stand right up and volunteer to induce vomiting every morning before dawn! No thanks." After a few awkward minutes of silence, and no shortage of dirty looks from our teammates, Coach Patino said, "Okay, you have to live with this on your conscience," and dismissed the assembly.

Rob and I both agreed that we could live reasonably well with such a huge weight to bear on our consciences. We did, however, have the wherewithal to lock our room door the next few nights, since our team would pound on it each morning in an attempt at payback. We did, after all deserve it.

The rest of the summer went by pretty fast. I attended another basketball camp out in Pittsburgh, but felt that I was getting worse at this game, not better. Oh well, I wasn't worried too much about it at the time. It was senior year and I was going to finally try out for the football team. I had always wanted to but had always been told that basketball should be the main focus as it held the most potential for me. Boy were they wrong! I loved football! I still had better than average foot speed, and for a big guy that made me either a tight end or defensive end. Well, I couldn't pay attention long enough to learn a play book so tight end was out. That left defensive end! My job was simple: crush the guy with the ball. "I can do that! I used to do it all the time back at St. Pet's in Glen Ellyn. Remember mawl ball?" I ended up doing fairly well for my first and only season playing the game! "Man, if I had only started out sooner in life! Who knows where I could've gone with this game?" I thought to myself. I didn't worry too long about that. I was too busy worrying about girls.

During the summer, Glen and I started spending a lot of time hanging out with two girls we'd known more or less since junior high. I'll call them Denise and Laura.

Glen had started seeing Laura, while I had a huge crush on Denise. After Denise displayed no real interest in me, I got bored and started looking elsewhere. A couple of my friends had told me that this girl Jennifer, not her real name, had a huge crush on me! "On me?" I asked. How could this girl be interested in me? She was, in a word, Hot! I eventually overcame my awkwardness and asked her out. Although we had very little in common, I being a wise-ass daredevil and she a very quiet, demure, nice Jewish girl, we hit it off pretty well. And besides, she wanted me! The latter being an obvious draw for me since I was a virgin. I know, pretty pathetic. Eighteen year old, big man on campus and I've never been to the "big game"! What can I say? By now my self esteem was so low, I would never have thought sex would be possible! Jennifer, sweetheart that she is, never let me worry about that.

They say you never forget your first time. I'm no exception. We had my house to ourselves. This was probably the only time in the eight years I lived in that house that the front door was locked! The anticipation was excruciating! As I moved in close to her, I could feel the earth begin to tremble at my approach! All the mountains and all the oceans of the world began to rise up! The Aurora Borealis shined brightly in the northern sky! The wind seemed to sing my very name! "Oh my God! So this is what it's like!" I thought to myself as my entire body flexed, every fiber of my being embraced this moment... only to be interrupted by Jennifer's voice, "Is it in yet?"

Oh well, practice makes perfect. Jennifer and I went out for a while, but that too didn't last for long.

While all this was happening, my friend, Alex, experienced a terrible loss. He had immigrated to the U.S. with his parents from what was then Yugoslavia. He was very young when they arrived, and a few years afterwards his parents divorced. His father remarried and moved away, losing touch with Alex. His mother also remarried and had a son, giving Alex a little brother. Alex's problem was that his step-father couldn't stand him and made no secret of it—so much so that he would often threaten to throw him out of the house when he turned eighteen. This torment went on over the years until the unthinkable happened. Alex's mother was diagnosed with terminal cancer. After a long hard-fought battle, she succumbed to the illness and passed away.

Alex was obviously devastated. Even worse, when the funeral was over his step-father made good on his threats and threw Alex out of the house! I'll never forget the day that Alex came to my house screaming with rage and sobbing uncontrollably at the same time! "How could he do this? That heartless son-of-a-bitch just threw me out!"

After catching his breath, my parents reminded Alex that they had said that should he ever need to he could come live with us. Glenn's parents had also said the same. So, Alex collected what little his scumbag step-father would let him take and lived with us for the first half of his senior year and with Glenn's family for the latter half. Things began to settle down some for Alex now that he was part of the family, and he and I shared my room.

As senior year got into full swing I felt unsure about the future. The football season had been a great experience, but by the time the basketball season started I felt all washed up. Whatever natural ability and talent I may have displayed in the earlier years of high school were more or less gone now. I became so obsessed with the thoughts of "Don't miss, don't miss!" that more often than not I'd miss the easy shots! Now I dreaded Friday nights! The thought of playing in front of the entire school and having everyone cheering for my friends and not for me was more than I could bear. "I should be an all-star by now!" I thought to myself. "I'm the one who made varsity when I was a sophomore, not them!" But my logical side knew the reason for all these feelings. There was no arguing the facts. They were playing better than I!

I vividly remember the moment when I knew I had had enough. During one of the games I had missed one too many of those easy shots and had become enraged with frustration. I was already in foul trouble when the referee called me for a three second violation. I exploded. "You've got to be kidding!!!" I screamed. All that outburst did was earn me a technical foul. When my coach called a time out, I stormed off the court. "God damn it!" I screamed, and kicked my chair halfway across the gym.

Normally an extremely forgiving man with always a smile on his face, coach Ron Livosi barked at me, "Pick up that chair and sit down!!!" Coach Livosi had only been with the varsity coach for three years, during which time he witnessed my deteriorating skills and attitude. For him, this outburst was enough, and he took me out of the game. Later we had a heart to heart. Having known me so long, Coach Livosi knew all about my other issues and had always offered to help whenever he could. I told him this was one thing not even he could help me with. As understanding as ever, he and I agreed that I should not be on the starting line up for the remainder of the season.

Once the season ended, we had the usual awards ceremony at the school. I'll never forget how coach Livosi handed out everyone's award saying, "I wish you luck with your college basketball career." When he came to me, he said, "We wish him well in his future endeavors."

"Well, that's it," I thought. "Even the coach knows it and isn't pretending anymore." The dream ended there. I would never play basketball again.

The year dragged on with the only bright spots being the time on the weekends that I spent with my friends. I had also now developed a liking for beer. Although it didn't pose any additional problems for me, this was still not a positive development.

I got a new part-time job at the Syosset House Movie theatre, one of the last single-screen, massive theatres on Long Island. As jobs went, it was pretty cool. We got to see all the movies for free, but the highlight for me was when Warner Brothers released the third film of a certain super-hero franchise.

Like any summer block buster, the pre-release hype for *Superman III* started early. The theater manager was trying to come up with a plan for the opening night. The ticket buyers would be on one side of the building, while the ticket holders would be on the other. The manager wanted to draw as many people to the theater as she could and needed a gimmick. Since the theater sat on a high point of Jericho Turnpike, one of the main roads that runs east and west along the northern portion of Long Island, its huge marquee could be seen for a mile.

"I've got an idea," I said, "Why don't we have someone rent a Superman costume and stand up on the marquee while people are standing on line?"

"Now where would we find someone who'd be willing to do that?" She asked, as if she did not know who would do it.

Come opening night this "Man of Steel" was waving to all the people in line, as well as to the passing cars that were jamming up Jericho Turnpike. I'll never forget the look on the poor Nassau County cop who was tasked with directing traffic into and out of the parking lot that night! He just looked up at me and shook his head. I didn't care. I was having a blast! I left no detail out on my costume. My sister Eileen, who was now a successful hair dresser in Syosset, had styled my hair with the trade mark "spit curl." When I took a break, I'd put on my usual navy blue jacket-and-tie usher uniform. Only that night I added a pair of black rimmed eye glasses to complete the ensemble. My friends all came and, knowing my previous affection for Superman, thought that this was the "perfect role" for me! Standing 6'4" with dark hair and blue eyes didn't hurt either! For that little kid who dove out that bedroom window back in Glen Ellyn all those years ago, this was a dream come true! Seeing the faces of all those little kids as their parents drove by the theatre that night was a sight I'll never forget! I could hear some of them in the line below. "Look Mommy! Up in the sky! Up on that building! It's a bird! It's a plane..." Nope. It's just a kid like them! Definitely a good moment!

With my senior year now coming to a close, I only had two concerns: graduating, and possibly going to the prom. The first problem was to find out if I had earned enough credits to join all my friends on graduation day. If I did not have enough credits, I'd be going to summer school, and only upon successful completion of that would I be given a diploma. This dilemma brought me to the main office of the school one morning in late June. I stood there, motionless, as the principal, Dr. Walter Yannett, and his assistant, Mr. Ron Barry, physically pulled all my high school records to do an actual count of my credits. Dr. Yannett wasn't a bad guy. He was a typical principal, all business. If you screwed up, he'd nail you. Mr. Barry on the other hand was everybody's pal! He'd go out of his way to make sure everyone was doing okay, and on this particular day he made no secret of the fact that he was as hopeful as I was! When Dr. Yannett finished counting, he looked up at me with a sly grin and simply said, "And without a single credit to spare!" Mr. Barry then smiled wide, and shook my hand without saying another word.

"Whew!" At least that's one thing my parents will not have to worry about anymore!" I said, as I walked out of the office and into the student lobby. Things weren't so grim after all.

The only thing I had left to conquer was to ask Denise to the prom. Although she had never shown any real interest in me, and I had found some distraction during the school year with other girls, I still had a thing for her. If I was going to ask anyone to the prom it was going to be Denise. When I finally worked up the guts to ask her she said, "No. But, why don't you ask Laura? No one's asked her yet, and I know she wants to go badly!"

Glenn had stopped seeing Laura, but she and I stayed pretty good friends. Although I thought the world of her, she was the last person I would've thought to ask to the prom. Besides, I really wasn't interested in going anyway. I had asked Denise just to see if I could get her to say yes. In the days that followed, I spoke to Laura and could hear the disappointment in her voice that no one had asked her to the prom. I was genuinely surprised at this since she was a very pretty girl with a fantastic personality! So I told her, "Hey, if nobody else asks you and you still want to go to the prom, I'll take you!" Laura then said, "No, you don't want to go," knowing full well that Denise was the only one I was interested in asking. So I said, "What, you don't want to go with me?"

"No, no! What, are you kidding? I'd go with you in a second!" She shot back.

"Fine. It's settled then." I said. As it turned out, I'd regret this decision, too.

Prom night arrived and I went halves with my friend Ricky on a limo for the night. Ricky wore a classic black tuxedo, while I, wanting to be different from the crowd, went for the "James Bond" look with white dinner jacket and black tie. When we went to pick up the girls, I was awe-struck! Laura was a vision. Now, I always knew she was pretty, but I always saw her as a pal, or just one of the guys. I could talk to her about anything, and usually did! Her smile was always so contagious it could easily pick people up. Now, tonight, Holy shit! She absolutely glowed! I thought to myself, "How did I not notice her before?"

The night began as planned. A limo ride to the Huntington Town House where the dance was held, then back into the limo for the hour long ride out to the Hampton's, and then to a party on the beach at Summer's Beach Bar. As soon as we arrived at the dance, Laura, being the social butterfly that she was, began hopping from table to table talking with everyone. That was the last I saw of her that night! I honestly don't know what I had expected from this prom thing, but I know I didn't care for this treatment at all! My other friends were also starting to get liquored up, but I didn't touch a drop because I didn't feel like it. I was just so pissed off at Laura for blowing me off.

As the night finally gave way to dawn, we all piled into the limo for the ride home. Almost immediately everyone passed out. Everyone but me. I was once again alone with my thoughts of self-doubt. Even though I was not at fault with Laura, the thought "What the hell is wrong with me?" kept echoing in my mind as I looked at Laura sleeping across from me. I couldn't help rewriting the script of the evening to play more favorably for me.

After the prom the plan was for everyone to go home, get showered and changed, and then meet up for breakfast at the diner. Then after breakfast we were to drive out to the Hampton's and stay at a house my sister had rented for the summer. "Yeah right!" I thought. Instead, when I got home I told my family to tell anyone who called for me that I was feeling sick and couldn't go out.

In the following days, Laura apologized about the prom, and I accepted her genuine sense of confusion about the evening. This made the bond between us grow even stronger.

For the rest of the summer we went from one party to another. Everyone knew where they were going to college and the future looked bright. Hell, even I was going to Nassau Community College in September! "Couldn't hurt to try, I guess."

The movie star in me was still there, but the knowledge, experience, and the focus to start working on that goal were not! "What else was new?"

I LEARNED ALMOST IMMEDIATELY DURING MY FIRST SEMESTER AT NASSAU COMmunity College that it would be another waste of time. Only now it was costing my parents money. They were just able to make ends meet. So, after stumbling through the first semester, I dropped out and started working.

I went from job to job working in a supermarket deli, delivering beer, etc. but nothing kept my interest for very long. This really worried my parents since they knew that a bad judgment call might get me into serious trouble. A friend having trouble finding his way had one such bad call that landed him in the Nassau County Jail. Bobby, not his real name, was locked up for three weeks for various larcenies. I'll never forget when I went to visit him one day. "This is not a pleasant place to be," I thought, as I looked at the various thugs and hardened criminals who were awaiting trial or transfers to the other various correctional facilities. And here was Bobby, stuck right in the middle of this nightmare! When I finally saw him he was surprisingly upbeat! His time was going by rapidly, and everyone was leaving him alone. The worst moment had been when one of the other inmates wouldn't shut up one night, and the guards took away the television the following night. Other than that, he made it through no worse for the experience.

When my parents heard that Bobby had been arrested and sent to jail they both cried. First for Bobby, since they always loved him as one of my friends, but also because they were worried that a similar fate might easily be mine. They didn't know it, but after that visit with Bobby I was never going to let that happen to me... EVER!

Well, as fate would have it, I would be wrong on that point.

On one fine day, a bunch of my friends and I decided to take a ride out to the eastern part of Long Island. Among them were Glenn, Ricky, his girlfriend Tara, Pete, and Laura. Pete and Laura were now dating, but she and I were still the best of friends. We took her car because it was a big old Chevy sedan that could seat all of us. I did the driving, since Pete and Glenn decided to do some morning beer drinking on the drive out. Okay, no big deal, I thought. That is, until Pete started taking the labels off the beer bottles and sticking them to the inside of the front windshield. Between them they had placed fourteen friggin' labels on the windshield! If that weren't enough, as we were driving through the town of The Hampton Bays, Pete leaned out the front passenger window and began screaming at some lady, "WWWOOOOOOOOOOOOOOOO!!!" A Hampton Bays Police cruiser pulled out behind us!

"Oh great job, Pete!" I said, just as the cruiser's emergency lights came on. After I pulled over, the two officers walked up and asked the usual, "Where are you going, what are you doing, why is your friend hanging out that window screaming at people?" As the officers took my license and Laura's registration and walked back to their cruiser, I just shot Pete and Glenn a dirty look. When the officers returned they ordered me from the car. Complying, they informed me that my license had been suspended for a previous unpaid ticket. The officers were as nice as could be, but they told me that they had to take me in because it was not a summons-releasable offense. Now, all of this was taking place out of earshot of my friends, so they had no idea what was going on. They really got worried when they saw me get handcuffed and put in the back of the cruiser!

Needless to say, once I paid the fine and was released I didn't speak to Pete and Glenn for a month. I needed that time to cool off, or I would have been arrested for something far worse!

As the year moved on my grandmother, "Mom" Brett, became ill and soon passed away. Mom had moved into a small apartment in Valley Stream to be closer to my aunts after the death of my grandfather. My father took Rob and me to visit her on weekends, but as we got older the trips with Dad became few and far between. In hindsight, it's something I regret.

I never knew my maternal grandmother, so Mom was the only grandmother I had. Being among her twenty-three grandchildren and two great-grandchildren, I was lucky to get thirty seconds with her throughout my lifetime! Still, Mom always remembered each and every one of us and never forgot a birthday! Not bad for anyone, let alone a ninety year old Irish immigrant!

I learned that when Pop passed away Mom was heart-broken. After spending so much of her life with him, she must have been close to him in ways that I could only imagine.

While in the hospital, the whole family visited her as much as possible. As with Pop, she had her good days. But as with Pop, they weren't many. The day Mom passed away my mother was in the room with her. She was able to hold her hand, and as my mother told us later, she seemed very much at peace. I know in my heart that Pop was waiting right there for her to finally mend her broken heart and take her home.

7 I'm Going Hollywood

Not too long after Bobby's release from jail, I decided to put real effort into pursuing an acting career, and I set a goal of moving to Los Angeles, California, by January 1986, come hell or high water. I still had no idea how to actually go about getting acting work out there, but that didn't matter at the time. Working steadily at a food service company, I saved every penny I earned for the big move! Tony, a high school friend, was attending the University of Southern California and had graciously offered to let me crash at his place whenever I was ready.

Meanwhile, Laura and I were getting closer emotionally—more than I might have anticipated. We even had our own song, "That's What Friends Are For," by Stevie Wonder, Dionne Warwick, Gladys Knight, and Elton John! In various phone calls and greeting cards that she would send me, she would end them with the words, "I love you!" This, coupled with the amount of time we were spending together, left me thinking and feeling that something very different than friendship was in the making. I brushed this aside, however, since Laura was still in a committed relationship with Pete, one of my closest friends! That friendship was definitely something I could never betray!

One night while hanging out in Pete's room with a bunch of his college teammates drinking beer, I went to get myself a fresh beer. While walking back to his room, I ran into Laura, who was feeling pretty good having polished off several Bartles & James wine coolers. She grabbed me and said, "Bill Brett, I love you!" laying one on me! Granted, it wasn't a deep, passionate kiss, but by no means was it a simple friendly peck on the cheek!

Okay, I was now really confused! Was it me, or did my best friend just kiss me on the lips in the apartment of my other best friend whom she happened to be dating? It had to be the wine coolers, I thought. Even though I knew in my heart I would never have her, I felt okay knowing she was with Pete. As corny as that sounds, I knew then that Pete would always take care of her and make her happy. Later that night, after Pete and I walked Laura home, he told me how happy she had been that I had come up to visit. "She talks about you all the time," said Pete. "Well, it's no secret how I feel about her, Pete," I replied, then added, "But I'll tell you, if I can't be with her, I'm glad she's with you." We never spoke another word about Laura, nor did I ever mention the kiss to him. No need to confuse things further.

CHRISTMAS LOOKED VERY BRIGHT THAT YEAR. MY FAMILY, SUPPORTIVE AS always, were behind my decision to move out to Los Angeles. My mother had even asked my Aunt Pat, who now lived in Oregon, to have her daughter, Peggy, who lived in L.A., look out for me. Well, Peggy did one better and offered to let me live with her until I got my feet wet. Man, I was really excited now! All my friends had given me California-themed gifts for Christmas, including the coolest collection of Tom Selleck/Magnum P.I.-type shirts. I guess they figured that L.A. being close to Hawaii everyone there must wear those shirts.

Laura and I were still spending a lot of purely innocent, quality time together. Although I was now in love with her, I kept it to myself.

My friend, Anthony, drove Laura and me to the airport to see me off. He gave me a big hug and wished me luck, fighting back the tears that were now welling up in our eyes. "I'll speak to you soon," I said to him, as Laura, taking my hand, walked me a few steps away. Unlike Anthony, Laura couldn't contain her tears. She hugged me for a few moments before speaking. When she broke our embrace, she handed me a cardboard box, saying, "Don't open this until you're airborne. Promise me!" We hugged again, and this time I looked directly into her eyes without saying a word. I then turned and walked down the hallway to my plane.

I felt emotional as I took my seat on the plane. What was in the box, I wondered, flipping it over to find a "People's Express" luggage label that read in Laura's hand, "I love you." As we climbed to cruising altitude, I opened the box. Laura had the lyrics to our song written in calligraphy and framed. "And then, for the times that we're apart, close your eyes and know these words are coming from my heart... and then if you can remember… keep smiling, keep shining, knowing you can always count on me, for sure, that's what friends are for."

That would have been a perfect bittersweet ending. Right? Too bad it didn't end there.

After what was the longest flight of my life, I arrived in the pre-dawn hours at L.A. International. Even though this was a major city airport, the place was empty. Even Cousin Peggy wasn't there! I was under the impression that she was going to meet me at the airport. As I waited, it became obvious that she was not going to come. So, I did what any kid in a strange airport at 3:30 am would do. I called Peggy.

"Hey Peggy, it's Billy!" I said to the obviously half-asleep voice on the other end of the line. "I just landed in L.A. Weren't you supposed to come and get me?"

"Oh, my god, what time is it?" she muttered.

"Um, just about 3:30," I said.

"Okay, give me a few. It'll take me awhile to get there," she assured me.

"Cool. Thanks again for taking care of me, Peggy!" I said, and we hung up.

I hadn't seen my Cousin Peggy since the summer of 1974 when my parents flew our whole family on vacation to Portland, Oregon. My Aunt Pat and Uncle Frank had moved there from Syosset around the same time we moved to Glen Ellyn. After Peggy finished school, she settled in L.A. An avid water polo player and all-around top athlete, Peggy had a great job with a fitness center that catered to the rich and famous. Perfect, I thought. Maybe I could get a job at Peggy's gym and make some connections.

Peggy arrived at the terminal in her little Mazda. "Oh boy!" I thought. "I hope my stuff fits in that little car!" It did. Returning to her place, Peggy said, "Make yourself at home, I'm going back to bed!" Her roommate had just moved out, so there was a vacant, albeit unfurnished bedroom for me to use. I crashed on the couch instead and woke up as Peggy was getting ready to head out the door for work. "I left my work number if you need to contact me, and there's a list of great restaurants in the kitchen," she said heading out the door.

The familiar feeling of being alone began to creep in again, only this time I was in a strange place thousands of miles away from home! "What was I thinking?" I asked myself, "I don't have the first clue as to what the hell I'm supposed to do next!" "Well, I'm not going to wait around here for the sky to fall into my lap. Let me have a look around this town," I said to myself.

A typical surfing/volley ball community in southern California, Hermosa Beach (literally, beautiful beach) had a huge pier that went out into the ocean. As I wandered around town I found, of all things, a comic bookstore. So, I figured I'd take a look. As if on cue, the first display case I looked into had the original issue of the first Superman/Spider-man team-up!

"I'll take this one, please!" thinking that it was a good omen for my first day alone in California! It turned out to be the only positive step that I took toward my goal in L.A.!

The next few weeks were a blur. I helped Peggy move into a more affordable one bedroom bungalow apartment further inland in Redondo Beach. I knew that I couldn't stay long with her there, however. "I've got to get out of Peggy's hair!" I thought to myself as I laid on the couch one morning. Then the phone rang.

"Billy, it's Peggy. Turn on the TV! The space shuttle just exploded!" she said excitedly.

I immediately turned on the TV. The sight of a shuttle taking off had become so routine that it barely generated any news coverage anymore. On this typical crystal-clear winter morning in Florida, however, the unthinkable had happened. As the Space Shuttle Challenger lifted off, a plume of smoke from the left side booster flamed out and the entire orbiter disappeared in a ball of fire! "God help those people and their families!" I thought.

The image that I still see clearly is the sight of the two boosters as they continued their ascent without the shuttle and main fuel tank. Other than the two boosters, however, I can't remember seeing anything else fall from the sky. Even after dozens of replays on the news that day, I thought how strange that something so huge could just disappear in a cloud of smoke! Years later in different circumstances I would make a similar observation

IN THE FOLLOWING WEEKS I WAS ABLE TO MOVE INTO TONY'S APARTMENT AND again crash on the living room couch. His roommate, Chad, a computer science major from Wisconsin who came from a well to do family was the most laid back individual I have ever met. Perhaps because he smoked weed like it was going out of style. That didn't bother me, however, since I was never into the stuff. I had enough to deal with without adding chemicals to the mix!

Since I did not know how to look for a job or an apartment, I was still not making any progress. While my savings dwindled away, I tried to earn my keep by keeping the apartment clean and running errands

One night while speaking to Laura on the phone and telling her about how I slept until noon on the couch, she dropped a bomb on me.

"Hey, I'm coming out there to stay with you for a week during my spring break!"

As if I didn't have enough troubles! She knows how I feel, Pete knows how I feel, and she's still traveling three thousand miles to visit me?

"Okay, but you know that I'm living on Tony's couch," I said.

"I don't care! I want to see you!" she fired back.

Tony and Chad were totally cool with it, "Hell, yeah! Have her come out and we'll show her around!" Chad said he would stay at his girlfriend's apartment for that week, and Tony was nice enough to offer his own bedroom for Laura to stay in when she arrived.

I was downright scared now. Not because I had not found a job or apartment, but because the girl I was in love with was coming out to California to see me! Since she hadn't mentioned anything about Pete, did this mean that she was making a move? Would she be expecting me to make a move?" I thought to myself, "Oh man, why can't anything important in my life ever go smoothly?"

Tony, who knew Laura and Pete well, agreed that she had something on her mind if not in her heart!

"We'll see," I said.

I did not confide my thoughts to Laura for fear that I might have misread her and that would end up spoiling things between us.

With Laura's arrival, Tony offered to sleep on the couch. Laura said that she preferred to sleep in the living room with me. Now, any normal man would have taken that as a sure sign of a move. My extremely low self-esteem, however, coupled with the fear of being wrong for making a move on my best friend's girlfriend, kept me from being "any normal man."

So, I just waited, and waited, and waited for Laura to spell it out for me. For five days we slept not six inches away from each other and she never said a word!

By the time Laura was to leave, the tension between us was thick in the air. When I drove Laura to the airport for her return flight, the good-bye was nowhere near as tender as the previous one two months before. It seemed more like a failed business venture and the parting of two potential executives.

I felt even more sadness this time, knowing that Laura and I would never be. In my heart and in my mind it was just another in a long line of failures in my life. As I watched her walk up the jet-way and out of sight, I remember thinking, "Well, that's it."

Two weeks later I was out of cash and had nothing left to fall back on. I knew then that it was time for me to go home. Any motivation I may have had was now long gone. I called my parents, and by the beginning of April 1986, I was back home for good.

I had no idea then that this was only the beginning of numerous changes that were about to take place in my life.

$\mathcal{8}$ Separate Ways

On returning home, I went back to doing pretty much the same old thing; staying up late, sleeping all day. Although I now worked with a landscaping company to make some money, I had no direction or real goals. My loving and supportive parents, with problems of their own that were about to surface, were also tired of my lack of motivation and of having no clear aim with being an actor.

My parents always seemed happy with their life together, going away for weekends or out with friends to numerous parties. Both drank, but I never saw either one of them really drunk. My mother was more of a social drinker, and my father would have his usual scotch at the end of the day and then fall asleep in his chair in our family room. Since there was always the constant feeling of love between them and us, I had no idea that their marriage was in serious trouble.

By the summer of '86, the trouble hit critical mass. Even I, not the most perceptive in these matters, had begun to notice the serious strain between them. Any doubt I may have had was put to rest one late afternoon. Rob and I were the only ones still living at home, but Rose, Eileen, and Chris had come by at my parents' request. I knew something bad was about to happen when my visibly upset parents called us all into the living room. They then told us that because of their inability to solve their differences they had decided to separate. My father said that when a relationship got so bad between a husband and wife that neither one even said "good morning" to the other, that it was time to end it. They reassured us that they still loved each other, but that they just could not live together. They expressed that their marriage wasn't a total failure since God had blessed them with the six of us.

Although not really surprised, I think the finality of actually hearing them say the words really hit my sisters hard. We all sat for awhile and talked, and my parents filled us in on the plans for selling the house. My father would move to New Jersey to be closer to his company's main office. My mother was looking at buying a townhouse a little further out on Long Island in Deer Park, only fifteen minutes further east on the Long Island Expressway from Syosset. Rob and I would stay with her until we were ready to move out on our own. Rob would be starting college that fall, and I was... well, I just was.

In August 1986, my parents in record time sold our great big house on Renee Road. The day we moved out was a little sad for me. So many memories. I guess I had always taken it for granted that my parents would grow old together in that house, and that the six of us would come to visit them with our spouses and children.

Never being a real fan of our dog, Casey, my mother tried telling me that dogs were not allowed in the Deer Park condo community. Seeing through her feeble attempt to convince me to get rid of the dog, I replied, "Oh, well, I'll keep her well hidden." That was the end of that.

Compared to the huge house we had just moved from, the condo seemed a little cramped at first, but I learned to adjust and we made things work. With Rob away at school and Mom and I on separate schedules, it was almost like having my own place! My only problem now was getting around. In Syosset I never really needed transportation because there was always a car available since people were always coming and going. Now, however, I needed wheels. As luck would have it, my brother John was getting rid of his old 1983 Mercury Cougar. My father said he'd pay for it, but that I had to get a job to repay him. Ok, I thought, no problem.

I was working occasionally now as a landscaper, but that was seasonal. I also tried furniture delivery for a custom home interior design place, but all that did was convince me that there really was no future for me. Although the owner of the company was an extremely nice guy, I never saw eye to eye with his sister, a typical north-shore, Long Island housewife with a very cross and dissatisfied attitude. It didn't take long for me to drift away from there as well. Things did not look good for me.

My father got me a job working in the warehouse of one of the companies with which he did a lot of business on Long Island. Although it was physical work, which I usually enjoyed, it was more often than not busy-work sweeping the floors—if I had nothing else to do, or sorting through boxes upon boxes of electrical fittings to ensure proper markings on shipping labels. I was convinced that my life was a waste.

"Is this all there is?" I continually asked myself.

I didn't want to disappoint my father again, especially since he had gotten me the job, but it didn't take long for me to start sabotaging myself by showing up later and later each day, some days not even appearing. I was at such a low point that I didn't think or fear the consequences of my actions. Finally, one day when I arrived an hour late for work, the warehouse foreman pulled me aside and said, "You're a nice guy Billy, but you're completely unreliable! You're fired."

It began to sink in. Outside of TV and stories I had heard from other people, I had never actually heard those words, "You're fired," especially directed at me! What am I going to tell my father?

When I got home I decided to call him and just tell him. He was less than enthused. After hanging up, I began what would become a life-long habit of soul-searching. What is so wrong with me? I come from a very loving family. My siblings are all very successful in their chosen careers. Why can't I find my place? In my heart I knew I could do more, but for reasons unknown to me at the time, I just could not get it together.

My physical health wasn't improving either. Although I was still an avid weight lifter, I would eat all the wrong foods and drink copious amounts of beer. My body fat sky rocketed! As fate would have it, while hanging out with friends at one of our favorite watering holes, Suzanne Tenore made me fill out an employment application for a job as a bouncer. I was now around 250 lbs and in need of a job. She made the prospect sound perfect. I could get paid and hang out with my friends! I never thought that getting fired from a job I hated would turn out to be a blessing in disguise!

THINGS BEGAN LOOKING UP FOR ME AS A BOUNCER. I STARTED MAKING MORE friends and meeting tons of girls. It's really amazing how the way you carry yourself can change the way people perceive you! While walking through the crowd in the main bar area one night, I actually had a girl grab my ass! Can you believe that? I mean, by now it should be pretty clear that I'm no "Don Juan," so this was pretty shocking for me. Especially when I turned around to see that the culprit was one of the most beautiful girls I had ever seen in my life! She was 5'10" with blue eyes, brown hair and flawless skin. She was in fact a model!

"Okay, who put you up to this?" was all I could think to ask, since I was convinced there was no way this vision would possibly be interested in me!

"Nobody put me up to it," she said simply, staring into my eyes. Then taking my hand in a genuine albeit gentle handshake, she said, "I'm Faith."

"I'm Billy," I replied as calmly as my screaming insecure ego would allow! We then got to know each other over the next couple of hours just talking about everything and nothing. Man, I hoped no fights or problems were happening that night—or an atom bomb being set off—because I wouldn't have noticed!

MICHAEL NIRACHS, ONE OF THE MOST DYNAMIC, ENERGETIC, GENUINE PEOPLE I have ever known, sold trees every Christmas and made good money at it. So when Christmas approached and he asked me to sell Christmas trees with him to make some extra money it was a no-brainer! Since my bar job was only hourly work, my boss had no problem with me taking a few weeks off. Despite the really long hours and no time off, selling Christmas trees was easy for me. I was making very good money—in fact more money than I had ever made before in my life—but I was becoming more distant, and felt oddly removed from the season I always enjoyed. By the time Christmas Eve arrived I was burned out.

I was supposed to spend Christmas at my sister Rose's house over in New Jersey. My parents and all of my brothers and sisters and their extended families would be there. I told them, however, that due to the tree lot schedule I would not be able to get there until well past ten o'clock at night on Christmas Eve. By the time I finally left the tree lot in Hicksville, it was already ten o'clock and the weather was rainy and miserably cold. I was not happy.

I caught the Long Island Rail Road from the Hicksville station and rode the thirty minutes into New York Penn Station where I switched trains to the New Jersey Transit southbound. It was well after 11:30 P.M. when I arrived at the New Brunswick stop in New Jersey, and the weather hadn't improved at all. As I waited for my family to pick me up, I huddled under a store front for cover from the rain. I couldn't help thinking of myself and that annoying, depressing, "Auld Lang Syne" song sung by Dan Fogleberg every New Year's Eve.

My family finally picked me up, and I made the best of it. I was definitely not in the "Yule Tide" mood, and I swore that I'd never let that happen again. As such, I tried to keep everything in better perspective the next two Christmas seasons that I worked with Michael. Michael later went into the stock market. After suffering the setback of the market crashing his first week on the job, he persisted and went on to become a millionaire!

LIFE CONTINUED TO GO FAIRLY WELL FOR ME WHILE I WAS WORKING AT THE bar, but I hadn't made any steps toward independence. I was still living at home and spending my income as fast as I made it. Since I thought I wanted to be an actor, I even started taking acting classes in New York City at HB Studios. With no clue as to how to actually get an acting job, I thought at least I could work on my craft.

I had a regular routine. I'd work four or five nights a week at the bar and on Saturday mornings I'd hop the train into New York City for classes at HB. Things were okay, until one night when I was closing up the bar early on a quiet week night. We were going to have a beer at another local pub to celebrate the birthday of one of the bartenders. I had always considered myself pretty smart about "knowing when to say when." I'm sure everyone says that at some point in their lives. This night was no different. After the celebration and reaching what I thought was my limit, I decided to call it a night and head home. I remember Michael asking me if I was okay to drive, to which I answered "Oh yeah!" I had no clue.

I jumped in my car and I had driven only a couple of miles when I noticed the police car behind me. The next thing I knew he threw on his emergency lights and pulled me over. Needless to say, I was scared shitless! The officer was very polite and asked the customary question, "Do you know why I stopped you?" "No sir, I don't ," I answered as respectfully as I could. He said that I had failed to signal when I changed lanes and that I had been driving beyond the speed limit. When he asked where I had been last I said that I had been at a bar with some friends celebrating a birthday. He asked me to take some sobriety tests, and I complied. I also agreed to a breath test, which to my dismay showed me over the legal limit.

I was placed under arrest and taken to the local precinct for processing. This was a life changing experience for me. While waiting to be processed in the precinct, I watched another "client" of the Nassau County Police demonstrate why they always tell you not to drink and drive! Aside from the obvious urine stains on his trousers, he proudly displayed his entire dinner menu selection on his shirt. He also verbally abused anyone with a badge, prompting one of the officers in charge to hit the "play" button on the precinct's loud speaker. A country western song, "You're an Asshole," cued for just such an occasion came on. As he was led off for booking, all I could think was what an asshole I was for being so stupid! How was I going to explain this one? This wasn't some teenage hijinks, this was real trouble!

After being processed and released, I called Glen to come and get me, vowing to myself never again to use such poor judgement. At my court appearance I was fined $500 and my licence was suspended. I had learned a valuable lesson. From then on drinking never presented a problem for me.

Coincidentally, my father also came to terms with his own drinking, took my mother's advice, and motivated himself to join Alcoholics Anonymous.

Things began to improve.

One night while at work at the bar, my friend Suzanne stopped by and happened to speak about the new nightclub she worked at over in Melville.

That simple conversation with her changed my life forever.

9 You Never See It Until It's Right In Front Of You

When I first walked into the Long Island Exchange I didn't know what to expect. Nothing could have prepared me for the sideshow that I saw before me. This nightclub was a two story, five bar, high energy disco that employed almost as many characters as it entertained. It had a legal occupancy of over one thousand people and would regularly triple that at any given moment on a weekend night. The second level overlooked a huge dance floor and stage area that would be the scene of many a knock down, drag out brawl, not to mention the occasional music act, such as The Village People and Latoya Jackson, just to name two of them.

The nightclub was attached to a brand new hotel called the Royce Carlin. The hotel boasted 305 executive guest rooms, a beautiful indoor grotto-style pool, weight room, outdoor tennis courts, and enough meeting space for any corporate or social function, backed by a five-star catering staff. In addition to the nightclub the lobby of the hotel also offered two additional restaurant/bar areas. The obvious cash cow for this monster, however, was The Long Island Exchange.

Every weekend the lines just to get in this place wrapped around the freaking building! Once you got to the front doors, you had to pay a ten dollar cover charge just to walk in! To this day, I cannot understand the attraction that compelled anyone to make that kind of sacrifice.

To give you an idea of the type of clientèle that frequented this place, remember the characters in films like *The Roxbury Guys* and *Goodfellas*, and then add a few steroid freaks. Everybody "knew" somebody, and every conflict was preceded by, "Do you know who the @$#*%! I am? If I make a phone call, you disappear!" Usually these statements were made by very short men wearing shiny suits, too much cologne, and gold chains that hung on their clothing. The women who hung out at this club were typical Long Islanders, big hair, short skirt, gum-snapping, guidette caliber: "Hey Carmine, you said you'd take me out ta dinna at an expensive restaurant befoowa go to da Lawngilynd Exchange!"

Not to be outdone by the customers, all the waitresses wore ultra mini skirts with very low-cut tops. One of the waitresses actually had a sock puppet she had made herself and used it to take drink orders! What a circus! None of that mattered, though. All I cared about was that I had a job paying ten dollars an hour keeping this place safe.

When I got a look at my coworkers, I knew I had nothing to worry about; weighing 250 lb, on average, they made me look frail! It's incredible that someone would be stupid enough to challenge such behemoths! But challenge they would, when they had too much to drink. The more they drank, the bigger their beer muscles seemed to get. But perhaps the main reason some of these idiots acted so stupidly was their delusion—if they had an Italian last name, dressed a certain way and threw a few names and catch-phrases around, this automatically made them one of "Scorcesi's crew." Oh well, I had job security.

The entire operation of this club was overseen by the executive staff of the hotel. Unlike the bars that I had been in and worked at, this place had a corporate feel to it. This would later prove to be a huge advantage for me! As the days became weeks, and weeks became months, things settled into a really fun and exciting routine for me. I was still going to acting classes at HB in New Yorl City on Saturday mornings and working nights at the club. I'd meet, and start seeing, the occasional girlfriend here and there. Every night we were all but guaranteed a full-fledged donnybrook! I was reminded one night, however, of how dangerous the job could be.

It was a typical Saturday night with the usual cast of characters coming and going. At one point there was a disturbance by the service area of the main bar. I had been over by the stage area with two of the other bouncers when we saw the commotion. We ran over just as four of our security staff launched two guys out the front doors. It turned out that these two "Rhodes Scholars" had decided it was too much trouble to walk all the way to the men's room so they had taken turns urinating in the ice bin. Where do people like this come from who, instead of walking thirty feet to a toilet, piss in the middle of a crowded room? And into an ice bin, for God's sake!

Unfortunately, that's not what made these guys memorable. After being ejected they promptly made their way around to the side patio door and convinced a customer to let them back in. They were immediately spotted by one of my teammates who had just thrown them out. These two mopes were physically unremarkable guys. Everything about them was below average, especially their judgement. My buddy Doug, however, was their polar opposite—6' tall and 245 lbs of lean competition-caliber muscle mass. His neck was thicker than my waist, and a physical attribute that would save his life.

When Doug tried to throw them out a second time, one of them grabbed a beer bottle and broke it on the side of the bar. As Doug grabbed him, the coward slashed the side of Doug's neck, nicking the artery. What followed can only be described as unmatched carnage. There was blood from Doug's wound and from injuries to the two patrons who would not leave.

After checking on Doug's condition, I went out front to see what had become of the two "professors." Until then I had never seen a dead body other than at the various funerals I had attended. When I first saw one of the men who had cut Doug, I was convinced that there was no longer life in the bloody mass of pummeled flesh now lying in the front parking lot of the hotel. His partner in crime was just as bloody. However, due to the amount of cocaine in his blood stream he was upright and somewhat talkative. While I tried to make sense of what I was seeing, my other team-mate, Mike, came out from the kitchen. He was not happy about what had happened to Doug.

Mike would, by all accounts, be described as the quintessential gentle giant. At 6' 7" tall, 340 lbs, he was by trade a professional wrestler. It was a rare night indeed that you would find big Mike without a very broad, warm smile on his face. Tonight was one of those rare nights. I watched in amazement as Mike walked up to the guy I thought was dead and kicked him slightly, checking for signs of life. You can imagine my surprise when we both heard the guy moan. What saved this jerk's life, though, was the belligerent mouth of his coked-up buddy. I've heard that you should never startle a predator in the wild when they're standing over or near their prey. When Mike heard this mutt running his mouth, it was all he needed to vent his anger. I barely saw Mike move before he had the mutt held high above his head. He then threw him head first into the side of a parked car.

By all accounts these two could easily have been killed. Instead, both were transported by the Suffolk County Police for treatment to their injuries and then taken to jail and charged with assault with a deadly instrument and trespassing. Doug was taken to the hospital and received numerous stitches to his neck. The doctors said that had it not been for the sheer thickness of neck-muscle, the jugular artery would have been cut completely through and Doug would not have survived. Needless to say, we were all a little shaken up by the experience.

We continued to have our share of major incidents from time to time, people shooting at one another, vendetta beatings with baseball bats out in the parking lots between customers. We dealt with the issues that occurred "in house," but once we got problems outside the building we left them in the capable hands of the Suffolk County Police. Each night we'd celebrate the fact that none of us got hurt, or that no one got killed, and then go have breakfast at the diner. I didn't think things could be any better in my life until I got to know the director of security for the entire hotel property .

Frank Sullivan was a retired detective from the NYPD, and like most cops after twenty-plus years serving the good people of New York City, he went into the private security field. Frank was a typical Irish cop. He smoked too much, drank too much, and definitely had a cynical view of his fellow man. He liked me though, and I definitely enjoyed listening to his war stories from his years in the NYPD. It wasn't long before he offered me a full time position on the hotel side of the security department. It was amazing that having started off as a bouncer I now had a chance at a real suit and tie job, something I could be proud to tell my family and friends!

The position was still an hourly, graveyard shift, but definitely a step in the right direction. The job came with medical benefits as well as travel perks! I was also starting to gain something that I really didn't notice at the time—my self-esteem. Without realizing it, the entire time I was working as a bouncer and dealing with people at their worst I was gaining skills in dealing with adversity. Perhaps Frank offered me the job because I was now carrying myself differently and asserting myself in direct but respectful ways. For whatever reason, it was making life good. I was happy. It's a wondrous thing, happiness. You don't realize how it can change your entire perspective on life. I was no exception.

I began to soak up the inner workings of the hotel and learn how the management handled different issues. I especially enjoyed hearing about the experiences of my coworkers on the hotel side of the security department, who were either active duty or retired law enforcement. I found their knowledge invaluable.

Then something happened that I never saw coming.

MY REGULAR SHIFT WAS FROM TEN AT NIGHT UNTIL SIX IN THE MORNING, AND during the slow week nights from Monday to Thursday only two of us from the security section worked the overnight shift. Six others in the front office and one or two engineers were the only other staff in the hotel on those night shifts, and I would hang out with them between my hourly rounds checking the floors and the area around the hotel. Where I could, I would try to help out in the front office, which kept me from getting too bored. Being naturally nocturnal, I always expressed my abundant energy at the times when the energy of most of the staff was beginning to lag. This high energy trait was particularly annoying to Jackie Prosa, the front desk/night audit supervisor. In spite of this, I was usually able to make her smile by doing something fun or unpredictable.

A very energetic, friendly go-getter who was steadily working her way up the hotel's corporate ladder, Jackie was born and raised in West **Babylon** and had graduated from New York Tech University majoring in hotel/motel management. In that way she was obviously more squared away than I could ever dream of being.

One night while she tried to ignore my usual cheeky antics, I began throwing peanuts at her from a dish in the audit office. As luck would have it, I landed one right in her ear on the first try. She, and everyone in the office, immediately burst out laughing at the silliness of it.

Although Jackie was extremely cute, with a smile and body to die for, she had a steady boyfriend. I was also seeing someone at the time, so I never thought about us as an item. One night, however, after I had completed my rounds, I was sitting with Don Rose in the switchboard operator's office just behind the front desk when Jackie walked out of her office. Don, a hard working bellman in his late fifties with the looks and personality of Sammy Davis Jr., turned to me and said, "I think that girl's sweet on you!"

"What?" I said. "No way! Besides, we both have significant others."

Don persisted, "Nope. I'm tellin' you man, she is definitely sweet on you!" I left it at that for the time being, but his remark made an impression on me.

A few months later my ongoing silly antics and fate laid the foundation for my future. It was a Sunday night, and as usual it was employee night in the nightclub. Since many of us on the hotel side were off on Sunday nights, we all would hang out at the bar and have a few drinks. I noticed that Jackie was acting a little preoccupied, so I asked her what was up with her. She turned in the direction of our coworkers at the opposite end of the bar and said annoyedly, "I can't believe they're staring at us!"

"Who's staring at us?" I asked, scanning the room with the tact of a tourist in Times Square.

"Don't look at them!" Jackie grunted.

"Who's staring at us? Oh, them." I said, finally spotting two coworkers looking in our direction. He had a crush on Jackie, and she had one on me.

At that very moment fate stepped right into my life.

Being the goof that I am, I said matter-of-factly, "I'll give them something to stare at!" With that, I grabbed Jackie and laid one on her. Even though she had not expected it, it happened to be a hell of a kiss, if I do say so my damn self!

"BILL!" she said in astonishment as I broke lip-lock with her.

"Hey, that was pretty good! Let's do it again!" I said, laying another kiss on her. This time Jackie kissed me back... and well! Needless to say, both of our coworkers stopped staring at us.

BEING AROUND JACKIE, I NEVER FELT ANY PRESSURE OF ANY KIND. I COULD always be myself and not worry about the consequences of my actions. Not even those times with Laura all those years ago did I feel this comfortable. It's funny how the love of your life can be right in front of you without you noticing right away! I began to understand then that things, events, happen for a reason. In time I would see how this principle also works on a larger scale.

Life continued at a steady pace, and I was gaining in experience. Lots of interesting guests stayed at the hotel from time to time, and I got to meet Perry Cuomo, Kenny Rogers, Jerry Orbach, Steve Guttenberg, Aretha Franklin, just to name a few.

My relationship with Jackie continued to grow, albeit I was still somewhat guarded since I had not been able to shake the feeling of inadequacy that dogged my life. I didn't want to fall in love and feel certain that she was the one for me only to have something, or someone, prove me wrong. So I did something that I had never done before, I remained patient and took it slow and easy.

By the following Christmas, Jackie and I were deeply in love! Jackie's mother, Geri, would tell me years later that she knew that I was the one for her daughter the night of our employee Christmas party at the hotel. Jackie had made a little too merry, and when I got her home she began living up to her high school nick name of "porcelain princess." As I held back her hair to let her get rid of the excess booze, her Mom said that she knew then that I was the one for her daughter.

In stark contrast to my huge Irish family, Jackie came from a small Italian family. Her father had died tragically of a massive heart attack a few years earlier. Fortunately for Jackie and her mother, Geri, and brother, Jerry, her grandparents lived right next door, and her aunt and uncle lived two blocks down the street. Extremely warm and welcoming, they made me feel like a member of the family from the first moment I met them. Not only did Jackie's Mom stuff me silly every time I came over, but whenever we'd stop by her aunt and uncle's house, they would see to it that I was well fed! Needless to say I started to put on a little weight after Jackie and I became an item.

Jackie's grandfather was a no-nonsense guy who busted his ass for a living, and made no secret of the fact that he came from a long line of proud Italians that would bust your head open if you messed with anyone in his family. He routinely told me stories of guys he'd thumped for doing something stupid, or who had pissed him off in some way. One story was about splitting a guy's head open using a pick-axe. After he "took care of business," he then sat down to a hot lasagna dinner without even a second thought. This particular story earned him the affectionate nick name, Jimmy Da Pick, from me, but I never shared it with him for fear of becoming a victim in one of his stories!

Although Jackie and I were together almost every waking moment, either at work or on our days off, we never let our love for each other affect our work. Jackie's job responsibilities had increased with a well deserved promotion to Assistant Front Office Manager which required her to work normal business hours. At first, this was a huge relief because she was feeling burned out from the overnight shifts and some of the chaos there. But, after awhile she felt that the hotel senior management was dumping too much work on her for the salary they were paying. She needed a change.

As it turned out, Jackie wasn't just venting when she said she was being overworked. After she left the hotel, they had to hire two people to do the work she was doing all by herself! This is the woman by which all others should be measured! Her organization skills and work ethic are second to none. Too bad for the hotel that they learned this too late!

Luckily, the company her mother, Geri, worked for was hiring, so Jackie took an office position with them. She quickly settled into a routine with the new job, and although we were on opposite schedules, we still had plenty of quality time together. Since we were now very serious about each other, we decided to find a place of our own to live. Our mothers did not greet this well, but I think even they realized what we already knew in our hearts. This was the real thing.

Our timing could not have been better. Just three years previously my sister, Rosemary, had bought a townhouse down the street from my mother's in Deer Park and had recently placed it on the market, but it wasn't selling. Rose, always the caring big sister, offered to rent it to us with the idea that we would eventually buy it from her. Jackie and I were thrilled, since it was an ideal place with one bedroom, a bathroom, dining room, eat-in kitchen, and a great living room with a fireplace and a loft overlooking the living room.

Life was looking very good indeed.

Just before his retirement from the hotel, Frank hired Rich Logan to replace him as Director of Security. In stark contrast to Frank, Rich was a young man in his mid-forties who had just retired from the Fire Department of New York after twenty-plus years as a fire fighter. He had spent his last few years there as an investigator with the fire marshall's office. Besides my father, Rich would become one of the most positive influences in my life.

10 DEEP WITHIN ME I HAVE A CALLING

Rich Logan is one of the most 'squared-away' people I have ever been lucky enough to call a friend. When he took the helm of the hotel security department, he promoted me to the position of Assistant Director. As such, I became part of the executive branch of the hotel management and received specialized training in fire safety and criminal law relating to the private security field. The hotel was doing so well that the owner bought into the Hilton franchise, and the hotel became The Huntington Hilton. In addition to giving the hotel a cosmetic upgrade, the security staff was also to change.

The night club was to be closed for several months during the renovations, so the general manager instructed Rich and me to interview and hire the new security staff. Our goal was to find the same quality personnel for the club that we would hire for the hotel side. We leaned towards a more professional image as opposed to the classic "body-builder in a tuxedo" presentation. This meant that we needed either off-duty or retired law enforcement personnel with basic training on how to deal with patrons within the guidelines of the law, and if needed, to place them under arrest. Gone, then, would be the days of thumping some drunk for getting out of hand in the bar.

After several weeks of reading resumes and conducting interviews, we put together a security staff that could rival the investigative wing of any law enforcement agency. Almost every branch of local civil service was represented, including the New York Police Department (NYPD), the Fire Department of New York (FDNY), Nassau, and Suffolk County Police, and the FBI! At the grand reopening of the night club, now called "The Savoy," the credentials of our new security crew were plainly in view.

The usual cast of gangster wanna-be's showed up, but if they got out of hand they were now handcuffed and placed under arrest for disorderly conduct and trespassing! Needless to say, things settled down in the club from then on, and we had a better clientele as a result. There was still the occasional brawl, but nothing like the blood-baths of old.

I was starting to feel differently about myself. More confident, perhaps. No, that wasn't it. I felt something stirring deep within me now—a calling. Not able to put a name to this feeling, I knew that the experiences I was having were guiding me.

I'll never forget seeing my first suicide victim. A hotel guest cut his wrists and bled to death in the bath tub. Distraught over some failed business venture, he had checked into the hotel the night before and had promptly drawn himself a bath. Before climbing into the tub, he consumed an entire bottle of pills to make sure he finished the job. He then opened both of his wrists with a straight-bladed razor. Instead of a suicide note, he made a tape recording of his final moments. On the recording he actually complained about the hotel service and about how surprised he was that it was taking him so long to die!

I've heard people describe the unique smell of human decay as a smell you never forget. Well, they are right! I was struck, however, by how peaceful the man looked. Other than the odor, and the complete lack of color in his skin, he looked completely at peace. I guess that was his goal. Rich later put it into perspective.

"He made a permanent solution to a temporary problem!"

His remark has stuck with me to this day.

Certainly there was someone somewhere who loved this man, and they would be heartbroken when they got the news of his death. Too bad he didn't just take an extra day, or an hour, or even just a moment to think about them.

I was becoming a full-time student of the human race. I was learning how to deal with all types of people during the best and worst moments of their lives. I became adept at listening to their problems and helping to calm them and to find solutions.

As a member of the executive staff, I was also involved in the Manager-On-Duty (M.O.D.) program. Being the M.O.D. helped me cultivate my people skills. Also, the M.O.D. was in essence the general manager of the entire hotel during those shifts.

The other department heads would regularly ask me to cover their M.O.D. shifts, because M.O.D. required us to stay in the hotel overnight. I had no problem with this since I was working nights anyway. I gained invaluable experience—with authority to sign off on surf and turf dinners for the entire overnight staff, as well as for local police officers working our area!

I was having fun. Soon, events would help me understand my calling—what my life was to be.

Around 9:00 p.m, I arrived at the hotel and saw that the hotel parking lot was packed as usual. There was a huge wedding reception in the ballroom, both restaurants were filled, and the club was promising to be a huge draw as usual. As I approached the front desk there was a whirl-wind of activity. Melissa Swanson, a hotel sales agent, was M.O.D. When she saw me walk in she said out loud, "Oh thank god, Billy's working tonight!" The front desk staff all smiled with a look of relief on their faces. Melissa told me later, "We always feel so safe whenever you're around!" "WOW!" I thought! "What a great compliment!"

Later, and in true nightclub fashion, I heard the dreaded "CODE RED" over the radio. One of the security guys who was near the stage and dance floor had seen several "disco-dans" begin a brawl, so he had called for backup. "CODE RED" was the radio signal we used for this purpose. By the time I reached the club from the other side of the hotel, most of the combatants had been ejected without much trouble. A few of them still hung around the front doors of the club uttering the obligatory, "They don't know who the @$#*%! they're messing with!" just to save face.

Then, one of these guys saw a car pull out of the front parking lot and shouted, "Hey, there he goes!" With that, three of these bozos charged after the car as it waited in line to make the turn out of the lot onto Route 110. When they got to the car they started jumping on it and trying to pull the driver out. As we approached them, I could see the driver's arm pointing upward... I thought to myself, "Hey, that looks like a..." POW, POW, POW!!! Shots rang out. "Holy shit!" I thought, "He just shot someone!" I was sure that I just witnessed someone getting their head blown off!

"SHOTS FIRED, SHOTS FIRED!" I yelled into the radio! "PBX, call 911 and get us some help!" I said, running towards the car without a gun! (I don't know what the hell I was thinking!)

Luckily, all my guys had drawn their guns and they took everyone down without another shot being fired. As it turned out, the driver of the car was an off-duty New York City cop, who had nothing to do with the earlier brawl. He had just been the victim of mistaken identity by these knuckle-heads. By the sheer grace of god, the moron who tried to pull him from his car saw the gun come up at the last second and dropped to the ground as the shots rang out. He did, however, require a change of shorts!

After everything settled down and I had typed up the incident report, Roger Waters, one of the security guys, pulled me aside.

"You know Billy," he said, "You really impressed me with the way you handled that! I've seen a lot of crazy shit in my time, and that was one of the craziest!"

Roger had spent over twenty years with the NYPD. To hear that from him really drove home this feeling of purpose that so often was a vague longing!

"You really ought to give some serious thought to becoming a cop!" he said. "You might not get rich and famous, but you'll keep food on the table, clothes on your back, and a roof over your head."

When I was a kid, besides idolizing super heros, I often thought of being a cop like my Uncle Jimmy. But over time I had become more ob-sessed with the thought of playing one on TV! Fame and fortune had been my only focus.

I can't describe the excitement of the adrenaline dump during the night's chaotic event, not to mention the feeling I had from knowing people felt safe with me around! Melissa had said as much earlier that night. Coupled with the night's events, I began to think, "I really love this work."

From that moment on, I was driven with purpose.

I certainly wouldn't be rich and famous, but I'd have a steady respect-able job with a great future, and I'd get to chase bad guys!

My family would need to be convinced, however.

Jackie supported my decision, but was concerned about the obvious risks involved. When I shared my revelation with friends and family they all seemed to agree that this was indeed the proper career path for me.

At the request of my colleagues at work, I applied immediately for a job at the well-known and highly respected Suffolk County Police Department (SCPD), which was accepting entrance exam applications. Suffolk Coun-ty Police officers are the highest paid police officers in the country. With

increased interest in police work as a profession and the good salary it offered, entrance exams were being held in numerous schools over the course
of a two day period to accommodate the many applicants. Each applicant
paid a fifty dollar "filing fee" to take the exam!

"Man, no wonder they're the highest paid cops in the country!"
I thought.

It was well known that the SCPD exams were no cake walk. Several
study groups and test preparedness classes were offered by different schools.
Although my family and friends were confident of my potential, I wasn't
taking any chances, so I signed up for classes. The classes were usually conducted by retired police officers at the cost of a hundred dollars per student,
and space was limited.

I was feeling an inner push forward. Jackie described me as being
"hyper-focused." I had her love and support, and I felt I knew where destiny was taking me. I poured every fiber of my being into preparing for the
Suffolk County Police Officer exam. I did not even bother to apply to other
departments, since I knew in my heart that this was what I wanted.

I'll never forget that morning in May when I arrived to take the exam.
I was so nervous I could hardly tell where the school was or what town
it was in! However, as soon as I sat down in the classroom the same old
familiar feeling of low self-esteem hit me square-on, "You must be kidding
yourself to think you could actually do well on a written exam!"

"Knock it off, asshole!" I said to my insecurities, "This IS where you
belong, and this IS what you're going to do!"

I settled down enough to finish the exam without thinking of my insecurities.

"That's it," I thought, "It's now out of my hands."

I knew that no matter what happened I had given it my best shot.

The hardest part was yet to come.

Like all civil service processes, the police entrance exams take forever to
score. Even with the use of the "Scantron" answer sheets, it's an arduous
task. To pass the exam, a 70% score was required. I knew full-well that
due to the high number of applicants and the few positions available, I had
to score 98% or better just to have a fraction of a chance. My friends reassured me that I was all but guaranteed of the job. I was hopeful, but the
doubt within me kept growing.

As days and months passed, I grew more and more anxious whenever I opened the mailbox. I'll never forget the day I finally received the letter of notification. As usual, I was home alone during the day while Jackie was at work. Grabbing the handful of assorted bills, coupon flyers, and the like, I quickly rifled through the letters and found the one addressed: "Mr. William G. Brett" from "The Department of Civil Service."

I sat there for a moment not knowing what to do. I had been waiting for what seemed like an eternity for this moment, and now I found myself afraid to open the envelope! "Well, here goes."

Like most government business letters, it began with the usual niceties, "Dear Mr. Brett, thank you for your interest in taking the application process".... YADDA, YADDA, YADDA. Okay, where is the... "You received a passing score of 70%. You will be notified should you be considered further for the position of police officer."

There it was. All that time and effort, and for what? 70%! I was devastated! Never in my life had I tried so hard or wanted something so much, yet failed so miserably. The *black cloud* from my childhood had followed me, and it probably would follow me for the rest of my life. It said to me that no matter how hard I try, or how much I might want something, the universe would see to it that the opposite came true!

I needed to hear a friendly voice so I picked up the phone and called Jackie at her office.

"Hello, Sweets!" she said in her usual bright way. "How's your day going?"

So I told her.

"Oh," she said solemnly, "Are you okay?"

At that point I lost it. Not since I was a kid have I cried as much. I felt so hurt and disillusioned. People had told me my entire life that if you want something badly enough, if you work hard and study for it, that nothing could prevent your success. Yet that rule obviously did not apply to me! "What is wrong with me?" I thought.

Jackie offered to come home, but I told her that I was okay. I just needed to vent. As we hung up, I felt better, but deep down I was sure that this *black cloud* would be with me forever.

I BEGAN TO THINK ABOUT WHEN TO PROPOSE MARRIAGE TO JACKIE! WHENEVER we walked through the mall she would always make sure I saw this one particular diamond ring in one of the jewelry store windows. The ring was hard to miss, with a three-karat center-stone that looked more like a car headlight—just a lot bigger and a lot brighter! "And only $7,500!"

Unbeknownst to Jackie, her mother had put me in touch with a family friend who was a jeweler. Based on my description, he custom-built the ring to look exactly like the one in the mall for half the price! (No, the ring didn't fall off of a truck, and it's not a cubic zirconia, thank you very much!) I still needed to save the money to pay for it, however, so my sister, Rose, was once again very understanding about late rent!

Jackie had previously warned me not to make any big proposal event that would embarrass her; no hot air balloons, no baseball game scoreboards, no big crowd awaiting her response. I got it, so I decided to give her the ring at home when she would least expect it.

It was a Saturday morning. While we were getting dressed I pretended to be in a bad mood and to act a little snippy with her. Jackie was of course in a good mood, but after I started in with my ill temper that all changed. Getting out of the shower, I asked Jackie to grab me a glass of ice water. Her response was less than loving. When I persisted she relented and went into the kitchen. A moment or two later I heard her call out, "BILL!"

"What?" I replied, with feigned annoyance, knowing that she had found the ring in its crystal box just inside the ice bin.

She walked into the bathroom with a smile that I had never seen before but have seen many times since.

"Oh yeah," I said. "By the way, would you marry me?"

"YES!" she answered.

The *black cloud* had no power to deny me her love then or at any other time since!

We didn't set a wedding date right away because we wanted to pay for the wedding ourselves.

My job at the hotel was going well, but it was becoming monotonous and it was not law enforcement! Also, the overnight and weekend shifts were getting old. Since Jackie and I were about to start our lives together as husband and wife, I needed to find something new with more normal hours.

Enter Charlie Gilardi, a rare individual I respect and admire. He and

Rich had worked together in the FDNY and had retired out of the U.S. Marshall's office at the same time. Charlie's full-time job was Assistant Director of Loss Prevention for Caldor, Inc., a large chain of discount retail stores in the northeast. He also worked part-time on the hotel side of the security department.

Charlie informed me that Caldor was looking for loss prevention managers for several of their stores on Long Island. The hours were flexible, and I would have my own office! He said that I would be perfect for the job and urged me to send them a resume. After discussing it with Jackie, she agreed it might just be exactly the change I needed.

After several interviews and meetings with various Caldor executives they offered me the job. Although Rich was disappointed to lose me at the hotel, he was happy about this new opportunity for me, but he also advised me not to give up on a career in law enforcement.

So, after five years of working in a "war zone," I started my new career in retail security. Man, what a mistake that would turn out to be!

Initially, the job appeared to be exactly what I needed. Daylight hours, my own office in the Babylon store, and I made my own schedule! I answered only to Charlie and his director, both of whom worked out of the district office over in Farmingdale! This was shaping up to be a pretty sweet gig. I hung my Superman prints on the walls of my office and put some of my collectibles on my desk. An array of twenty video screens on the far wall showed the view of dozens of various surveillance cameras placed throughout the store. How cool was that?

I soon discovered, however, how useless that camera system was!

Not long after starting at Caldor, our department name was changed from "Loss Prevention" to "Asset Protection." Instead of concentrating our efforts on watching the merchandise for possible theft by customers and/or employees, we now focused on the in-house theft/shortages via weekly and monthly inventory audits. In short, all we did was take computer readouts of what the store should have had on the shelves and in the store rooms, and then physically confirm that the items were in fact there. If they weren't, the department manager would be brought to task. Meanwhile, we were getting ripped-off blind with merchandise literally being carried out the back door! Being too new to feel that it was my place to say anything, I kept quiet and did what I could until I felt more confident to openly address it.

A year or so later, I was offered the position of handling the Huntington store in addition to the Babylon store.

Although I was doing well with Caldor, I still yearned to be a police officer and had taken three more entrance exams for various police departments. I managed to pass two of them—my test-taking skills had not improved.

JACKIE AND I DECIDED TO MARRY ON MY TWENTY-EIGHTH BIRTHDAY ON A Saturday in September 1993. Since we had connections at the Hilton where we met and fell in love, we thought it only appropriate that we book it for the reception. In June we also bought a house next door to my sister, Rose.

My favorite feature of the house was the most perfect specimen of a Colorado Blue Spruce right in front of the front walkway. All I could think about was how it was going to look when I covered it with Christmas lights! Once again, I was reminded that at least this part of my life was untouchable by that *black cloud*.

Before we knew it, it was September.

Jackie did not plan the traditional "Girls night out" bachelorette party, being more content with a nice quiet bridal shower. She told me it was perfectly fine for me to go and tear it up for my bachelor party if I wanted, but that there had better not be any strippers, and that I had better behave!

Since my younger brother Robert was to be my best man, he was organizing the party. I immediately instructed him NOT TO HIRE ANY STRIPPERS! and he agreed.

I don't know if it was payback for all the times I beat up on him as a kid or for the Christmas morning in Glen Ellyn when I switched the gifts around under the tree, but not only did he hire a stripper, he hired quite possibly the ugliest I had ever seen! When she tried to convince me to take my clothes off for the traditional "Lap dance," I vehemently refused. Thinking that it might be funny she then planted her face right in my lap!

Two factors were now against me. One, I had committed the classic fashion *faux pas* of wearing white pants after Labor Day and two, she had applied her make-up with a spackle knife. Make-up, combined with her vivid red lip gloss, made my lap now look like a crime scene!!! When she lifted her head, my pants revealed a carnage! All I could do was look at my brother and say, "If I go down, I'm taking you with me!" As far as I was concerned, the party was over. Envisioning Jackie's reaction, I spent the majority of the evening in the clubhouse kitchen pouring gallons of club soda on the front of my now-ruined slacks.

I managed to conceal my feeble attempt to clean the "Hazardous Materials Waste" covering the front of my pants by un-tucking my "Tom Sellek/ Magnum P.I." shirt. This simply made me look like a drunk Magnum P.I. wanna-be who had visited a sloppy hooker! What a freaking mess!

By the time I got home it was "O'Dark-thirty." Thankfully, Jackie was sound asleep. I thought about waking her up and telling her about the evening, but for some reason I decided not to do so. "Maybe I could wash the pants before she even sees them, and she won't be the wiser?" I thought. So, I buried them at the bottom of my hamper. A few hours later I woke up with the sense of being watched. Sure enough, there was Jackie holding up the offending pants with a look on her face that I had never seen before and never wanted to see again!

"I thought you told me there weren't going to be any strippers at this party of yours?"

I did what any self-respectful man would do in that situation. I threw my baby brother right under the bus!

"But hon," I groveled, "Rob hired one after I had told him not to! How was I supposed to know?"

I should've left it at that, but didn't. "Besides," I didn't do anything. I was good!" Oooooo, that last comment did it!

The term, "Hell hath no fury like a woman scorned," no doubt came from a man who enraged an Italian woman!

Jackie exploded, "Oh, you thought you were being good?!!! The wedding is off!" she said, storming out of the house.

"Well," I thought, "now what are you gonna do?" I had just managed to screw up on the one positive beacon of light in my life and all because of a pair of pants with lipstick. "Just perfect!"

I got dressed and went over to Rose's house where my brothers were just waking up. "Well, Rob, thanks to you, I'm a bachelor for good now!" I said matter-of-factly. I knew, however, that he meant no harm.

Jackie calmed down after a few hours and came home. She gave Rob an earful, but we all eventually got to laugh about it. To this day though, if

I even talk about wearing white pants, Jackie will give me the evil eye! Oh well, white makes me look fat anyway.

THE BIG DAY FINALLY ARRIVED. I COULD NOT HAVE ASKED FOR A BETTER BIRTHday present! The weather was flawless, seventy-two degrees and not a cloud in the sky! I stayed in the hotel the night before to prevent jinxing tradition by seeing Jackie prior to our meeting at the altar. Rarely do weddings go exactly as planned, but ours did. My *black cloud* must've overslept that day!

We celebrated mass at Our Lady Of Miraculous Medal in Wyandanch, a beautiful little Catholic church where my sister, Rose, was married. Because of my mother's connections with the church, my cousin, Tommy Harold, a Catholic priest, was able to perform the ceremony.

As we waited in the sacristy, a room behind the altar, I noticed that Tommy seemed unusually nervous. Having known Tommy my whole life, I always saw him as a pillar of calm wisdom from having dealt with the life experiences of so many people that he served.

"It's one thing to say mass in front of the usual crowd of parishioners, but that's our whole family out there! You know what a tough crowd they can be!" he said.

Needless to say, Tommy brought his "A" game and did a fantastic job!

You always hear men say how beautiful their wives look as they walk down the aisle and they see them in their wedding dresses for the first time. Well, Jackie far exceeded that! She looked radiant! Any butterflies I may have had prior to the start of the ceremony completely disappeared when I saw her. Tommy kept us on track and guided us through the ceremony without missing a beat. Before we could even get flustered over our vows, we were pronounced man and wife! The rest of the day flew by quickly as Jackie and I greeted over two hundred invited guests!

Because it was my birthday, my friends invited a "Special Guest" to the reception to wish us well. Everyone who knew me knew about my lifelong infatuation with a certain superhero. Every birthday and Christmas I received at least one gift with his familiar insignia on it. In fact, Tommy even mentioned him in his homily during the mass!

During the reception Jackie and I were called by the DJ to the middle of dance floor where my groomsmen seated us in chairs. The DJ then got everyone to sing "Happy Birthday" and announced that a special guest had just "flown in" to wish me a happy birthday.

"Look! Up in the sky! It's a bird! It's a plane... It's Superman!"

The doors to the ballroom swung open and my friend, Anthony, dressed as "The Man of Steel", was carried in by the wedding party as though he was flying above them! It was a perfect day.

Jackie and I spent our honeymoon in Montauk, a quiet Long Island beach town with the genuine feel of a New England fishing village, yet without the crazy, trendy East Hampton crowds. It was a perfect, relaxing week.

"I am truly blessed!" I thought.

11 Is This All I'll Ever Amount To?

To an outsider, my life might have looked pretty good, what with my new home, a beautiful wife, a steady job, and a big family that loved and supported me. Yet, I felt more and more trapped in my job. In my heart I knew I could excel as a police officer, but fate seemed to be frustrating that dream. The frustration was made even worse by the fact that others I knew who were taking police entrance exams were getting jobs. Two of my store detectives, and an asset protection manager from Caldor, were hired by the NYPD. I knew in my heart there was something wrong. My conviction to be a police officer was so intense, it felt like an irresistible force. Fate, however, was proving to be an immovable object. No matter how hard I tried, no matter what steps I'd take, I could not break through the impasse. There had to be something at work here. There had to be some reason. All I could see was the *black cloud*.

Due to financial losses, Caldor, Inc. was making company-wide cuts. I had been given the responsibility of the Huntington store specifically because of the record losses from the previous inventory. Now, I was instructed by the district office to cut back security coverage of one of the two entrances and exits at the store. Needless to say, we were getting ripped off blind! Prior to the cutbacks, we had begun to make some progress.

As with most of the stores, the general managers did not like the fact that we, the asset protection department, didn't answer to them. We were sort of the "Internal Affairs" of retail. The general manager at the Huntington store was no exception. At any opportunity, he'd call the district office to complain about something he thought that I should, or should not, be doing. Even with my dark frame of mind, I could handle this. What I could not handle, however, was the unrivaled incompetence displayed by the executive decision makers who were based out of the home office in Connecticut. They would make a habit of showing up in the stores with all their local middle management lackeys in tow and try to impose their will upon us, the witless line employees.

One day I arrived mid-morning, since I was scheduled to work until closing. I was informed by one of my detectives that several of the executive posse were in the store conducting one of their "wisdom-sharing" tours. When I got to my office I could see the visitors, via my closed circuit surveillance system, walk to the mall side exit door. A second later the so-called head honcho picked up the house phone and summoned me via the public address system to come to the mall entrance. "Ok," I thought, "Here we go."

As I approached the aisle near the exit I could see about eight managers standing there, including the general manager who did not like me. Two of the men with the senior executive were from the executive section of asset protection and directly responsible for implementing all of the cutbacks. Before I even got near him, the senior executive began tearing into me. Not since my math teacher had made a fool of me in the seventh grade had anyone humiliated me or made me feel so shitty!

"Who's supposed to be covering this door?" he asked condescendingly. Before I could finish answering him, he interrupted me.

"Let me ask you this, how much loss is too much?" Before I could answer him, he barked, "Until you find someone to cover this door, you will stand here and check the receipts of everyone who walks out! Do I make myself clear?"

Even as I write this, I can feel my emotions of rage all over again. I stood motionless for a moment and contemplated the worse case scenarios of stepping into this guy and "cancelling his check" with a left-right combination! Thankfully, logic won out, and I swallowed hard. What really bothered me, however, was the fact that two of my so called supervisors just stood there and never said a @$#*%! word! I just looked at them as they walked off following that jerk like the rest of his sheep!

My blood was boiling. As a kid I would have naturally lashed out verbally and/or physically, but as a grown-up now I coped with this kind of insult by keeping it all bottled up. This practice can be extremely stressful to the psyche of someone who is wired the way I am! While I got through the rest of the day, the damage was done. I knew that my time with Caldor would soon be over.

The stress was taking its toll on Jackie as well. She couldn't stand to see me always feeling dark and gloomy. This was not the man she'd married.

On the night of Fred Varacchi's thirtieth birthday everything reached "critical mass"! Jackie wasn't feeling well, so she stayed home in bed while I went to the party. I enjoyed being around Fred since a sophomore in high school. He always made me feel confident about myself. Fred always teased me by saying, "When you become a big movie star, you're going to buy me a racing team so I can quit my job and drive on the pro circuit!" Fred was a self-made man who was always working for the things he had. He also knew how to save money when he had to. When he and Eileen started dating, he said he knew that she was the one he'd spend the rest of his life with. He was right. I was always in awe of Fred's ability to focus on the things he wanted and his ability to work toward achieving those goals. Although I was his polar opposite in this regard, he never spoke down to me or belittled me in any way. It's amazing how so many people in my life were wise beyond their years! You'd think some of that would have rubbed off on me! Being around Fred was just what the doctor ordered for my current state of mind!

When I returned home from the party, Jackie was still awake. She looked pissed.

"What's wrong?" I asked.

"You got a call from the general manager at the Huntington store this afternoon," she said. "He was unbelievably rude and nasty to me. He wanted to know where you were and why there wasn't any security coverage at the store! He then said that you were to call him immediately when you got home and then hung up. What an asshole that guy is!"

I apologized for her having to deal with the call and reassured her that I would put things right first thing in the morning.

"You're not going to do anything stupid or crazy, are you?" she asked.

"Now you ought to know better than that," I said.

"That's what I'm worried about!" she zinged.

The next morning as I was driving to work I was struck by how calm and relaxed I felt. Maybe deep down I knew that I was now about to eliminate the source of so much stress and depression in my life. Certainly, rational adults did not do what I was about to do. I felt more like the kid I was with an irresistible force bending destiny to my will and telling fate, "Oh yeah? I'll show you! I'll just quit this place!"

I felt that I was on auto-pilot. I calmly walked into the store, grabbed my store detective, Peggy, and said to her, "Come with me."

"What's going on?"

"You're going to watch me pack up my personal belongings from my office, then you're going to escort me out of the building."

"WHAT?" she replied. "You can't quit!"

"Watch me," I said, simply. I then told her of the previous night's events, which helped her understand my actions. Although Peggy persisted in trying to convince me to stay, my mind was made up.

After I loaded up my belongings, I thanked Peggy and walked out of the store, closing that chapter of my life forever.

Fate began to shift to allow my irresistible force.

12 Keep Dreaming, Pal!

I 've heard that the human body has numerous ways by which it reflex-
ively deals with physical and emotional stress. When we physically
overheat, the body's sweat glands activate, producing sweat that causes us
to cool. Conversely, when we're cold the body will begin to shiver to create
warmth for our core to keep the blood running warm from our heart out to
the extremities. On the emotional side, there are several schools of thought.
A universal belief is that when the human psyche becomes overloaded it
uses the pressure relief valve of dreams to find balance.

We've all heard about the dream where someone finds himself on a
stage in front of a large crowd only to discover that he is naked! This dream
suggests a fear of something or a subconscious apprehension towards an
upcoming event. Or, there is the dream where a person finds himself at one
end of a long hallway and he tries to run. The harder and faster he tries to
run the more he finds that he cannot even move! This suggests the feeling
of being trapped. Another common one is when people envision themselves
in flight. This indicates the brain's method of dealing with a stressful situation.

The psyche sees dreams as a way of breaking the bonds of earth and
leaving all worries below. It's believed that you can tell a lot about a person
by the dreams they have.

Like most people, I've had these dreams. Although I felt genuinely
relieved at quitting Caldor, I was stressed out by future uncertainty. Needless to say, I was doing a lot of "night flights"!

In descriptions that I've heard, no one talks about the actual sensation
of being in the air. Their descriptions are usually vague recollections of
"floating in the air". Whether due to excessive emotional stress or just my

overly abundant imagination, every time I wake up from a flying dream, I can remember every detail! My dreams are also in color, and because of my infatuation with the Man of Steel, whenever I fly in my dreams I'm always dressed in the primary red and blue!

The actual sensation of taking to the air without mechanical assistance is a feeling I can hardly describe! The slight pull of gravity as I accelerate upward, the wind passing around me. To change direction, I simply arch my back, tilt my head and reach out with one of my hands toward the direction I want to go. It is as simple as that! The dream usually begins with me standing on the ground in street clothes. At some point I find myself still standing there, but my feet are no longer touching the ground! In those moments when the laws of gravity do not apply to me, I am overcome with the most amazing sense of invulnerability, and skyward I soar! There were times, however, that even in mid-flight I feel a sense of doubt as to what I am experiencing. As though my logical conscious mind is telling me, "This is not possible! Humans cannot fly without mechanical assistance!" I then immediately start losing altitude, then fall outright. Amazingly, I don't wake up right away. I can vividly recall the sensation of "my cape" enveloping my torso as I plummet toward earth. When I see this happening I always regain my "powers"and rocket back into the air! I have yet to hit the ground in one of these dreams.

Okay, enough already. What's this obsession with Superman? I have to admit, it is a little unusual. I can't explain it. As a kid I guess it was just the "Faster than a speeding bullet, more powerful than a locomotive, able to leap tall buildings in a single bound" thing. But as I grew up and developed my own sense of right and wrong through my own life experiences, I begin to wonder what the world would be like if such a man existed. Although he's just a fictional comic book superhero, his ideals have made him an American icon! Even with seemingly limitless physical powers, in every story those powers are used to help humanity and never for personal gain! Further, no matter how evil the villain might be, he is never killed by Superman. "Fighting the never-ending battle for truth, justice, and the American way!" However corny, I've always felt this statement to be very profound. Superman's defiance of gravity also kept me drawn to him as an ideal. Maybe I wanted to soar above the *black cloud* that kept dogging my life.

A FEW WEEKS AFTER LEAVING CALDOR, I GOT A CALL FROM RICH LOGAN. FOR health reasons, Rich had left the Hilton not long after I did. After recovering, he took the position of Director of Security for Danford's Inn out in Port Jefferson, a beautiful little landmark hotel that was right on the water next to the pier for the Connecticut ferry. Rich called to offer me an hourly paid graveyard shift, and I accepted it.

During these shifts I did a lot of soul searching. Every night I'd end up on the second floor of the hotel in the old nautical-themed pub that overlooked Long Island Sound. The pub had not been open for a few years, so it was a perfect place to sit with a cup of coffee and reflect. As I looked out over the water at the lights on the Connecticut side of the sound, I found myself silently asking God for guidance. I knew in my heart that I was capable of so much more. I truly felt that there was something I was supposed to be doing with my life, but the signs were not yet obvious.

I SOON BEGAN TO NOTICE A SERIES OF SIGNS IN MY LIFE.

Being a recovered alcoholic, my father attended daily meetings at Alcoholics Anonymous. One day he pulled me aside and said, "Wait until you hear this one!" He told me that one of the guys he had sponsored was a psychic medium, and that on that morning they had been talking about the topic. Apparently this guy was supposed to be the real deal. All he had to do was stand near someone and he could read them. Being skeptical, my father asked, "Do you get anything off me?"

"Oh, you're easy to read, Buddy!" he answered, confidently.

Keep in mind that he had only just met my father that day, so he had no opportunity for having any information about my father.

"Let's see," he began. "You come from a large Irish Catholic family. You've got six children: two girls and four boys. Their names are John, Rosemary, Eileen, Christopher, and... uumm, Stephen, and Robert."

"Well you were doing great, but you missed one!" my father told him, genuinely impressed. Without telling him my real name my father said, "I don't have a son named Stephen."

Looking very confused, the man persisted, asking, "Are you sure he doesn't have a nick-name or something, like Slick, or Sam, or something?"

"Nope," My father assured him, "You're not even close!"

Still looking very confused, he told my father, "This is strange. I could've sworn his name was Steve, or something... I'm seeing this big red letter "S" right there over his chest."

My father almost shit his pants!

"Isn't that amazing?" my father said to us.

I was completely taken aback! I mean, how the hell could this guy have picked up on something like that just by being near my father? "This had to mean something, right?" I thought to myself. Now more than ever I was convinced that all of the events in my life must be leading me towards something, exactly what I still had no idea!

13 A Real Life Pet Detective

In the spring of 1996, while I was still at Danford's Inn, I got a call from Tommy O'Brian, whom I had once hired for the security staff at the Savoy. A retired NYPD officer, Tommy was now Chief of the Law Enforcement Division of The American Society for the Prevention of Cruelty to Animals® (ASPCA®). Until then, I knew of the ASPCA only as an animal welfare group. I had no idea that they actually had a police force!

Based in Manhattan, the ASPCA had been founded in 1866 by Henry Bergh, who was Ambassador to Russia under Abraham Lincoln's administration. Modeled after the Royal SPCA in the United Kingdom, the ASPCA was the first agency of its kind in the United States and was one of the first law enforcement agencies in the U.S. with agents authorized to carry firearms. As New York State Peace Officers, these "Agents," as they are called, have full jurisdiction throughout the state and are charged with the duties of investigating reports of animal cruelty and, if necessary, arresting offenders.

Tommy told me that the ASPCA had a position available and suggested that I apply. A private non-profit organization, the ASPCA receives authorization via the State and is regulated by various state agencies. As such, it was not bound by the local department of civil service. It could interview and hire people on a case-by-case basis without entrance exams. This was good news for me since I do not test well!

I eagerly submitted my resume and application while thinking, "If this is my only chance at a career in law enforcement, then I'll take it!" I soon got a call for an interview. Having the new chief as a friend was a stroke of good luck for me for a change!

I arrived at the ASPCA an hour early, not taking any chances with delays on the Long Island Rail Road! Located on East 92nd Street on the upper east side of Manhattan, the building was only five stories tall but stood out with its ASPCA stainless steel letters emblazoning the top of its red brick wall.

My interview went beautifully. After meeting with the Director of Human Resources and various members on the Board of Directors, I was told they would be in touch shortly. Shortly indeed! Before I even got out of the building, Tommy caught up with me saying, "Congratulations! You're working for me now, "Agent" Brett! Get yourself together and be back here Monday morning!"

"Holy shit!" I thought, I finally landed a police job! Well, sort of.

I couldn't wait to tell Jackie, who was thrilled albeit leery of my working in New York City. My parents both welled up with tears when I announced to them, "You're now speaking to a Special Agent with the Law Enforcement Division of the ASPCA!" My father grabbed me in a bear hug, kissed me on the cheek, and said, "I'm so friggin' proud of you!"

I had finally done something to make them really proud! "This is a nice place to be!" I thought to myself. Things were looking up!

MY CAREER IN LAW ENFORCEMENT BEGAN DIFFERENTLY THAN I EXPECTED! At that time new agents at the ASPCA received only a few weeks of on-the-job training with a senior agent! "Okay," I reasoned, "this is a private agency, so they do things differently." I concluded that they must know what they were doing since they'd been around for over 130 years! I didn't care, really, I was too caught up in the thrill of it all! "Just call me Ace Ventura, Pet Detective," I mused.

My senior agent trainer was a guy named Mike. I won't give his real name because he hates being in the spotlight and would probably track me down and shoot me! Mike had spent more than twenty years with the NYPD working in the Bronx. Short in stature but with a huge personality, Mike coupled his singular wit with a very cynical but funny view of the world. A "cop's cop," Mike kept things in perspective with bits of wisdom that we labeled "Mike's commandments," such as, "Turn off the @$#*%! siren, I'm trying to sleep, you rookie scumbag!"; "Any large amounts of money in brown paper bags we find, we split 50/50, or you commit suicide!"; "Admit to nothing. Deny everything. Demand proof!"

When he was being serious, Mike told me to never stop planning for the future. "Everything you do should be focused on the long term goals you set for yourself," he said. "The ASPCA is a great stepping stone to a future, and a nice place to retire as I'm now doing. But you don't want to make a career out of it!" he warned me. I listened to him, but right now being one of only eight agents working for a nationally known law enforcement agency was exciting for me. There I was, Billy Brett, conducting investigations into reports of animal cruelty in the greatest city on earth!

I eventually ended up on the evening shift working from four to midnight with steady weekends off. On my daily round I would arrive at the office, get my assigned case load for the night, and put on my uniform that was identical to the NYPD except for the lettering on the shoulder patches. Then I would head out into "the naked city".

We drove the typical Ford Crown Victoria/Police package cruisers. Painted charcoal gray with bright blue stripes down each side, they had the ASPCA Law Enforcement crest on the front doors and red state trooper lights and sirens. But I quickly learned that the ASPCA did not have the resources to spend on state-of-the-art cars for its law enforcement department. As a matter of fact the newest Crown Vic in the fleet was then four years old, and the cars were constantly in the shop. This didn't matter to me because it was all so cool!

New York City is an amazing place that can overwhelm you with its sheer size. There's a good reason the song goes: "The Bronx is up, and the Battery's down!" Once I saw that it was laid out on a grid, it became second nature for me to find my way around it.

Towards the end of each shift I'd stop in Central Park, near Grand Army Plaza. Directly across the street from the Plaza Hotel, hack lines start for the tourists to catch the horse and buggy tours through Central Park. In addition to investigating reports of animal cruelty, the care and condition of these draft horses is a founding fundamental of the ASPCA. While Ambassador Bergh was visiting Russia, he witnessed an enraged man brutally beat a horse with a club until the horse dropped from exhaustion. When Bergh returned to the U.S. he launched the ASPCA. The scene of the horse beating was made the emblem of the shoulder patch on the ASPCA uniform.

The laws protecting the health, welfare, and working of these horses are amazingly strict. There are numerous rules and regulations for the operation of the horse cabs in New York City. For instance, they are restricted to operating in and around the immediate area surrounding Central Park. The only other area of the city where they are permitted is the theatre district, but only for a limited time each night. If the outside temperature reaches ninety degrees or higher, the horses cannot be made to work. As such, we kept our eye on the temperature reading on a regular basis.

At the time, I felt the majority of the drivers were hard working stiffs who genuinely cared about their horses and generally played by the rules. As elsewhere in life, there were those among the cabbies who wanted to push the rules. They'd sneak into the park when they saw us coming, wait for us to leave, and then sneak back out. More often than not we'd catch and fine them. Or, when we pulled up on them in our cruisers, they'd turn around and return to the stables. Occasionally, we even went "hands on" when they challenged us.

One of them decided to test agents Joe and Debbie on one of those typically miserable, hot New York City summer days. Joe and Debbie had dispatched all the drivers back to their respective stables after confirming that the air temperature was well over ninety degrees. However, this driver claimed that the thermometer reading was flawed, and that being the case he did not have to comply with the law. The fact that these particular thermometers were authorized, approved, and endorsed by every agency in the city from the board of health to the American Meteorologists Association didn't faze him one bit. He was not going to comply, and he went so far as to push Joe!

Just to give you a little "tale of the tape," Joe is 6'1," 225 lbs of lean muscle mass and a golden gloves boxer. And Debbie is the embodiment of a female cop! Besides having the mental toughness of any seasoned officer, she was built like a brick house. Unlike most women, she knew how to throw a punch, which earned her the nick-name, "Knuckles"! The driver, on the other hand, a recent immigrant from Ireland, was physically unremarkable. So they quickly introduced "Mr. Scofflaw Hooligan" to the sidewalk and taught him the error of his ways. The story spread quickly through the ranks of the hack line. Needless to say, whenever Debbie and Joe showed up at Grand Army Plaza they were met by the most respectful group of handsome-cabbies you ever saw!

A huge drawback with our job was that we were routinely sent alone into areas of the city where even the NYPD feared to tread, equipped only with first generation Nextel direct connect cell phone radios that were not connected to the NYPD system! Our best hope if we ever got into trouble was for someone to hear our call for help and know where the hell we were!

Although it was standard procedure for agents to operate single cruisers, my partner, Annie, and I kept tabs on each other just in case one of us needed help.

On one four-to-midnight shift, I had been working over in Brooklyn and didn't finish up until 11:00 P.M. As I came over the Brooklyn Bridge, Annie called to say that she was already at the gas station on the corner of East 92nd Street and was about to head into the office.

"Are you on your way in yet?" she asked.

"Yup. Be there in five minutes," I assured her.

As I made my way north up Franklin Delano Roosevelt (FDR) Drive, I suddenly heard Annie yelling into the radio, "Billy get up here quick, I need help!"

I should interject here that we sometimes had to respond to crimes against humans!

"Where the hell are you?" I yelled back, activating the lights and siren.

"I'm on 92nd in front of the office. Some guy is beating the living shit out of a woman right in the middle of the street!" she said, the adrenaline dump clearly audible in her voice.

Physically, Annie was my polar opposite, only 5'4" and weighing 115 lbs. A former beauty queen, she looked more like a spokes-model than an ass-kicking cop!

I was only ten blocks away, but it might as well have been ten miles! "Holy shit!" I thought to myself. "This is the real thing!"

As I flew up 2nd Avenue and came screaming around the corner of 92nd Street, I saw Annie draw down on this clown as he moved towards her. As drunk as he was, however, he seemed to know what Annie's Glock would do to him if he got any closer.

As I jumped out of my cruiser and ran towards the couple, he ran directly into the path of an oncoming minivan! The driver stopped in time, but the moron kept on running anyway, slamming into the hood of the van and falling to the ground. I could tell that he wasn't hurt but was playing possum lying there moaning, so I ordered him up on his feet. When he resisted I moved him to the sidewalk by the lapels of his very expensive looking wool overcoat. He began kicking his legs in my chest as if he were pedaling a bicycle. I yelled for him to stop but he kept on doing it.

Now, I have never considered myself a tough guy of any kind. In fact, I've always seen myself more as a Clark Griswold than a Clark Kent! Yet, I had to bring this guy down quickly before someone got hurt. So I dropped all 250 pounds of my weight on him while drawing back my right hand. I hesitated hitting him since the angle of my arm with the idiot's head might have smashed it into the concrete and killed him! I did then what any responsible superhero-crimefighter would do, I cocked my wrist, put my fist within four inches of his nose, and gave him an old fashioned sedative.

"Lights out, Buddy!"

My new friend now "resting comfortably" on the sidewalk, I rolled him over and handcuffed him. During the chaos, his lady friend had slipped away into the night.

"Perfect timing!" I thought, as the calvary then arrived from the NYPD's 19th precinct.

"What happened here?" one of the patrolmen asked as he came running up.

"You guys okay?"

"Holy smoke! Who shot that guy?" another asked.

I noticed then that blood had pooled on the sidewalk around my "client's" face. It amazes me how delicate the human nose is. All I had done was give him a tap from four inches away.

"No one shot him," I assured them, "He just has a nose bleed."

The patrol lieutenant, a little guy perhaps in his early thirties with a typical "Napoleon Complex" look about him, walked up to us. Doing his best to make us feel like third string water boys, he said, "Is there any good reason this man took such a beating?"

Shocked by his attitude toward us, I blurted out after a second or two, "No sir, no one beat him. He suffered a bloody nose after I was forced to subdue him."

"Okay then, your cuffs, your collar!" And without another word, he turned and walked away.

With the genuine disdain that some of these cops showed toward us that evening I realized that maybe I did not have a well-regarded position in law enforcement as I thought I did. I later discovered that a lot of rank and file police officers do in fact look upon ASPCA officers as "wanna-be's"... Dog catchers with guns! I guess this is what Mike was trying to tell me when he advised me not to settle into the job as a career. "Great," I thought. "This is just great."

Once again, my self-esteem was in a familiar low place. I began to rationalize that by attempting to force fate to allow me a career in law enforcement, I might somehow have started a chain reaction of going "tit-for-tat" with the universe. At the time, I had no clue how profound my theory was!

I BECAME RESIGNED TO THE FACT THAT THIS JOB WAS LIKELY TO BE THE PINNACLE OF my professional career in law enforcement. Still, it certainly could have been worse.

As an agent with the ASPCA, I not only investigated animal cruelty but conducted various inspections involving animals. This included the numerous movie shoots, TV shows, and the circus, to name a few. I have to admit, it was neat meeting actors such as Mary Tyler Moore, Bernedette Peters, and Matthew Broderick.

Whenever the circus came to town, we, along with the NYPD, would escort the animal trainers as they marched the elephants from the train yard in Queens to Madison Square Garden in Manhattan. Always done in the middle of the night in order not to add to the already insane traffic in New York City, on-lookers gathered to watch the event, many of them with their children.

I once had the task of driving Roger Carras, then President of the ASPCA, to ABC studios where he was to give an interview regarding the death of Jacque Cousteau. Upon our arrival at the studio, Roger suggested that I not wait in the cruiser. "Why don't you come upstairs? It would be silly to wait in the car." Nice guy!

Roger was scheduled for a pre-recorded interview that would air on Nightline. The studio was pretty quiet with only a handful of people working. Roger, a former ABC news correspondent, was right at home, of course. Noticing the "Goofy kid" look on my face, he said, "Yeah, it is kinda cool, isn't it?" He also noticed that I was staring at a certain desk and chair located in the center of the studio. He said, "Go ahead. Sit down. He won't care, we're not on the air."

Granted, I was not yet the superhero I had dreamed of becoming as a kid, but sitting in Peter Jennings' chair in the ABC Newsroom studio was definitely a Clark Kent moment for me!

FROM CASES OF NEGLECT TO INTENTIONAL ABUSE, THE NEW YORK ASPCA office averaged between 400 and 500 cruelty complaints each month. If we needed a search warrant, we would go through the same process followed by the NYPD. Agents collect evidence, investigate crime scenes and take photographs, just as with any CSI show on TV today. Photographic evidence is really important in ASPCA cases because the animals cannot talk and tell their stories.

Many complaints we received were unfounded. Whenever they involved the care and condition of an animal we issued a "Notice To Comply" to the owner/guardian to correct the issue. The majority of the time this action corrected the problem. There were times, however, when the owner/guardian did not respond, and the animals were seized and brought back to the ASPCA's state-of-the-art hospital for any needed treatment. Treatment needs were common when landlords of abandoned buildings, or even local drug dealers, would lock pitbulls in buildings to guard their property and/or their "stash".

Timmy Kelly and I would finish our jobs for the night, then he'd say, "Come on Billy, let's go find a raging gun battle to get into!" Ironically, one night one found us! We had parked our cruisers next to each other on the upper east side near the FDR. A former cadet with the NYPD, Timmy knew to sign out a radio from the 19th precinct each night in case we needed help. We were finishing up paperwork when we heard the distinctive "POW, POW, POW" of gunshots nearby, followed by some patrolman screaming over their radio, "10-13, 10-13, SHOTS FIRED!"—10-13 being the police radio code for "officer needs emergency assistance".

We immediately sped in the direction of the shots, but before arriving we heard the dispatcher's voice over the radio say, "All units disregard, it was just some juveniles with fireworks!"

"Oh well, maybe next time," said Timmy.

Timmy came from an atypical NYPD Irish Catholic family. A live-wire who could never stay anchored for long, he quickly made plans to brighten his future by going to law school. Coming from a family of cops, Timmy was a self-proclaimed expert on any and all things police-related. He knew the inner workings of every department from New York to Los Angeles and everything in between. I had no idea that this skill of his would eventually change my life forever.

Besides Timmy and Annie, my other close friends on the night shift were Paul Romo and Rob Lopriano. A young man in his twenties with a good education and two older brothers in law enforcement, Rob Lopriano was a proud Long Island Italian. He was also the only one of us who could go toe-to-toe in a game of wits with Mike. With his rapier-like wit, Rob would be all over us like a cheap suit if we were foolish enough to stammer or to antagonize him! Although I knew Rob liked me I did my best to keep my mouth shut around him! I can truly say I've never laughed so much while working with anyone!

Paul Romo on the other hand had spent many years working in Starret City in Brooklyn. I could make him almost pass out from laughter from my childish antics. Paul always kept an unbelievably optimistic outlook, and so never gave up on me or let me give up on myself with his positive view of the future! His friendship while at the ASPCA was invaluable!

Working with Paul, Rob and Timmy helped to keep the job fun and interesting while providing me with unique insights into life.

In 1998 and 1999 I participated in two specialized ASPCA training programs. One was a three day swift water rescue school in Maryland. We spent an entire day in the roughest part of the Potomac River getting slammed into granite boulders! The next day we learned how to repel down a cliff at Carter Rock. What any of this had to do with animal cruelty, I had no idea. But, I wasn't about to say anything! I was having a blast!

For the second training program Annie and I spent four weeks at a defensive tactics instructor school conducted by the FBI! The program was two weeks of classroom instruction and two weeks of twenty cops beating the snot out of one another!

This was one of the most memorable, life affirming experiences of my adult life! I truly felt that I had excelled at something!

During the classroom portion, the instructor made a point to compliment Annie and me. Based on our comfort level in front of the class he was convinced that we had been instructors before. I guess those years of acting school had paid off!

The tactical portion was even better! In addition to the daily physical regimen, the two weeks culminated with a practical team-building competition. We were divided into several teams. Starting at various positions on a huge obstacle course laid out over a US Army camp in upstate New York, each team was assigned to carry a shotgun and large steel ammunition case. The first team to complete the entire course won the competition. Each team was evenly matched. There were some hard core physically fit cops here! This was not going to be a cake walk.

The defining moment for me came when our team approached "the tower," a twenty-foot wooden wall with a platform at the top. Each team had to climb to the top without any ropes or ladders. Needless to say, there were no openings in the boards to place your hands or feet. As we made our approach to the tower, the instructor on scene started asking us, "Okay, what are you guys going to do? You've got a man up there that needs help! How are you going to get to him?"

I honestly don't know how I thought of this, but at that moment I shouted "human ladder!" and placed myself at the base of this wall. Right on cue, my teammates knew what to do and immediately climbed on my shoulders forming a ladder. Everyone scaled the wall, and once on top, teammates pulled the rest of us up! We won the competition!

The instructors pulled me aside later and asked me how I knew to form a human ladder. I gave them an honest answer... I had no idea.

Throughout my life, it seemed that if I tried my best at something and worked hard towards that end, I would somehow screw it up. But, if I just did something without prior thought, I could complete it without effort—as if I were in a zone.

I went back to work a new man after this training.

A lot can happen when you feel on top of the world. The world might just come knocking!

14 WATCH OUT WHAT YOU WISH FOR

My physical regimen while working at the ASPCA for four years trimmed me down from a hefty 270 lbs to 205 lbs of lean muscle mass. I felt and looked better, and Jackie approved of my new eight-pack abs! This, coupled with my recent achievements at the FBI school, left me feeling that my life was on the upswing.

I also decided that if I could not make it as a "real" police officer, I'd try my hand at acting again. I needed some new head shot photos to send to the casting agencies around the city. A young photographer named Jimmy was riding with me for a few days to chronicle the daily routine of an ASPCA agent for a class assignment. Jimmy helped me by taking extra photos of me to send to the casting agencies.

One day towards the end of an uneventful shift, Jimmy and I were heading back to the office when the chief called to summon me uptown. The FDNY was fighting a huge fire in a twenty story historic apartment building in Harlem, and the city's animal control center had been asked to help evacuate the pets abandoned by the residents.

When we met up with my unit, the FDNY scene commander said that they had successfully "knocked down" most of the fire, confining it to one side of the building. He asked us to conduct a room-by-room search of the areas that had been extinguished, assuring us that it was safe to do so. Because the fire had done extensive damage to the lower floors, both the elevators and stairwells were destroyed. As such, the entryway to the building was to be an eighth floor window using the FDNY's tower truck!

"Terrific! Sure! Let's not do anything dangerous! Sorry, Jackie!" I thought.

Jimmy was thrilled since he would be getting shots too good to be true—his "agent" being hoisted eight stories into the window of a burning building! Television news cameramen were also at the scene! I imagined the caption beneath Jimmy's photos reading, "Look, up in the sky! It's a bird! It's a plane!" but, I quickly replaced it with one that read, "Dog-cop goes into burning building!"

"Oh well," I thought, "It's too late to turn back now!"

I must admit that going through that building was unlike anything I could have imagined: the absolute destructive power of fire is so unreal! An historic building built of steel and stone, its interior had been reduced to rubble by the fire. I understood then why my firefighter friends, Rich and Charlie, loved the thrill of fighting something so powerful and surviving it. "No thanks!" I thought to myself as we finished up our search.

Sadly, we were unable to find any animals alive beyond those that were taken by their owners when they left the building.

IN TIME MY PHOTO DISTRIBUTIONS BEGAN PAYING OFF WITH CALLS FROM CASTING agencies. I even got some bit parts with my brother, Chris, and his friend, John, who were doing some independent films. Although they didn't pay much, well no money at all in fact, I felt that they would be good experience. I was a featured player in the minor films *YAW-NYC* and *Dance*—which I had a lot of fun doing. I also played one of the Bernham Woods soldiers in background shots for *Macbeth in Manhattan,* a 1999 independent film that was shot uptown near St. John the Divine Cathedral. I didn't care! This was the real deal—a paid acting job with real actors!

As soon as I arrived on the set, I saw how real it was! The first person I ran into was John Glover!

"Holy shit!" I thought to myself! "This guy's been in everything!" A classical thespian, John Glover had done everything from Broadway to major motion picture roles. This guy had worked with Burt-friggin-Lancaster, and here he was walking up to me and the other extras!

"How are you, fellas?" he asked with a genuine grin that said, "Yeah, I'm just a regular guy too."

"Uh, good Mr. Glover," I answered, sounding every bit the dork that I must've appeared to be! Still, I was on the set of a real movie that I would be appearing in with John Glover! Cool!

The day went by in a blur. I remember watching Mr. Glover do his scenes just before we "goons" got to do ours. We were dressed all in black— the medieval equivalent of modern day sniper gillie suits—with branches and leaves stuck to us for camouflage. We were then given huge Celtic swords and told to slowly creep up the hill inside the wooded area adjacent to St. John the Divine, giving the illusion of a covert attack. Very cool!

I finished my scene and headed home... well, I tried to anyway. Returning to my car, I discovered it had been towed! In the excitement of getting a real acting job, I had missed the "No Parking After 4 P.M." sign posted thirty feet away! "Great!" I thought. "Looks like I'm taking the subway to Penn Station tonight!" Oh well.

Although I was pissed about my car getting towed, I was too happy with my day to let this event ruin it for me. Besides, there would be more paid acting jobs to cover the towing.

The real deal came with some background work—an official actor's term for being an extra—on a new HBO series called *The Sopranos*. I'll never forget the day I arrived nice and early at Silver Cup Studios in Queens. After signing in and filling out the obligatory Central Casting tax forms, I waited around with the other "extras" to be led to the set. Here, in a huge space like a warehouse was an amazingly real living room set designed for a cocktail party scene!

When the actors entered I thought to myself, "That guy looks familiar. I know I've seen him before. He's a character actor, and he's been in a ton of films..." I subsequently learned that he was James Gandolphini!

Before the cameras rolled, one of the actors standing next to me joked about how long it was taking, and that with the lighting we'd all die from heat stroke before completing the scene. Yes, it was Edie Falco, but how the hell was I supposed to know that when the show hadn't even hit the air yet!

I was called for another day of shooting, but acting could not compete with my real interest in being a cop, so that shoot turned out to be my last as an actor.

NOT LONG AFTER JACKIE AND I BEGAN DATING JACKIE'S MOTHER, GERI, remarried and moved to Charlottesville, Virginia, with her new husband. Since Jackie and her mother were very close, Geri kept trying to convince us to move there as well, but being typical New Yorkers we dismissed the idea saying that there was nothing in Virginia that we couldn't get in New York! Boy, were we wrong!

We reconsidered the idea of moving to Virginia after I had been with the ASPCA for a couple of years. After all, Virginia's real estate market, property taxes, and overall cost of living seemed extremely attractive and affordable! The money that we could make from selling our small two bedroom townhouse in Deer Park would more than cover the cost of building a brand new four bedroom single family home in Virginia! However, it wasn't until my in-laws mentioned the numerous police departments in the Charlottesville area and that most, if not all, of them were currently hiring, that I sat up and took notice!

Given my record with the New York law enforcement agencies, I thought I'd have nothing to lose by looking into this prospect. So, Jackie and I headed down to Virginia on a fact-finding mission.

As soon as we arrived we both felt a positive vibe from the rustic landscape and its beautiful heavily wooded areas! Try as I might not to get my hopes up, in my heart I started to feel that maybe this was finally going to happen for me and that one of these police departments was going to snatch me up.

Sure enough, a few weeks after our trip I received a notice in the mail from the Charlottesville Police Department indicating that I was to report to their headquarters in three weeks for an orientation!

"Holy shit!" I thought. "Maybe this really is going to happen!"

The orientation was uneventful, with the "acting" chief just giving us a brief overview of the history of the department and saying how wonderful it was to live and work in Charlottesville.

"Okay," I thought. "This is still looking good. After all I now have the credentials of a New York State Peace Officer! Surely that will carry some weight!"

Although I remained cautiously optimistic, as the weeks went by with no word from Charlottesville my optimism began to fade. Finally, after two months had passed, I called to learn of my status.

"Brett, William G. … Okay, here it is," an obviously uninterested desk sergeant answers.. "Yeah, William, you were listed as not qualified. We're looking for people with prior experience."

"But I'm currently an investigator with the law enforcement division of the ASPCA in New York City!" I insisted, hoping to convince him that it was a legitimate police job! It didn't.

"Well," he said. "They may consider dog-catchers to be law enforcement in New York City, but in Charlottesville we don't. Is there anything else I can help you with?" he asked dismissively, hanging up before I had time to answer!

"Well," I thought, "That's it."

I was so used to being rejected for not being qualified that I did not feel my usual acute sense of disappointment. Even with the sergeant's blatant disrespect on the phone, I felt strangely okay, as if something was telling me, "Don't worry, it'll come."

"What the hell are you doing wasting your time in Podunk? Why don't you apply to the Fairfax County Poice Department?" Timmy exclaimed upon hearing about my experience. "Fairfax is right outside Washington, DC. They're a nationally ranked department for personnel and training, and they pay fairly well!"

As I've mentioned, Timmy is THE authority on every police department in the country.

At first, I dismissed the idea of one more department that would tell me to get lost. But with Timmy's persistent pestering I filled out an application and mailed it in with my resume. When I called with a question regarding my application a nice woman in human resources said, "Oh, Fairfax County isn't hiring right now, but we'll keep your application on file for future reference."

"Yeah, right!" I thought to myself.

"Patience Jackass, Patience!" Timmy said to me.

Two weeks later I received a notice in the mail from the Fairfax County Police Department.

"Dear Mr. William G. Brett," it began. "Thank you for your interest in applying for the position of Police Officer with the Fairfax County Police Department..."

"Okay," I thought. "Here we go again."

"... You are to report to the Massey Building located at 4100 Chain Bridge Road, Fairfax, VA for the entrance exam."

"Wait a minute!" I thought. "They're telling me to report down there for testing??? Holy shit!"

I don't know why I felt so excited this time. I mean, they weren't giving me a job, they were just telling me to show up and take a test like all the others had. Something felt different this time, however. Unlike prior experiences in which I could almost feel the presence of the *black cloud*, it was now absent. Perhaps it would eventually show up as it always did, but for now I set aside the thought of it and went through the motions for the exam as if the cloud did not even exist.

The test was scheduled for a Wednesday evening at 6:00 P.M. I had been so routinely rejected in the past that I didn't invite Jackie to come with me. Besides, it was a long day's drive just to sit around and wait for me. Timmy, however, insisted on coming with me! I guess he was so tired of hearing me bellyache about my previous failures that he wanted to help me with my confidence.

We made it to Fairfax in record time, arriving so early in fact that we had enough time for a late lunch.

"Good luck, Jackass!" he said jokingly after he dropped me off at police headquarters.

"Relax!" he reassured me, seeing me tighten up, "You've already got the job."

"Thanks, Asshole! Jinx me, why don't you?" I snapped back.

He laughed as he drove off to visit family living nearby.

As I walked into the lobby of the twelve-story glass tower, I was struck by how few people there were for the test, some forty by my estimate, all of them looking like former military men with the customary "high and tight" haircut and the confident bearing of the US marines.

"That's just great!" I thought, my poor self-esteem taking over, "What chance have I got with these guys?"

"What the hell," I thought, convinced that this was a wasted trip, "But since I'm here, I might as well take the test."

After completing the test, one of the detectives escorted me to his office upstairs for a post test interview. When we sat down he asked me to tell him about myself.

"This is different!" I thought to myself, "A police department actually taking the time to get to know the person applying for the job, instead of just looking at a cold number."

After we spoke for a few minutes, he said that I should receive my test results in the mail in a few weeks and thanked me for my time.

Timmy was late returning from his relatives' house, so I found myself standing in front of the building alone, my low self-esteem no longer allowing me to imagine for a second a successful future in law enforcement.

"I can't keep doing this to myself," I thought, "It's certainly not fair to Jackie either! She has to live with my constant hopes and inevitable failures. She deserves more than that."

When Timmy finally showed up, he asked, "So, how'd it go?"

"Oh, you know, the usual," I replied.

"Patience, Jackass, Patience!" he counselled.

15 WHEN IT RAINS IT POURS

Film director and producer Paul Berriff gained approval to make a documentary about the daily workings of the law enforcement division of the ASPCA. Paul and his cameraman were to spend several weeks riding with and filming agents as we conducted our investigations throughout the city. The documentary, *Animal COPS*, (later renamed *Animal Precinct*) would be aired on *Showtime*, and if well received they hoped to use it as a pilot on the fledgling Animal Planet Channel. I was very apprehensive at first since I did not want the whole world to see what a dork I was. Jackie saw it differently, saying that perhaps some casting director would discover me and I could give up trying to be a cop.

Paul Berriff was from England, and aside from being a film maker he had written several books about the RSPCA, Great Britain's main humane organization. We hit it off right away. Having had previous experience with the RSPCA, Paul was able to get almost anything he wanted for his project. It didn't take him long to seek an upgrade of our working conditions, equipment, and training. Things improved considerably after Paul was with us for two weeks. Paul got approval to use footage of some serious cruelty and neglect cases and of some of our more basic care and condition checks. For certain cases we worked in pairs. Annie and I were followed while we conducted an investigation into a cock-fighting organization in the Bronx. We were filmed gathering information on a suspect, tracking him down and making the arrest. We also raided two separate locations in the Bronx where we seized dozens of fighting roosters and drug paraphernalia. I have to admit, I was enjoying the filming.

In the final weeks of filming, I got the call for which I had been waiting for nearly ten years! I had already received notice in the mail from the

Fairfax Police Department that I had passed the written exam, but I had dismissed it assuming that they had just put me in the "circular file." You can imagine my excitement when I was told to report to the Massey Building in a week for a polygraph examination! Granted, it wasn't a job offer, but it was still a lot further than I'd gone with any other application!

After taking the polygraph test, I was called back a few weeks later for a physical agilities test, and a physical and psychological evaluation. After passing these with flying colors, I finally got the call that I'll never forget.

"Hello. Is this Billy Brett?" the voice on the other end of the phone asked.

"Yes it is," I answered.

"How ya doin' Billy? This is Detective John Sheehan with the Fairfax County PD," he said with a flawless Brooklyn accent.

After asking me if I was still interested in the job, he informed me that he would be my background investigator, and if I had any questions regarding the process from that point on I should call him immediately.

"Billy, I've been down here twenty years," he said, "And I've never looked back. I'm hoping you'll be the first in a long line of success stories for my record here!"

DUE TO THE HECTIC SHOOTING SCHEDULE WITH THE FILM CREW AND MY frequent trips to and from Virginia, Jackie and I kept missing each other like two ships in the night. One night after the film was completed and I was working in Brooklyn near Coney Island, I got a phone call from her.

"Guess what?" she said excitedly, "I wanted to wait until I saw you in person, but God only knows when that would be!"

I hesitated.

"Come on, guess!"

"You're pregnant!" I said, feeling my heart open beyond every failure in my life.

This was perfection. And my life had changed forever with the realization that I was going to be a father.

JACKIE WAS LESS THAN ENTHUSED ABOUT THE POSSIBILITY OF US MOVING TO Virginia. Being pregnant while I'd be away at a police academy, she was even less enthusiastic.

Our entire squad was working the day shift that day before Thanksgiving so we could all get home to our families for a long weekend. I was riding "Shotgun" with Annie in Brooklyn when I got a call from Detective Sheehan.

"Hey Billy!" he said in his now all too familiar upbeat manner, "You all set for Thanksgiving?" he asked.

"Yes sir!" I answered.

"Good deal! Hey listen," he continued, "I just wanted to be the first to congratulate you! I want to officially offer you the job... You do still want it, don't you?" he said jokingly.

"YES SIR!" I answered!

"Okay, cool. I'll let the commander of personnel know I already spoke to you. He wanted to wait until Monday, but I figured I'd give you something you could share with Jackie so you could really celebrate tomorrow! You have a great Thanksgiving, Billy!" then hung up.

"Thank you, sir!" I barely managed to say. "Holy shit!" I thought. "This is finally it! I'm finally going to be a real police officer!"

"You got the job?" Annie asked already knowing the answer by the tone in my voice. "Congratulations! You see? You never had anything to worry about," she said matter-of-factly.

"Yeah, right," I said. "Now all I have to do is tell Jackie!"

When I got home later that night Jackie was busting her butt cooking and preparing for Thanksgiving, difficult for her now that she was six months pregnant. Since she was not in the best of moods, I decided to postpone my "good news" until the following day. At least that way there'd be plenty of witnesses present when she tried to kill me!

When an in-law at the gathering brought up the subject of my being a policeman, Jackie said that we had not yet made a decision about it.

"Besides," she said turning to me. "Bill hasn't even been offered a job."

In that instant she saw the look on my face where I attempt to lie or keep something hidden!

"You heard from John Sheehan, didn't you? When?" she asked, coldly. Then before I even got the words out of my mouth, she said emphatically, "We are not moving to Virginia!"

"This one would take some time to work through," I thought to myself, since it would be a decision that was second only to deciding to be parents. She later discovered that it was the best decision we ever made!

In spite of the frustration of feeling "trapped" for some time at the ASPCA, when 1999 drew to a close and I was preparing to leave for my new job in Fairfax, Virginia, I felt a little sad about leaving the agents with whom I'd developed such good friendships. But life was calling me on.

Fairfax, here I come!

16   WHO CAN? WE CAN!

Jackie and I decided that during my six months at the police academy she would remain in New York. She was then eight months pregnant and it seemed ridiculous to relocate and try to find another OBGYN in Virginia. Besides, we still needed to sell our house on Long Island.

Throughout my life, whenever I thought about failing at something, I usually would. This time was different. Although Jackie and I took the precaution of keeping the house until I graduated, I was not going to entertain the thought of failure! I had never felt like this before, and I liked the feeling. I began to think that maybe things happened for a reason. Maybe all those years of perceived failure were God's way of using fate to guide me. Either way, I thought, "This is my time!"

Not surprisingly, both our families stepped in to help. Jackie's mother, Geri, volunteered to stay with Jackie for the final weeks of the pregnancy and after the baby came. With my mother living right next door, I knew that Jackie had a strong support system. As well, Timothy Farrell, my brother John's brother-in-law, graciously offered to share his house with me. Timothy lived in the Franconia district of Fairfax County, but his work for the U.S. State Department in Washington, D.C. often took him abroad. I stayed with Timothy from Sunday through Thursday and headed up to New York when my classes ended on Friday.

So, on Sunday, January 17, 2000, my adventure began!

My first day on the job was both terrifying and exciting. I did not want to screw up, so I arrived two hours early. Not surprisingly, some of my classmates did as well. When everyone was present a very serious looking academy instructor directed us to a classroom.

In addition to training Fairfax county police officers, the academy also trains Fairfax county sheriff's deputies, police department recruits for the towns of Herndon and Vienna, as well as recruits for the animal control and fire marshall offices.

When all sixty of us took our seats, the rest of the academy staff filed in. After various commanders made brief introductions, the chief of police greeted us. To this day, I'm totally convinced that the county got him from "Central Casting." He had the looks of a movie star and was obviously an accomplished public speaker. What struck me most, however, was something he and almost all of the commanders said: "Some of you will not make it!"

They used the words "will not" rather than "might not," which I thought was strange. Statistically, I know that some recruits don't make it through, but I thought to myself, "These guys don't know me! They don't know how hard I've worked to get here, or how long I've waited to finally get this chance! How dare they tell me I won't make it through!"

I wondered if any of my classmates felt the same way.

After the chief finished, he left with the other commanders. The second lieutenant in charge of the academy program took over. Standing about 6'3" he was one of the most serious looking human beings that I had ever met. Not since I had been a kid with Fr. Martin had I felt so intimidated by another person. And like Fr. Martin, he had that look—as if he could read your mind.

The second lieutenant covered our responsibilities as recruits and told us that we'd be responsible for electing a class president, a vice president, and a treasurer to act as liaisons to the instructors. As well, the class president would be expected to address the entire academy class, instructors, command staff, friends, and family at the graduation ceremony in June.

"God help that poor bastard!" I thought. "Whoever he happens to be."

At one point each recruit was asked to read aloud the General Orders for officers and basic training. When it was my turn, I read my portion to express the seriousness of the General Orders using all the proper voice inflection from my years of training to be an actor. When I finished reading the section, I could feel the second lieutenant glaring at me. A deafening pause followed.

"What, did you work as a reporter with WTOP Radio?" he said, making fun of my apparent fearlessness in the face of public speaking.

The class had a good laugh at that, and my classmate Ricky whispered to me, "I think we've found our class president."

I laughed as if he were kidding. It turns out that he wasn't!

The rest of that first week went by in a blur. We were issued our navy blue academy uniforms and photographed for identification. We also filled out endless paperwork.

Before completing the forms, the academy staff had given us specific instructions on exactly what to fill out and when. True to form, out of shear excitement of wanting to do well, I hadn't heard a word of the instructions and filled in sections that we had been told to leave blank. I didn't feel too badly when I discovered that some of my classmates had made the same mistake. After collecting the forms, the lieutenant called me and the other "non-conformists" to the front of the class.

"Were you, or were you not told to leave these sections blank?" he asked. "Don't you think it's important for police officers to be able to hear and comply with instructions? Each of you will write a 500 word essay on the importance of following instructions... Due on my desk Monday morning!" he concluded.

"Terrific!" I thought to myself. "I'm not here a week, and I'm already in trouble! How the hell am I going to come up with a 500 word essay in two days?" The most I had ever written were love notes to Jackie!

I spent the next five hours pondering what to write about as I made the drive home to Long Island. Before I arrived home, I had the essay all but written in my mind. It would be about Sir Robert Piel, the founder of modern police science. Jackie described me as "hyperfocused" while writing my essay, but I had no idea of the significance of the term or its meaning.

I returned on Monday with renewed confidence. When I got to know my classmates, more and more of them began hinting that they wanted me to be the class president!

"No way!" was my standard response to their running joke. "Besides," I said. "I've got too much going on anyway. I've got a baby only days away and a house to sell up in New York. No thanks."

The following Friday, I spent the entire five hour drive home thinking about the possibility of actually being elected as class president.

"There's no way!" I thought. "Things like that don't happen to me."

I felt that I had "forced fate's hand" enough by landing this police job. Dreaming of such a thing as class president would only be pushing my luck.

"Still though, what if?"

The following week my classmates elected me class president!!!

"What the hell?" I thought to myself! I felt that somehow I was living someone else's life. "These things just don't happen to me!"

But somehow I knew that I could handle this responsibility. I knew that it wouldn't be easy, but something was pushing me forward. Perhaps it was the thought of being responsible for leading my classmates and seeing that we help one another get through the academy, or perhaps I had forgotten to worry as I usually did. Either way, when we finished up that day, we gathered as a class to discuss our goals. I remembered then what the chief and the other commanders had said to us at orientation. I decided to share my views with my classmates.

"First, I want to thank you guys for having this kind of confidence in me." I began. "I still don't know what you were thinking about!" I joked. "Do you remember what all of those "white shirts" said to us on the first day? They said, 'Some of you will not make it through this academy!' Didn't that piss some of you off a little? Maybe it's just me, but after I heard that it just galvanized my resolve to succeed here! How did they know what I could, or couldn't do? Since we need to support one another in our time here let me propose this to you. Whenever we're doing P.T. (physical training), or D.T. (defensive training), and we're starting to feel fatigued, someone will shout out "WHO CAN?" and the rest of us will answer "WE CAN!"

I concluded by letting them know that they could call me with any problems they might have, and that we'd try and solve them together.

As we closed, someone seized the moment and yelled at the class, "WHO CAN? "

"WE CAN!"

"You see? This is why I said to you when we first met that you would be the president," Ricky said, winking at me as he filed out with the rest of the class for the day.

I COULD NOT BELIEVE HOW WELL THINGS WERE GOING. FOR ME, THE ACADEMIC portion of the academy was certainly no cake walk, but due to study groups and my nightly ritual of burying myself in the books, I managed to do okay.

As the weeks went by, I was feeling more and more at ease with my responsibilities. Just when I thought nothing could ruin this, Jackie called.

She was hysterical. She had just come from the OBGYN. There might be a problem with the baby. The doctor had noticed some irregularities with certain hormone levels and wanted her at the hospital to induce labor as soon as possible. I told her not to worry, that I was on my way. Hanging up, I tracked down my squad leader.

A very athletic and attractive woman about my age, Master Police Officer Virginia D'Ceser had been a cop for almost twenty years. She had an extremely nurturing attitude toward us, which earned her the nickname, "Mom." Being a mother herself, she didn't hesitate for a second when I told her what was going on.

"Go home!" she told me, "We'll get you caught up on anything you miss."

When I returned home that Thursday night, it was the beginning of a long Presidents' Day holiday weekend. Jackie was a little bit calmer and felt fine physically. I tried to be as calming and reassuring as I could be, but I did not have a friggin' clue as to what she was going through.

When we arrived at the hospital, Jackie's doctor started her on an I.V. drip and tested with Petocin to see what, if any, negative reaction the baby or Jackie might have to the drug. Before long both Jackie and the baby began having adverse effects. Pulling me aside the doctor said, "Tonight, probably. Tomorrow, the latest," meaning that was when the contractions would begin.

"Wow!" I thought to myself, "that quickly!"

So we went home to wait as ordered. I felt confident. I still had three days until I was due back at the academy, and I would only end up missing the one day of classes.

"This is going to end up being perfect timing!" I told my mother-in-law.

The baby, however, had other plans.

As Friday dragged into Saturday and Saturday into Sunday, the baby was still no closer to joining us "on the outside!"

I finally told Jackie, "You know I'll have to go back to Virginia tomorrow night, right?" as though this statement would somehow coax her and/ or the baby to get things moving.

"I know. I'll be fine," she said with a calm tone in her voice that I had not heard all weekend.

As I drove down I-95, I felt a subtle calm which in some sense I was always aware of, and which often allowed me to predict events before they actually happened! I could see ahead that the baby would be blessed with a healthy and happy life!

When I spoke to Jackie that evening she sounded tired but assured me that she felt fine. Early Tuesday morning Jackie's mother called to say that they were on the way to the hospital. Rationalizing that part of my training would be the safe operation of emergency vehicles at extremely high speeds, I sped back to New York in record time!

Jackie was hooked up to several monitors in the delivery room. I could only imagine the pain she was in from the look on her face! As the day wore on, the pain worsened so she received an epidural.

Finally, after twenty-six hours of labor, our daughter, Emily Caitlin, came into the world.

Having never seen child birth in person before, I can honestly say, it is an experience that I'll never forget! Emily was without doubt the most beautiful thing I'd ever seen in my life!

In that very moment my life changed irrevocably for the better!

Until then I had only identified myself as "Billy." Now, I would forever be known first and foremost as "Daddy"! I think that even Emily knew that she would forever have me wrapped around those perfect little fingers!

By the next day our entire family had converged on the hospital to meet the newest member of the Brett clan.

While I wanted nothing more than to stay there with my wife and new daughter, I had to get back to Virginia for a big test coming up. Fortunately, my instructors helped me come up to speed for the upcoming test.

Throughout my life I have been blessed to know a lot of hard working and considerate people, but none more so than my classmates of the 36th session of the Fairfax County Criminal Justice Academy! Our strength as a team galvanized as the weeks progressed. During our daily runs, for example, as the squads neared the end of the route and before crossing the finish line, the entire unit would turn around and run back to meet the slowest runner, and then we'd all run past the line as a unit saying "WHO CAN?" "WE CAN!"

I CAN REMEMBER ONLY ONCE BEING TRULY SHAKEN UP WHILE AT THE ACADEMY.

After covering the do's and don'ts of how to inform families of the untimely death of a loved one, the instructor played an actual recording of a 911 call received at our dispatch center:

"Fairfax County 911. What is your emergency?" the operator asked in the usual professional, cool tone.

"There's a man in my house who just raped me!" the obviously traumatized female voice on the other end whispered. "I don't know if he left yet, but I need help!" she said, her voice now barely audible.

"Okay Ma'am, I'm sending help right away!" the 911 operator assured her. "I need you to stay on the line with me, Okay?"

The caller then tried to answer questions being asked by the operator before suddenly stopping.

"Wait a minute... I think I still hear him... OH MY GOD!!! NO!!!" she screamed!

Between her screams the muffled sound of a male voice could be heard. He had returned to the room because he thought he had dropped something. He had discovered his victim on the phone. He then began stabbing her, the sound of which was clearly audible over the phone. The sickening "thump" of the impact of the knife and her screams for mercy seemed to go on for an eternity. Then the screams stopped. The killer had disconnected the line.

If there was ever a question as to whether or not evil truly exists in the world, it was answered for me that day! How could a human being even conceive of such a violent act on another human being, let alone actually commit it? We were then shown the actual crime scene photos of that grissly night.

I was overcome with sadness. Clearly this was a young woman in her twenties who had a family somewhere that loved her. A father would have to identify his little girl. All I could think about was my new daughter, Emily.

"What kind of a world had we brought her into?"

I knew then why fathers call their daughters "their little girls" no matter how old they are! I felt enraged and then frustrated that there was nothing I could to do for that girl.

"This is why I have chosen this path," I thought, hardening my resolve. "If people this evil actually exist, then they're going to answer to me!"

"Everything's going to be just fine," I told Jackie and Emily silently whenever I looked at a photo of them that I had taped to the top of my desk at the academy.

AS THE FINAL DAYS AT THE ACADEMY CAME TO A CLOSE, MY CONCERN WAS what I was going to say in my address to the graduating class and all our families, not to mention the entire command staff and the government officials of Fairfax County! Somehow, it was a lot easier than I had imagined. Remembering the daily examples of dedication by my classmates, the words seemed to flow easily enough. We then presented the academy staff with a shadow box with all sixty names of the 36th Session, and the badges of all four agencies represented in our class.

After the presentation, my classmates and the instructors had a surprise for me.

"In recognition for dedication, leadership, and positive attitude, the 'Instructor's Award' goes to Officer William G. Brett".

"Holy shit!" I thought, "Could all this really be happening to me? After all those years of feeling so inept, was I actually now receiving an award from other police officers for being positive?"

I could never have imagined this, and before my entire family, too. It was my proudest moment. I had accomplished something that would make them truly proud of me. Instead of testing their love for me, I had reaffirmed it! Not only were my parents overcome with emotion, but my oldest brother John, usually the stoic rock of calm, had this huge smile on his face that I had never seen before!

"I can't tell you how proud I am of both of you!" he told Jackie and me. Hearing that from John meant more to me than a hundred awards!

As I made my way out of the auditorium, I was stopped by one of the instructors who had been with the department for over twenty years and had the reputation of being a no-nonsense cop with no patience for incompetents. A bear of a man, he was (and still is!) one of the most intimidating men I've ever met! I thanked him for all of his help during the academy session.

"Mr. Brett, the success of this class is due in large part to your efforts here. Now get away from me, you carpet-bagging, Yankee-dog!" he said smiling as he walked away from me.

If I did nothing else with my career, at least I'd have that memory to take with me!

"Tomorrow, Metropolis, here I come," I thought to myself, "ready and prepared to protect all who need it!"

17   BILLY ON THE BEAT

I was assigned to the Franconia District Station in Alexandria and would be working the evening shift from 1:30 P.M. to 1:00 A.M. Since this was the most sought after shift, I was all too happy to have it.

The patrol schedule was—and still is—the greatest concept ever! Instead of the old rotating schedule, officers are assigned permanent eleven and one half hour shifts. The day shift is from 5:30 A.M. to 5:00 P.M., my evening shift was from 1:30 P.M. to 1:00 A.M., and the midnight shift was from 7:30 P.M. to 7:00 A.M. We worked two days on, then two days off with every other week-end being an off duty three day weekend! This worked out perfectly for me since I would still be commuting for the next two months to Long Island to help Jackie get the house packed up.

As a rookie officer, I was required to complete a probationary period in which I was trained by a Field Training Instructor—a senior patrol officer who observes and evaluates new officers and offers guidance and/or correction when needed.

I was fortunate to be assigned to Master Police Officer (MPO) Wesley McNiel. A former Marine, he was about my age and still practiced the physical regimen of a "Jar-head."

We hit it off right away! Fresh from the academy, I always answered him with a "Yes sir" or "No sir," to which he would respond, "Cut that SIR shit out, you're a cop now!"

We spent each shift trolling for bad guys, jumping on calls so I could get good experience, and going over the usual "what, when" scenarios. After hearing about my previous incarnation as a "Pet Detective," he told me that it had been bugging him for the longest time that he thought I looked familiar. It wasn't until I mentioned the "Animal Planet" pilot episode that he realized where he had seen me. I had hoped that no one had seen that show for fear of the ridicule that would inevitably follow. Not until I mentioned it to MPO McNiel, however, had anyone realized that I was in it.

One night after finishing up my shift, I was in the locker room while the rest of the squad was gathered in the report writing room with our sergeant and second lieutenant. The sergeant paged me on the intercom to come to the report room immediately.

"Uh-oh!" I thought. "That doesn't sound good!"

As I entered the report room, my bosses were at their desks with a serious look on their faces.

"Officer Brett," my lieutenant said in a cold tone that convinced me my career as a cop was over, "Why didn't you alert us to your status before now?"

"Oh shit!" I thought, "What the hell did I forget to do?"

Being new, and with a lifetime of making mistakes, I automatically assumed that I had screwed up something! While these negative thoughts raced through my head, my lieutenant began giggling.

"So there I am flipping channels last night, and there's Big Bill on my TV!"

My sergeant joined him in laughter. Subsequently, I could always tell when the show had aired, because the cruiser's computer would light up with messages from all over the county that read, "Hey dude, I saw you on TV last night!"

AS PART OF MY TRAINING, I WAS ASSIGNED TO A SECONDARY FIELD TRAINING Instructor on the day shift to give me exposure to the different types of complaints/cases that were unique to those time periods. PFC Phillips was also a native New Yorker, born and raised in the Bronx. He had moved to Virginia as a teenager with his family. Before joining the Fairfax County Police Department he was in the Air Force. A few years younger than I, he reminded me of my older brother, Chris, in many ways. Like MPO McNiel, he treated me as an equal and never spoke down to me.

PFC Phillips was also one of the most proactive police officers I have ever known! We'd walk down the hallways of seedy motels and inevitably come across rooms where mopes were up to no good. PFC Phillips would use what I came to call the "Jedi Mind Trick" on these "pillars of society," and they would almost always give themselves away! It was really amazing how easily their guilty consciences betrayed them.

As the new guy, I was constantly worrying about missing something or forgetting to do something. As a result, I was constantly missing and forgetting things. So PFC Phillips began calling me "Mr. Magoo."

JACKIE AND I HAD DECIDED TO RENT A BEAUTIFUL NEW TOWNHOUSE JUST outside historic downtown Fredericksburg, a forty minute drive south of Fairfax. I was immediately smitten with Old Town Fredericksburg, the famed boyhood hometown of George Washington. It had all the charm of Glen Ellyn that I had enjoyed as a boy but twice the history! And just as with Glen Ellyn, the town threw a parade for pretty much any occasion! I knew that this was where I wanted Emily to grow up. So, by the beginning of September, we packed up and left Long Island forever. I had all but forgotten that the *black cloud* ever existed.

By October 2000, I had completed my field training and was "cut loose" to patrol on my own. I ended up being permanently assigned to the day shift on PFC Phillips' squad. I could not have picked a better group of hard-charging cops to work with, nor the funniest bunch of wise-ass juvenile delinquents I have ever known!

During the day we'd handle the calls for service and go hunting for drug runners in the motel parking lots or at traffic stops out on I-95. Afterwards, we'd hang out to "research" the effects of beer on the tired and angry police officer and to have bitch sessions to release stressful days.

Aside from "choir practice," we frequently played practical jokes on each other to relieve stress. PFC Phillips and I were usually the ones to do so. Our roll calls were also the verbal equivalent of a Ultimate Fighting Championship cage match. God help the poor bastard who screwed up a report or just plain stammered when asking a question! If you weren't sharp, you were dog meat! One particular afternoon, PFC Phillips was being particularly brutal with one of the men in our squad. I felt that he had crossed the line.

"Okay, enough is enough!" I thought as he hammered this kid. Clearly it was time for a little street justice!

Now, as practical jokes go, you can do the usual fake arrest sheet with your "victim's" academy photo in the arrest column and attach it to the roll call boards, or you can move their cars from the station lot, or even move their lockers out into the parking lot. But for some reason I had decided that PFC Phillips, being the hard-charger that he was, deserved the grand-daddy of them all. I had been told of this practical joke a long time ago, with the stipulation that it should be used only as an absolute last resort!

Of course, I went straight to that last resort. "The ATOM Bomb!"

While PFC Phillips was finishing up his paperwork, I walked out into the rear parking lot where all the cruisers were parked. He had made the mistake of leaving his running with all his gear still inside. Once the coast was clear, I climbed into his cruiser, killed the engine, turned on the air conditioning and set the controls on "High." Carefully opening his crime scene processing kit, I took out his unopened jar of fingerprint powder.

If you're not familiar with this substance, fingerprint powder is made from talcum powder and volcanic ash. It is so ultra-fine that you need to handle it with latex gloves. If it gets into your pores it takes weeks to completely wash out.

I opened the jar of fingerprint powder and emptied its contents in every vent, making sure that they were all aimed at the driver's seat. I then looked around carefully again. Good, nobody in sight, so I got out and closed the door behind me as if nothing had happened. I then moved out of sight and waited. A few minutes later, PFC Phillips walked out of the station and got into his cruiser. As soon as he turned the key in the ignition, it happened! The interior of the Ford Crown Victoria immediately filled with the black cloud of death, and PFC Phillips leapt from it as though the car was on fire. Covered from head to toe in the powder, he resembled a coal miner who'd just been rescued from a mine collapse! The screams were incredible. The rage in his voice was all I needed to hear to know it was time to leave. The mission was a success.

The next day at roll call, however, PFC Phillips knew right away that there could only be one person capable of perpetrating such a heinous act. He looked right at me as soon as he walked in and said, "That was real funny. Just wait 'til you see what I do!" The tone in his voice let me know that I was toast!

PFC Phillips is one of the few people who is patient enough to wait for the perfect time to repay a good practical joke. As it turned out, he stalked me for several days to find the perfect moment to strike. And did he ever!

Taking the day off, PFC Phillips followed me to my usual lunch spot driving a car that he knew I wouldn't recognize. After watching me go inside the building, he used his fleet key to gain entry to my cruiser. When he had taken care of business, he got into his car on the other side of the lot and waited for me. On returning to my cruiser I looked at my air vents just as I turned the key...

"OH SHIT!"

Although not nearly as explosive as when I got Phillips, the effect was just as devastating. I sat there for a moment, stunned.

"This really is the mother of all practical jokes," I said aloud. I then laughed, knowing that I had deserved it for what I had done to him.

When I got to the station I quickly went to the locker room and tried wiping off the powder without much effect. I soon learned that the fine powder's color shows more when you add water! The more water I splashed on my face, the more I looked like a coal miner! "Oh well." I thought, "Payback is a bitch!"

We both received a little talking to by our lieutenant and had to clean up both cruisers. It took us forever to get that freaking powder out of the upholstery, not to mention our skin! We also agreed never to unleash that kind of wrath on each other ever again. A word to the unwary, this really should be the absolute last resort when it comes to practical jokes.

ON MY DAYS OFF, JACKIE AND I BEGAN LOOKING AT EVERY MODEL HOME IN the greater Fredericksburg, Spotsylvania, and Stafford area. We kept coming back to a neighborhood in Fredericksburg with model homes for construction, one of which had a living room with a twenty-foot ceiling and a gas fireplace. The first thing I imagined in that room was the fifteen-foot Christmas tree that I would no doubt have to get every year! Also, with the number of families with small children living there, I was immediately reminded of a Norman Rockwell print with children running everywhere having the time of their lives!

"Perfect!" I thought.

After a lot of number crunching, we decided to steal from Peter to pay

Paul to pull it off—a decision that which would come back to haunt us—and went to contract in January 2001.

Our entire family from New York visited for Emily's first birthday in February, and we drove them across town to show them our new neighborhood and our plans for construction! It all seemed so perfect.

By June 2001 construction was completed and we were handed the keys to our dream home! I could not believe in my good fortune after so many years of thinking that I would be forever over-shadowed by the *black cloud*. I felt truly blessed! The skies seemed forever clear and blue.

18 HAPPY BIRTHDAY, BILLY

I've always heard that it's a common male *faux pas* to forget ones wedding anniversary, but since mine is on the same day as my birthday, it's almost impossible for me to forget! If I had any lapses in the past, my thirty-sixth birthday put an end to forgetfulness.

That September morning began beautifully. Like the rest of the east coast, Virginia woke up to a picture perfect day with mild temperatures and unlimited visibility. It was a glorious day, our eighth anniversary, and I had the day off.

Because Emily likes the Disney Channel, we'd normally be watching it or Nickelodeon all morning long. But as fate would have it, that day I was able to watch the *Today Show* while I drank my coffee—a rare treat for me since I rarely get to watch any grown-up news in the mornings, and I can only handle just so much Spongebob Squarepants!

As Jackie read the morning paper with her coffee in the kitchen, I caught the tail end of an interview that Matt Lauer was doing with Harry Bellefonte. I guess it was around 8:45 when they went to a commercial break.

What we saw next would forever imprint in our minds exactly where we were and what we were doing in that moment.

Seeing the live video feed and listening to Matt Lauer try to report it, my mind wasn't really grasping what it was receiving. "What you're seeing is a live shot of lower Manhattan where a plane has apparently struck the north tower of the World Trade Center!" he said, his voice clearly shaken. Smoke and flame that only jet fuel could create plumed from a monstrous hole in the upper floors of the north face of the building!

My thoughts immediately went to my friend Fred, who over the last several years had busted his ass working his way up the corporate ladder at Cantor Fitzgerald and was now their Chief Operating Officer. With the title came an office befitting a C.O.O. "Holy shit!" I thought.

"Hey Jackie!" I shouted, even though in my heart I already knew the answer to my question, "Didn't Fred tell us his office is on the northwest corner of the 104th floor of that building?"

Like everyone else on the planet, I stood motionless in my family room and watched helplessly as his building burned out of control. So many thoughts raced through my head. How could the FDNY begin to even fight a fire like this? How could a pilot possibly hit a building so big on a day that is so clear? I had remembered seeing the old news footage of the bomber that struck the Empire State Building back in the 1940's, but that was during a storm and the top floors of the building had been covered by clouds! Besides, that was sixty years ago! Surely our more advanced technology today would prevent such a thing from happening! I guess I was still too naïve, but I couldn't even think that someone would intentionally fly a plane into a building.

Soon, every TV channel had cameras aimed at the trade center carrying the signal live. Reporters were talking to witnesses on the street who recalled seeing a large commercial jet liner just before it hit the building! As one of the witnesses spoke about what she had seen, her voice changed drastically. "Oh my god! What are they doing? Oh my god, they're jumping from the windows!" Even as she said it, I was watching it live. My mind couldn't grasp it. Countless people were now leaping from the upper floors above the impact zone! "Could one of them be Fred?" I wondered. I'll never know.

At that moment the little kid inside of me hoped for a miracle. He hoped that somehow all of this was just a dream, and that at any moment that familiar red and blue streak would rocket skyward and save those people...

Not today. This was one dream that would just go on and on. While watching this nightmare I noticed what I thought was another aircraft. I remember thinking, "Man, that other plane looks like it's getting too close to the..."

Then the second fully fueled jumbo jet slammed into the south face of the south tower! Any naïve questions I had vanished in that instant.

At that point there was no doubt. The only question was who was doing this? Why were they doing it? What was their next target? It didn't take long to get an answer. The reports were now coming in from Washington, D.C. that the Pentagon had been hit and that the White House, Capitol Hill, and numerous other landmarks were being evacuated because there were several hijacked aircraft that were inbound. In fact, as it turned out the entire country began evacuating all the major landmarks and high rise buildings. In an unprecedented move, the federal government ordered all air traffic grounded, and all inbound international flights were instructed to turn around or redirect to Canada or Mexico. For the first time since Orville and Wilber Wright took off from the dunes in North Carolina, the airspace above the United States was devoid of any aircraft!

All of this was too much for Jackie to bear. "I'm taking Emily outside. I don't want her seeing this," she said. Maybe it was Jackie's voice that started my brain to fire again, and I started making phone calls. Hoping for a miracle, I tried Fred's office phone, but all I got was some automated voice telling me that all the circuits were currently overloaded. I then tried calling his wife, Eileen, at home. She was in a state of shock. She told me that Fred had managed to call her from his cell phone after the initial impact to his building. The FDNY had told them to hold on while they did everything in their power to reach them. But before Fred was able to say anything else, they had been cut off. I told her to hang up immediately in case he tried to call back.

I then started calling my family. My brother, Rob, had already left his office in Times Square and was en route to his apartment on the upper east side. Rob told me that our brothers, John and Chris, were out of town— John on a speaking engagement and Chris in Long Island. "Thank god!" I thought. My immediate family were all safe. I then spoke to my sister, Rose, who told me that Cousin Jimmy Haran also worked in the north tower. I never knew that my cousin worked for Cantor Fitzgerald. I later discovered that he had actually worked in the same office with Fred!

After hanging up with my sister, I called the ASPCA. Annie told me all the agents were accounted for and were safely back at the office in upper Manhattan. I told her to stay safe and hung up.

It was at this point that I watched in horror as the inconceivable happened... the south tower of the World Trade Center collapsed! "How can this possibly be happening?" I thought to myself. These two buildings were icons of the New York City skyline. Now, both were hit by modern day jumbo jets and one was now lying in rubble at the foot of its twin. "How much time does the north tower have left?"

As helpless as I felt watching this, I couldn't imagine what anyone still inside the north tower was feeling! Some continued to jump. Some never got the chance. Like its twin, the north tower simply collapsed into its own foot print. How many lost souls? 10,000? 50,000? 100,000? As the cloud of ash, smoke, and pulverized concrete completely enveloped lower Manhattan, I could only imagine how many people were dying.

As catastrophic as all of this was, only divine intervention and superior building engineering kept those buildings from falling over on their sides after being struck. I'm sure that was the intention when this horrific act was first conceived. How could anyone even think of committing such a heinous crime? Where would this kind of hatred come from? These were not military installations. Those were not soldiers jumping out of windows. They were just everyday citizens who had shown up for work on time that fateful Tuesday morning. I started to get that feeling again. Like that day in the academy after hearing the recording from the 911 dispatcher. "If evil such as this can exist in the world..." I remembered.

I began thinking like a cop again, because when Jackie came back into the house later that afternoon I told her I'd probably be going up to New York City to help out. Obviously she did not want me to leave the house. "Jackie," I said, "you know Fred and Jimmy were murdered today, don't you?" Maybe it was the tone in my voice, but this statement ended any discussion on the matter. Here was a crime scene the likes of which the world had never seen, and there were brother cops and fire fighters who needed our help.

The next day I reported for work and with little more than a look from the rest of my squad, I knew we were heading to New York City. Because of our proximity to the Pentagon and Washington, D.C., we had issues of our own to handle first. Most of the Fairfax County Police and Fire Department emergency response resources had already been deployed to the Pentagon. That left the rest of the county issues in our hands. Aside from the numerous paranoid 911 calls of suspicious looking middle-eastern males lurking about, the county was very quiet. We had been told in no uncertain terms that the Fairfax County Police Department would not officially sanction any resources being deployed to the scene in New York. We didn't care. We would go on our own time! So when we finished up our shift we packed light overnight bags and headed up to Union Station.

As we drove along I-395 through Arlington, we passed within a few hundred yards of the Pentagon. Apparently the hijackers had used the interstate to guide them straight to the building. Looking like a movie set for a disaster film, the scene before us seemed unreal—until that smell hit us. Yes, the unmistakable odor of jet fuel... and something else. This was a stark reminder of where we were heading.

Upon arriving at D.C. Union Station, we were escorted by a uniformed officer from the Amtrak Police Department and placed aboard the next train bound for New York City Penn Station. Considering that all air traffic was still grounded throughout the country, the train was fairly empty. Perhaps it was still the basic fear of the city coming under another attack that kept everyone away. The ride north was a solemn one. The looks on the faces of the few passengers on the train with us said it all. They all knew who we were and where we were heading. As we arrived at Penn Station, some of them actually approached us and thanked us, wishing us well as they walked off the train.

We made our way upstairs to the driveway between Madison Square Garden and Penn Station where we were met by two more Amtrak officers. They told us that the OEM (Office of Emergency Management) had established a staging area for all out-of-town emergency service personnel over at the Jacob Javitz Center on the west side of Manhattan. Graciously offering to drive us there, we piled into two marked police vans and raced across town.

When we arrived, we observed what could only be described as controlled chaos. There were cops and firemen from all over the country standing around waiting for direction. After I made my way over to the liaison trailer, I was instructed to fill out some paper work that consisted of name(s), date(s) of birth, and all the basic next of kin information of all our personnel. Then I was told that they'd call us up when they needed us. Since this wasn't good enough for us, the senior of the two Amtrak officers said, "Don't worry, we'll get you downtown right now!" and with that we all piled back into the vans and drove with lights and sirens to the Trade Center.

It was surreal. Only two years earlier I had driven through lower Manhattan almost on a daily basis, but now I couldn't get my bearings. With the exception of the glow of the emergency lights, lower Manhattan was completely blacked out. What we saw as we got closer was indescribable. And there was that odor again—jet fuel and something else.

The Amtrak officers dropped us off as close by as they could, but we still had to walk five blocks down the West Side Highway. As we made our way through the inner perimeter near the front entrance to the Financial Plaza Building of Merrill Lynch, we could see that the rest of the West Side Highway was buried from that point south. Even with our training and combined experiences, nothing could have prepared us for what we were seeing! Here it was two days after the towers fell, and there were still pockets of fires that had yet to be fought because they were still out of reach!

We didn't have the first clue as to where to begin, so we cut through the lobby of the Merrill Lynch Building and found ourselves in the marina area at the west end of Liberty Street. Stashing our gear under a trailer, we made our way over to the southwest corner of the Trade Center. Without a word, we jumped into the bucket lines that were now going full force. We worked into the late hours of the night until a huge thunderstorm rolled through dumping a massive amount of water. You could feel it in the air. It was as though everyone was thinking the same thing. "Maybe god was trying to wash off the dirt from this injury to fight off infection." It didn't matter. The fact was that the scene was becoming much too dangerous for anyone to continue working around those jagged metal beams that were now slick from the rain.

It had been such a long day that none of us had stopped to think about food or where we might find a place to sleep. We were soaked through to the bone from the rain and were now freezing since the temperatures had dropped with the passing storm. Trudging back to the marina we grabbed our gear and walked into the lobby of the financial building where several hundred other cops and firefighters had also sought refuge. There had to be at least two inches of water on the floor from a combination of rain and countless fire hoses that were running in every direction as far as one could see.

As we walked through the huge atrium lobby of this building, I remembered the day years earlier that my brother, John, had given me a tour of it.

I remembered saying how beautiful it was, and how it would make a great movie setting. In fact, Eddie Murphy had used it for a scene in the film, *Boomerang*. Tonight, however, it looked like a scene from a very different movie. Huge sections from one or both of the towers had crashed through the eastern portion of the glass roof rendering the entire lobby unsafe. As such, several uniformed officers from the New York Police Department advised us to keep moving.

We finally found an unlocked door in the hallway of the adjacent building's lobby that led to a sushi bar restaurant. It was now pervaded by the aroma of two-day-old unkempt fish. Still, it was warm, dry, and had soft couch-like booths where we could lie down for awhile. I was just dozing off for what seemed like five minutes—it turned out to be three hours—only to be awakened by two uniformed New York police officers.

"What the hell are you guys doing in here?" they shouted. "Don't you know this building is still unsafe?"

As we all began sitting up, we noticed several other heads poke up as well. It seemed that while we slept, several other cops and firefighters had made their way into the restaurant. Gathering ourselves, we headed back outside.

In stark contrast to Tuesday morning, Friday was gray, overcast, and cold. To our amazement, we saw dozens of volunteers handing out boxes of brand new clothing and boots that had been donated by all the major New York City retailers. These volunteers directed us to several locations where hot meals were available for all the emergency response personnel. Too tired and hungry to go searching, we picked the closest one, a catering ship named "The Spirit of New York" now docked at the end of the marina and serving hot meals 24/7. After grabbing something to eat and stowing our gear on its upper floor, which we were allowed to make our base of operations, we returned to the dig site and jumped back on the bucket lines. We'd dig, we'd load, we'd pass the bucket of debris down the line.

As the days went by, that odor only got worse, but there was no time to even think about it. The thought that someone might actually still be alive under all of this rubble had all but dwindled. Whenever we'd come across anything, the pace would slow to a crawl in an attempt to recover as much of the person as possible. Rarely more than one emergency worker was needed to remove them from the rubble. At least the families of these victims would have some kind of closure. How many hundreds, even thousands would not? I remember thinking to myself, "Come on Fred, show me where you are!"

I never got an answer.

As the reality began to sink in, I found myself one day standing in front of "The 10 house" on Liberty Street. It is a relatively small FDNY fire house located directly across the street from where the south tower once stood. I was standing there in a daze, facing the dig site when suddenly I began to notice all the different uniforms working on the pile. There were cops and firefighters from all over the world standing next to each other with their sleeves rolled up working side by side—Los Angeles Police Department; Fire/Rescue units from Boston, Chicago, Nashville, Philadelphia, and Pittsburgh; the Royal Canadian Mounted Police; Scotland Yard; firefighters from Mexico and France—all had made their way to New York to help in any way they could!

Through my sadness, I couldn't help feeling a surge of pride. This was, after all, what our job is all about—people had needed help and first responders had answered the call without a second thought. What brave souls these people were who answered the call that Tuesday morning!

This feeling of pride was stirred again about a week later while we were working the dig site in the middle of the plaza between the two towers. This once beautiful courtyard now looked more like that game we played as kids called "Don't Break the Ice". When the buildings collapsed, the falling debris broke through the floor of the plaza revealing the several levels below. Numerous precarious foot bridges were all that remained of the plaza floor and were the only access to and from the dig sites. The only recognizable feature in this grotesque landscape was the sculpture of "The Sphere" located in the center of the plaza. The falling debris had cut a huge gash in the top of the sculpture, but it was otherwise intact.

I had been working just under the sphere when one of the Port Authority Police Officers located a victim not five meters away from me. As was now the routine, the digging around that specific area stopped while all but two or three workers slowly dug to recover the victim. This time two heroes, a Port Authority Police Officer and a fire fighter, were found not ten feet away from each other.

"This is the reason we all came here!" I thought. "Two more families would no longer have to anguish over the whereabouts of their love ones."

Where is my friend in all of this? Where is my cousin?

As the FEMA (Federal Emergency Management Agency) techs cleared the debris freeing our "brothers," one of the huge cranes lifted their stretchers out one at a time. There was no way to safely carry them out manually due to the exposed lower levels of the plaza. As they were both lowered to the street side of the plaza, a contingent of six members from both of their departments took charge of carrying them the rest of the way. Before picking them up, there was a moment of silence. We all lined up to form a gauntlet, which was promptly taken charge of by a Port Authority sargent who shouted, "DETAIL."

On reflex, we all snapped to attention. As we did so, a flag was draped over the bodies and they were lifted up. "PRESENT ARMS!" the sargent shouted. Several hundred cops and firefighters held their salute for nearly ten minutes as our brothers' bodies were carried out. Beaten, filthy and exhausted, it was the finest honor guard I had ever seen!

As was now the standard, whenever a member of service was recovered the ambulance would be escorted by four NYPD Motor units and taken to the temporary morgue. Even as the ambulances pulled away, men were still holding their salutes on the other side of the street! Everyone had broken down. This scene repeated itself countless more times.

As time passed, however, the bucket lines shut down permanently in favor of heavy equipment since the hope of finding anyone else alive or dead was unrealistic.

We left New York City the following day feeling that we had made a small contribution to the recovery effort. As we walked towards the marina I got a really good look at what remained of the once iconic skyline that has been a backdrop for countless films, post cards, and wedding proposals. There was now only a lingering plume of smoke where the two towers stood just two weeks earlier.

In that moment I was finally able to grasp the reality that I would never see my friend or my cousin again. "Goodbye Fred. Goodbye Jimmy."

WHEN I ARRIVED HOME LATER THAT DAY, JACKIE MET ME IN THE DRIVEWAY.

Maybe it was my filthy exhausted appearance, but there were tears welling up in her eyes and she had a look on her face I had never seen before.

"You're not going to go join the Marines now, are you?" she asked finally with genuine concern in her voice.

I laughed. "No!" I reassured her. "What would make you think that?"

"I know you!" she said, "You'll be taking this personally! So you'll want to go after the bad guys yourself!"

I couldn't argue with that observation. However, my priorities were now and forever with Jackie and Emily.

"My love," I said. "I am home for good. By the way, happy anniversary!"

"Happy birthday, Bill," she said smiling, as we walked into the house.

19 THERE ARE NO SUCH THINGS AS MONSTERS

Do you remember how often as a child you'd check under your bed to see if there were any monsters? Can you recall how long it would take you to fall asleep even after your parents reassured you that there were no such things as monsters? How old were you when you didn't need your bedroom door left open to let the power of that forty-watt force field shine in from the hallway light? I guess like most people, it was what I couldn't see that scared me the most. I can remember being told by my parents, "Close your eyes, Billy. Now, what do you see?"

"Nothing," I said.

"Okay, now open them."

Of course, when I opened my eyes my room was exactly the way it should be. No hideous large creatures with blood red eyes or razor sharp fangs stared back at me from the darkness.

"You see? There's nothing in the dark that isn't there in the light!"

LATER IN LIFE, HOWEVER, I DISCOVERED THAT THERE REALLY ARE MONSTERS. The terrifying thing is that they don't look like monsters at all! By all outward appearances they look just like human beings. Yet inside, they're something else—something so sinister that even adults are afraid. Some monsters can't be seen by their victims until it's too late. Others can't be seen at all!

I wonder how many passengers aboard flight 93 that fateful Tuesday morning on September 11 suspected that there were five monsters among them? What I've heard is that although they must have been frightened by the knowledge of monsters on the plane, they were able to overcame their fear, like the little kid being empowered by that hallway light, and fight back.

Faced with the fact that they would probably not survive, they still acted to ensure that no one else on the ground would die that day!

And what of the monsters that never show their face? The ones that strike from such a distance that the victim has no time to react.

Even as the smoke from lower Manhattan still lingered, another monster decided to attack. This one, however, never made a sound nor showed its ugly head. No, this one used the United States Postal Service to deliver its deadly strikes. Somewhere on this planet, a human being packaged up several envelopes containing anthrax and mailed those envelopes to numerous locations throughout the United States including network television news offices and Capitol Hill in Washington, DC. Several people died as a result. What kind of a cowardly creature is this? Why? To this day, noone knows who or why.

THE THREAT THIS POSED TO EVERYONE PUT US ON RED ALERT. NOT ONLY WERE we chasing 911 calls of "suspicious looking" middle eastern males in connection with September 11, but now, every letter delivered by the U.S. Postal Service without a return address or appearing to have something inside it other than a piece of paper required police response. In addition, there were "copy-cat" letters with baby powder that someone thought it was funny to mail! As a result the next few months were hectic for us. Then the letters stopped coming, we got through the holidays and work returned to normal. Throughout, we tried to keep the mood light even when we weren't having a good day.

One day after working on some six cases, I was swamped with paperwork. Most of my reports were multiple-page narratives, with a burglary report being four pages long! Everyone had already turned in their case reports and were changing to go home. Always looking out for me, Luis offered to make copies of my reports to disperse to their appropriate files.

"Oh dude, you're a life-saver!" I said. "Thanks brother!" and handed him the reports.

Now Luis is quite a character. Built like a silver-back gorilla with a heart twice as big, he beats all the statistics for being alive, let alone being a super-hero crime-fighting cop! Born in the Bronx to a drug dealing couple who had made enemies throughout the five boroughs of New York City, Luis was just a toddler walking down the street holding his mother's hand while she carried his younger brother in the other, when a man attacked and brutally stabbed her to death! Tragically, his father also met a similar fate. Luis and his brother were then shuttled from one foster home to another throughout their early childhood before they were adopted and raised together in northern Virginia in a very loving and nurturing environment.

As Luis walked off, our lieutenant stopped him and handed him several reports that were to be shredded since they were old cases and/or had sensitive information. A few minutes later Luis returned with a quizzical look on his face and asked me, "What did you give me, Bro? Did you want copies, or was I supposed to shred them?"

My heart sank. I was hoping that he was just kidding.

"Why? What did you do with those reports I just handed you?!"

My multiple-page reports were now confetti. Most of my squad had returned to the report room to await the supervisor's official dismissal. Almost in unison they shouted, "Oh my god! What did he do?"

I was in shock. I barely remember one of the guys standing behind me screaming in my ear, "OH MY GOD, CLUB HIM!" But I was too tired to think, let alone reach for my baton!

Needless to say, Luis offered to stay and help me write up the reports. Luckily, I had good notes from the cases. From then on, however, Luis was officially known as "Shredder."

Shredder and his wife had recently bought a house right near ours, so he and I started car-pooling together to work.

WE WERE JUST BEGINNING TO ESTABLISH A NORMAL RHYTHM TO OUR DAYS again, when —BANG, another monster showed up on a beautiful day in early October 2002.

The news first reported a series of shootings in Maryland that had all occurred within a short distance of one another. Initially thought to be a case of random violence, we soon realized that this was the work of one person. With no apparent connection to one another, the victims had been shot with a high caliber rifle from a considerable distance. Some witnesses thought that they had seen a white box truck leaving the area after one of the shootings. Needless to say, people started seeing white box trucks everywhere and were calling 911 to report them.

This monster didn't confine himself only to Maryland. Over the next few days, he struck several more times between Washington, D.C., Fairfax County, and as far south as Richmond, Virginia! The media quickly dubbed him, "The Beltway Sniper." Unlike the "Son of Sam" murders in New York City during the 1970's in which girls or couples were targeted, this guy was going after everyone! Not even children going to school were safe!

A multi-jurisdictional task force was activated consisting of every local law enforcement agency as well as the FBI. This action generated a ton of overtime hours as the task-force started posting officers to the access points of all the interstates as well as mall parking lots and the like.

Even on my days off, I constantly stood vigil with my daughter while she played with the other neighborhood children. Living on the corner of a cul de sac, I felt that, even with the steady flow of construction trucks in my still growing neighborhood, I'd be able to spot a strange vehicle and control any problem should it arise.

My vigil was proven to be a wise decision. As the kids were all playing in our driveway, I saw a Spotsylvania County Deputy Sheriff fly up my street and turn north up towards the homes that were still under construction. I told all the kids to go inside and cautiously made my way up the street. Normally, when I'm home and I am off duty, I secure my weapon in the house, but since this nightmare began, I was never without it! As I crossed the street, the deputy drove back towards me driving more slowly and looking from side to side as he did so. When he approached me I held up my shield and ID to put him at ease.

"What are you looking for?" I asked.

"We just had a lady get shot over by the mall! Someone just called into the dispatch center saying that they'd seen the suspect truck come into this neighborhood!"

"I've been out here for awhile with the kids, and I haven't seen anyone come in here matching the vehicle description," I assured him.

Now this is starting to get scary! This guy was right in my town. He shot a woman loading her car in the parking lot of Michael's craft store! "That store is one of Jackie's favorite places to shop! What if she had been there today with Emily?" I thought to myself.

Unbelievably, there were still no solid leads. Everyone was still being told that the suspect vehicle was a white truck or van of some kind.

I thought that meant it was some kind of pickup truck with a bed cap on it. Whoever it was, they were able to get in and out of heavy traffic areas, line up a shot, shoot someone, then get out of the area without being detected! There's no way anyone could do that out in the open without being seen! Yet he was escaping every time!

A couple of days later, Shredder and I were scheduled to work the task- force overtime when a second shooting took place in Fredericksburg. A man from Philadelphia had been traveling through Virginia with his wife when they decided to stop in Fredericksburg to get some gas at an Exxon gas station just off of I-95. While filling up his car the man was shot, and as in the previous shooting, the assassin had disappeared into heavy traffic without a trace.

News was traveling very fast now. One of my neighbors at that time was an operator with the FBI/HRT (Hostage Rescue Team). I saw him come running out of his house and start throwing his gear into his un-marked Crown Victoria. After he told me what had happened, I imme-diately called Shredder and told him that we had better get moving north because I-95 would be a nightmare, if not completely shut down, as a result of the shooting. Since we didn't have a take-home cruiser, we wore our blue windbreaker raid jackets with their hidden "POLICE" panels secured by Velcro. Affixing a "POLICE" panel to one of the sun visors of Shredder's personal car with its high beams and four-way flashers on, we made our way northbound on I-95.

As expected, I-95 was a nightmare. Traffic was virtually at a standstill. Little by little, however, we inched our way northward and were able to sneak past as much of the traffic as our make-shift "POLICE CAR" would allow. Every mile or so we'd see a pair of marked cruisers from the vari-ous jurisdictions, one on either side of the highway facing south—no doubt hoping to spot a suspicious vehicle.

As we approached the exit for Quantico, however, we saw a lone Prince William County Police cruiser that appeared to have a large gray Ford van stopped on the right shoulder. He appeared to be trying to get the driver out of the van. Since the officer was all alone, I told Shredder to get behind the cruiser. When we identified ourselves as officers, there was genuine relief in his eyes. He told us that his nearest backup was still a ways off with all resources stretched beyond their limit. He said that he had pulled the van to the side of the road, but that the driver was unresponsive to his attempt to contact him using his cruiser's loud speaker. Since there were no windows in the van, we could not easily see the driver. Nor could we see if he was alone or if he had a weapon.

The officer made another attempt at calling out the driver over the loud speaker. As soon as he said, "Driver! Step out of the van," the driver put the van into gear and took off!

"Holy shit!" I thought, "This is the guy!"

I jumped into the cruiser with the officer while Shredder ran back to grab his car. We chased the van for approximately one-eighth of a mile before pulling it off to the right shoulder. Shredder pulled up behind us. This time when the driver was told to exit the van he did so without incident. An Asian male in his forties emerged from the van. I can safely say that he looked more frightened than anyone I had ever seen. He told us that he was alone in the van, and after the Prince William Officer and I cleared him, we knew this was not our suspect. As it turned out, he had stopped on the shoulder to check his map and had no idea that the officer had pulled up behind him. Since his van's radio was blaring loudly, he didn't hear the officer when he was called out by the loud speaker. Not until he had pulled back into traffic had he noticed us in pursuit and had become frightened. After finding no irregularities with his driver's license, the officer sent him on his way.

Right then the cavalry arrived in response to the officer's initial radio call.

"Well," I thought, "better late than never!"

The officer thanked us for our backup, and we continued on up the highway to work.

AS THE DAYS WORE ON, THE NIGHTMARE CONTINUED WITH SEVERAL MORE people being assassinated. Then on the afternoon of October 23, 2002, as I was getting ready to end my shift, I heard an initial radio call alerting us that state police were running code to a shooting in our district. There had been reports of shots fired near I-95 in the southern end of the county. Needless to say, as soon as we heard that call, every cop in Fairfax County ran code to the area. As I was driving and listening to the updates over the radio, I heard one of our senior detectives call out for everyone to slow it down. There had been a bad vehicle wreck on the southbound side of I-95, and the state police were already on scene.

When I pulled up on the adjacent roadway, I was directed by supervising officers to divert traffic away from the scene. As I set up my flare pattern fifty feet away from the fatal motorcycle wreck, I could see officers from both the county and the state covering up the body of someone lying on the shoulder of the road. Only then did I notice the blue flashing strobe lights of his wrecked motorcycle.

The motorcycle trooper had been running code to the initial call of a shooting when he came upon the I-95 southbound afternoon rush hour traffic jam. In an effort to move more quickly to pass the traffic, he had tried to move over to the right shoulder. Simultaneously, a tow truck driver, talking on his cell phone and not paying attention, also pulled onto the shoulder to pass the traffic ahead. The trooper never had a chance!

The irony of this tragedy was that the officer died responding to a bogus call about shots being fired by the "Sniper" when the Sniper had been nowhere near Fairfax that day.

Later that night, the nightmare finally came to an end.

After countless false leads, the Task Force got solid information on the suspect's vehicle. The incident commanders decided to release the information to the media in hopes of tightening the net around the assassin.

Sure enough, an alert truck driver at a rest stop in Maryland spotted the dark blue 1980's Chevy Caprice with New Jersey tags and called 911 immediately. While waiting for the police to arrive, the alert truck driver risked his own safety by blocking the exit of the rest stop with his truck in case the suspect tried to leave.

Within moments of the call, the entire area was crawling with Special Weapons and Tactics (SWAT) operators from every department in the area. Fifty "Ninjas" yanked two suspects from the Chevy Caprice and handcuffed them without firing a shot. To everyone's complete surprise the trigger man was a sixteen-year old kid!

I remember thinking about the adult suspect, Mohammed, as I watched the story being reported on every network news channel later that night, what an evil monster he must be to convince a sixteen-year old kid who idolized him to kill innocent people at random!

CLIMBING THE STAIRS TO EMILY'S ROOM THAT EVENING TO TUCK HER IN, I FELT a huge sense of relief that the ordeal was now over. While kissing her good night as she drifted off innocently into sleep, I couldn't help but think of all the times I had told her that there were no such things as monsters.

In that moment I wondered how old she would be when she discovered the truth.

20 CAUGHT UP IN THE FLOW

Even with the insanity of October's events, my job was getting easier and my confidence grew with each call I handled. My responses to any situation, no matter how volatile, were reflective and calm. Dealing with domestic disputes, I was often able to calm both parties by simply pointing out the obvious to them: "Hey, you might not love him/her anymore, but you both did something right. You both helped make that perfect little person over there," pointing to their child. "Remember, your number one priority in life is the health and happiness of that perfect little person! Everything else is secondary." This usually had the desired calming effect, and both parties would be able to find a peaceful resolution.

Sometimes, however, talking was not enough.

One morning I was covering a slot for an officer who worked on the day squad opposite mine. Around mid-morning dispatch received a suspicious event/911 hang up call. Whenever the dispatch center receives calls via 911, hang up or not, we always respond to confirm whether or not the police are actually needed. This call was a perfect example of why we always adhere to this policy.

The call had been placed via a cell phone. Using the dispatch center tracking technology we were given an address in the Springfield area. I was close by so I marked myself enroute to assist. Arriving at the house, I met up with three other officers and we all took up the standard safe approach to the house. The window shades were drawn and the front porch light was on, giving the appearance that no one was home.

After the contact officer received no response from within the house, we did a quick sweep of the exterior. Just as we were beginning to think that this was a wild goose chase, we heard some movement from within the house.

I returned to the front of the house and joined the contact officer at the front door while two of the other officers covered the back. We were informed by the dispatcher that there had been no response from the cell phone. So we knocked on the door again, and this time heard a woman scream, "Oh my god, help me! He's gonna kill me!"

In an instant I was back in the academy classroom listening to that 911 recording of the girl being brutally stabbed to death in her own home. "Not this time!" I thought to myself.

Before realizing it, I had blown past my partner and kicked the front door off its hinges! When we entered we were met by a frightened six-year-old girl. We directed her to the waiting arms of several more officers now arriving at the scene. From a point of cover, I shouted a challenge to anyone inside the house: "Fairfax County Police! Anyone inside the house come out now with your hands out in front of you! Do it now!"

"Yes sir! We're coming out now! Please don't shoot!" a male voice came from the basement.

The first person up the stairs was the woman, who had clearly been beaten about the face and neck. She was hysterical and bleeding. As soon as I saw that the "offender" coming up the stairs was unarmed, I holstered my pistol and promptly introduced him to the hardwood floor of the house. With the scene secure, we tried to get information from his victim but were quickly interrupted when he shouted, "Shut the @$#*%! up, bitch! Don't you say nothing!"

That was all I needed to hear. I escorted my new friend to an awaiting blue and white limousine, which took him to Fairfax County's "Gray Bar Hotel and Resort" for booking.

I had done all this very naturally, responding as needed to the flow of events. I discovered that when I responded with my heart everything fell perfectly into place, and I did not have to think. My body just responded, and my gifts of strength and problem solving were a matched pair.

THE CARNIVAL WITH THE USUAL ATTRACTIONS—COTTON CANDY, FUNNEL cakes, roller coaster, ferris wheel, over-priced games of chance where you really have no chance at all—was in town at the Springfield Mall, set up on the outskirts of its parking lot. A chain-link fence secured to the ground by interlocking concrete blocks surrounded the carnival. Sections of the fence were secured to each other with galvanized steel couplings. The only opening in this "fortress" was the main gate where there was a cover charge to enter.

On a warm night I was working an overtime slot protecting the fences. As with most police departments, we have our share of street gang issues. These small carnivals tended to draw gangs who saw them as an opportunity to show their "colors" and display gang loyalty. To discourage trouble, we provided an overwhelming show of uniforms at these events in addition to placing plain clothes officers in the crowd.

Our gang unit had been busy dealing with some "clients" out in the parking lot throughout the night; ironically, the carnival area was the quietest place on the entire mall property! I had just finished locking up a DUI "Rhodes Scholar," who had decided to drive by a bunch of uniformed cops while drinking a beer (he had eight empty bottles on the passenger side).

Returning to my post at the fence with my partners, Sweeney and Grif, we were standing outside the carnival's fence line about a hundred yards from the main gate when Rich walked up to me. A detective with the gang unit, Rich was wearing the customary black tactical gear normally worn by SWAT. In addition to our standard uniforms, the tactical look has the desired psychological effect on would-be bad guys as well.

As we stood there swapping recaps of the night's events, we heard a huge commotion from within the fences. A carnival employee came running to us from the opposite side of the fence screaming, "There's a bunch a gang-bangers in here punching and stabbing some dude!" Sweeney and Grif immediately started running toward the main gate. Rich started to run as well but stopped when he saw me grab the fence. Now, I'm not a metallurgist, so I don't know the exact stress pressure of galvanized steel. I'm not a structural engineer so I have no idea what the structural integrity of concrete is. I simply knew that I needed to be on the other side of that fence.

I grabbed the fence and started to lift it. At first, it was the proverbial immovable object. Nothing seemed to be happening. Then everything came apart at once! The steel coupling holding the section together began to fail and the concrete footing broke free from the bottom of the fence posts.

Rich told me later that he didn't move at first because he thought it was so cool to see me tearing that fence apart!

We were soon on top of those clowns and had them cuffed and stuffed!

I can't say that I knew what I was doing, I just got caught up in the flow in a sort of "knee-jerk" reaction based on needs at the time. The one thing I do remember is that as we escorted our handcuffed "clients" out of the opening in the fence that I had just created, the carnival staff had these quizzical looks on their faces while repairing their "secure perimeter."

21 SHROUDED IN DOUBT

Again, just when I felt most optimistic, that *black cloud* of mine would inevitably show up. I had a great job, great wife and daughter, and a beautiful house. Even so, the smallest negative issue could rattle my self- esteem.

We were starting to get "FINAL NOTICE" letters in the mail, as well as constant phone calls from creditors. I became so preoccupied with the thought of losing everything, that I began second guessing myself on even the most mundane task. My efforts to focus within this clouded funk were time-consuming to say the least. Yet, I still had moments of clarity when I could become distracted by my work and momentarily forget my problems.

While routinely checking vehicle registrations in the parking lot of one of the county's less than stellar motels, I discovered a beat-up minivan about fifteen years old with a license plate that belonged to a newer Lincoln Towne car. So I decided to investigate the discrepancy. Walking up to the empty van and looking inside, I saw in plain view an open plastic bag containing a large amount of green leafy material and two cell phones. I called for an additional unit and my friend, Gene, responded. I asked him to keep an eye on the van while I spoke to the motel staff. Having dealt with this motel before, I knew they were pretty good at keeping tabs on what vehicles belonged to which guests.

The front desk clerk informed me that the car belonged to guests in room 52, which was just above the front office on the opposite side of the building from where the van was parked. The clerk also informed me that there were at least four guys in the room. A typical two-story building just off of I-95, the motel had no enclosed hallways.

I called Gene, giving him an update and saying that I was going to do a "knock and talk" on the room. After requesting another backup unit, Gene blocked the van with his cruiser and joined me at room 52. We listened momentarily but heard no noise coming from within. Since it was still fairly early on a Sunday morning, we assumed that the men were probably sleeping off their night's activities.

I knocked on the door and was promptly met by a young man who's face went from semi-consciousness to absolute horror at seeing me. He jumped behind the door to hide, while his friend stood up and spoke to me in his best rehearsed voice.

"Is there a problem officer?"

After getting the first young man to step out in the open, I informed them that there was a "problem" with their vehicle and requested permission to enter the room. Gene and I counted four guys in the room, none of whom were comfortable at being awakened by members of Fairfax County's finest! When I asked who owned the van they replied, "What van? We don't have a van. We got dropped off here last night," obviously forgetting that they had provided vehicle information to the front desk clerk when they checked in.

While maintaining good officer safety with contact/cover, I asked these gentlemen if there were any weapons or illegal substances in the room, to which they said, "No." After a cursory pat-down for weapons, I was given permission to search the room. I checked everything including the toilet tank in the bathroom. Initially I found only a small marijuana roach, but it was enough to make a charge. More importantly, it was enough to make these men extremely nervous.

As I continued my search I found a backpack on the floor next to one of the beds. The kid who had originally opened the door said it was his and gave me permission to search it. Inside, I discovered dozens of unused small clear plastic zip-lock baggies.

"What are these used for?" I asked.

"For transporting jewelry, man," he answered.

"Oh, are you a jeweler?" I asked.

"Naw, man," he said, almost immediately regretting his answer.

The large amount of "green leafy substance" in the van and the possession of the marijuana roach and baggies indicated evidence of a potential possession-with-intent-to-distribute, which is a felony.

One of them then asked to use the bathroom. Having already checked him and the bathroom, I gave him permission. On his return he sat down on the bed, and I went back into the bathroom. The keys to the minivan were now in the toilet tank!

As I returned to the room I held the keys up in an obvious manner and said, "Hey Gene, look at this! That bathroom must be magic!"

Now they were really nervous.

"Can I speak to you outside, officer?" asked the kid who had said he was not a jeweler.

By this time Gene had gone down to the cruisers to confirm their information, while Wayne, our third backup officer, covered the remaining three subjects.

As I stepped out onto the open hallway with this kid, he did what any healthy young felon would do… he took off running! I couldn't help thinking, "Where the hell's he going to go?"

As I caught up with him at the end of the balcony/hallway and grabbed at his shirt, he totally surprised me by jumping twenty-five feet to the parking lot! I was awestruck at the length he was willing to go to get away from me! I was more impressed that Gene, who had seen him begin to run, could catch-up to him and blind-side tackle him!

With me gone, the other three men became extremely uncooperative and began to advance on Wayne. With three against one, Wayne drew his weapon and instructed them to get on the floor. At this point I returned and also gave the order to get down.

"@$#*%!! You ain't doin' sh…," stated the subject who had attempted to hide the keys in the toilet.

Important safety tip here for the uninformed: never make a statement like this to any police officer when another officer's safety is at risk!

Before he could even finish his thought, I grabbed him and drove my knee into his diaphragm. Placing his left arm into a hammer-lock, I drove his face into the concrete floor of the hallway and handcuffed him. When I re-entered the room, the remaining two gentlemen offered no resistance.

Meanwhile, Gene had a problem of his own. I didn't know it then, but when Gene tackled the man in the parking lot the momentum had carried them both into the doorway of one of the lower-floor rooms. Gene's head had struck a concrete threshold causing a three inch gash on his forehead that momentarily stunned him. In the interval the suspect had escaped. However, Gene was able to call in a description of the young man to other responding officers and to our K-9 unit.

In many cases, the barking of a K-9 dog is sufficient to convince an escapee that the game is over. But a few suspects think they can actually outrun a full- grown German Shepherd—who's sole purpose as a chosen breed for police duty is to chase down fleeing suspects! This young man tried, but in just a few minutes he was in custody.

Of the four men, three had various warrants and were sent to jail. The jumper admitted to owning the van and the weed inside. It turns out that they had been partying so hard the night before that he had forgotten about the big bag of marijuana in the van!

As I left the jail, one of the young men who was still sitting handcuffed to the bench waiting to be processed called over to me.

"Hey Officer Brett, you got a second?"

"Yeah, what's up, man?" I asked, walking over to him.

"Look," he said, "I just wanted to apologize for the way I acted earlier. I know we were wrong, and I don't usually behave like this. I'm going to college, and I'm trying to get my life straight, so I should have known better. Besides, I have never been slammed that hard in my life! I will never mess with another Fairfax County cop as long as I live!"

I smiled as I shook his hand and wished him luck. And I meant it.

Gene ended up with several stitches in his head, and we both received the certificate of valor for our efforts in the case.

Even with this accomplishment, however, I couldn't shake the feeling of my ineptitude. When I wasn't careful, this feeling would snowball, and I'd get so distracted that I'd schedule different appointments for the same time.

For example, I had taken a day off to go to the Fairfax county tax office to clear up a notice that they wanted to put a lien on my salary. Records still had me listed as living in Fairfax County, and according to the tax office I owed back taxes on personal property! While I was getting dressed, I got a call from our court liaison office reminding me that I was supposed to be in court that day! After a frantic trip from Fredericksburg to the Fairfax court house, I arrived just in time to be told that the case had already been heard and that the judge had held me in contempt for missing it! As I walked out of the court house with a $50 fine imposed by the judge, I was convinced that my life would be forever over-shadowed by the *black cloud*!

Jackie and my family also began to notice that I was sullen and quick to dismiss people. It just seemed that we had worked so hard to get where we were that it was unfair to have these financial setbacks occur. My attitude was so defeatist that I began to dismiss all my successes as the result of a fluke or "dumb luck." Instead of concentrating on success, I was consumed by my sense of failure.

Jackie's humor helped me whenever I got too caught up in my negative zone, as did Emily's sweet little voice, which could pierce any dark mood of mine when she said, "I love you, Daddy." Or the sound of her laughter when I tickled her to the point where she'd plead for me to stop, only to say, "Tickle me again, Daddy!" Then on June 23, 2004, Jackie gave me another beautiful gift—our daughter, Sarah Catherine.

Although my "dark side" seemed permanently ingrained in my out-look, Sarah would prove to be every bit as powerful as her older sister at keeping it at bay!

22 Every Super Hero Needs A Cool Pair Of Boots

I never gave serious thought to changing any aspect of my career as a policeman. I didn't want to be a detective since I don't have the patience for that kind of work! When I looked into the SWAT team, I found their schedule to be very restrictive. With two little girls at home and a wife who had already put up with years of my odd work hours I figured, "If it ain't broke, don't fix it!" This effectively eliminated any option with the narcotics or street crimes units as well.

Besides, I was having too much fun in patrol! Then my friend Jeff entered the picture with another option for me to consider.

Jeff had been with the department for more than twenty years, spending most of them in the traffic division motor squad before moving to the accident reconstruction unit. From there he was promoted to sergeant and assigned to work day patrol supervising my squad. A true southern gentleman, Jeff is one of the few cops in my department who is actually from Virginia! He had grown up in the area that I now patrolled! He and I hit it off from the first day we met. Being a movie buff like me, Jeff constantly quoted obscure movie lines during roll call, causing the rest of the squad to scratch their heads in disbelief. As far as Jeff and I were concerned, every aspect of life could be summed up by a line from *Caddyshack*, or any Mel Brooks film!

Not long after we got to know each other, Jeff tried to convince me to put in for the motor squad. Like Rich in New York, Jeff always looked out for me like a big brother, and I trusted him as such. Yet, of all the options in law enforcement, being a motorcycle cop was the one that I swore I'd never take. First of all, I had never ridden a motorcycle in my life! Second, being a policeman was dangerous enough without having to do it on two wheels!

I had seen a trooper's fatal wreck, so it was a job I was never going to do and that was that!

Jeff persisted, however, hitting me with all the advantages of being a Fairfax County Motorman; weekends and holidays off, cool leather jacket and boots, a take home Harley Davidson!

Slowly I began to break down under his pressure, trusting that he wouldn't try to talk me into something that he didn't think I could handle or wouldn't enjoy. Since my financial position suffered a setback with the loss of one of our cars, I began to seriously consider the proposition.

"A take home vehicle would be a huge help right about now, wouldn't it?" Jeff reminded me.

"Yeah, but I've never even ridden one before!" I persisted.

"Don't worry, dude!" Jeff reassured me, "That's to your advantage! You don't have any bad habits that we're going to have to break! We'll show you the correct way to ride a motorcycle!"

That sounded logical to me since they were the best riders in the country. If anyone could teach me to ride a motorcycle it would be them! The question now was whether or not Jackie would agree. Predictably, she wasn't thrilled with the idea but said yes to my trust in Jeff.

Thus began my journey towards the motor squad. It took me two attempts to do well enough on the entrance process to get into basic school, but I finally made it.

I'll never forget my first day in basic motor school. I was very nervous! One would think—or hope in my case—that a beginning rider would be introduced slowly to the fine art of motorcycle riding, let's say with a Schwinn bike, or a moped, or something like that. Not so! Fairfax County doesn't mess around with anything less than the grand-daddy of all motorcycles—the Harley Davidson Electra Glide.

For those not familiar with this motorcycle, it weighs about 900 pounds and has a full fairing covering the front handlebars and blue strobe lights on all sides. I'd never been a "motor-head" so I knew nothing about engines, but this bike was LOUD and had some serious "giddy-up" as I soon discovered!

All of the instructors were senior motormen on the squad, and each of them held numerous titles from the various competitions that were held throughout the country. Several times a year police departments throughout the U.S. and Canada host motorcycle safety competitions, and the Fairfax County Motor Squad routinely "clean up"! Competitors ride their motorcycles through a series of obstacle courses made up of orange road hazard cones. There are usually two sets of identical courses. One is un-timed and designed to measure the basic skills for negotiating the course, and the other is timed for speed. The goal is to clear the courses as fast as one can without touching any of the cones. The cones would later prove to be the bane of my existence, and the catalyst for a future life-changing event in Charleston, South Carolina.

Basic motor school is set up much like the competitions, or "Rodeos," with the difference that courses are much wider to accommodate the unskilled riders. Initially the team wants to see how new members can handle a motorcycle. Having had no prior experience, I only knew that the right hand was the throttle, the left hand was the clutch, the left foot was the gear shifter, and the right foot was the brake. Most people might think this was pretty simple, right? Wrong!

My first mistake was thinking that I could muscle this 900 pound behemoth to do what I wanted. As soon as I got on the bike and tried to pop up the kickstand, I leaned too far over to the other side and the bike just kept on going and fell. I ended up on the ground next to it.

"Okay," I thought. "Let's try this again."

I managed to get the bike up on the side stand and to give myself another shot. This time I even got it started and into first gear! I soon discovered, however, how much "giddy-up" this bike has! As soon as I gave it a little throttle and released the clutch, that monster took off like a pissed-off bull! Thankfully, I managed to stall the engine before it got to any speed, but then I promptly dropped the bike again. I couldn't help thinking that I had made the biggest mistake of my life coming here!

At that moment one of the instructors walked over to me. He had been watching me and saw the frustrated look on my face. With a crooked smile on his face, he said to me, "Okay Bill, if you're done messing around we can get started now!"

His comment brought me out of my familiar negative train of thinking. "Just relax, and let the bike do all the work. The trick to riding this bike is just finding the fine line where the friction point of the clutch meets the throttle."

I began to relax, then listen, and I heard what they were trying to tell me.

"Okay," I thought, "Here goes..."

I started off nice and slow, and sure enough, the bike did exactly what they said it would do and also what I wanted it to do! I then began doing some nice wide circles, nothing crazy, since getting the bike to turn was the goal. When I was beginning to feel a little comfortable with the wide circles, the instructors had me enter one of the cone courses. Although the distance between the cones was the same as for the much wider circles, the circle was now so tight they might just as well have told me to make a turn on a man-hole cover!

"Just relax and trust the bike," they said. "Use your head and eyes to turn... whatever you turn your head and look at, the bike is going to follow."

"Okay," I thought. "Clear your head and do what they told you!"

To say that it took every fiber of my being to keep looking where I wanted to go would be an understatement! Entering the circle, I immediately locked the forks to the right and leaned into the turn. I kept my head and eyes locked over my right shoulder even as the reflexive urge to look down was screaming at my subconscious! What happened next was something that I had never expected. I had the bike leaned so far over that the foot board on the right side of the bike began scraping the ground! This sound was and still is the coolest thing I had ever heard! As I completed the turn and came out of the circle, I was amazed at what I had just done! Seeing that amazement in my eyes, the instructor walked up and said, "You see? I told you!"

That was it. I was hooked. "Jeff said I would love it, but... Holy shit, this was incredible!" I would never doubt him afterwards.

The basic motor school went on for two weeks, and although it was the most mentally and physically demanding two weeks of my life, it was also the most fun I'd ever had! Jeff was also right about my inexperience being to my advantage. I ended up finishing the final riding test with the fastest time! This meant that I would be the first one from the basic school to come up for the six weeks of field training with a senior field training motor officer.

Jeff had seen potential in me that I could not see in myself since I always focused on the weak points of my positive accomplishments. Throughout my training period I was plagued by the feeling that someone would walk up to me and bluntly say, "You're not supposed to be here!" However, in October 2004, four years after I started as a patrol officer at the Franconia District station, I completed the basic motor school program and began my training with the motor squad.

I was assigned to ride with Dan, whom I had originally met at Franconia when I first graduated. Dan had been a career Marine who upon retirement joined the Fairfax County Police Department. He then quickly made a name for himself and joined the motor squad. Dan also lived near me, which was a real bonus. Normally, new motormen-in-training aren't allowed to take their bikes home, but Dan was able to convince the supervisors that if they would allow me to ride home to Dan's house, instead of leaving my bike at the office, I would have that much more training time in the saddle! That was a huge benefit, if for no other reason than the experience I gained from riding to and from Dan's house in the unpredictable Virginia autumn weather! I can honestly say I had never known fear until I got on a motorcycle and rode at night through the winding country roads of Stafford County, Virginia, in cold, driving autumn rain!

Most of my training went well, although I didn't always see it that way —being so hyper-sensitive about disappointing Jeff. I would mentally beat the hell out of myself!

Dan always encouraged me, however, pushing me further each day than I'd gone the day before. As for the rest of the motor squad, I could not have picked thirty-two better men with whom to ride, let alone call my friends! Each of them brought something unique to the squad, yet all of them were exactly the same about one thing—they loved to bust each other's balls!

I found this out first hand on my first day. Wanting to make a good first impression, I had arrived nice and early. When I walked into the office, only one other cop was in the room.

"Hey, I'm Joe!" he said. "Nice to meet you. You must be the new guy."

"Yeah," I said, "I'm Billy"

"Welcome aboard, Billy! Hey listen, in case you were wondering, the Dunkin' Donuts is right up on Route 50 in Fairfax City. Make sure you get enough for about thirty-two hungry cops! I know you want to make a good first impression!"

If I had any previous doubts about these guys, Joe put that to rest!

Throughout the course of my training, if any one of them saw me having a problem with something, they would take the time to check on me or to offer constructive advice. As soon as they saw that I was okay, they would promptly bust my balls! In fact, the first time they all saw me in full uniform—helmet, glasses, jacket, and boots—they nicknamed me "ROBO-COP".

ONE OF THE BIG DIFFERENCES BETWEEN THE MOTOR SQUAD AND WORKING FROM A cruiser is that you're not dispatched to calls every five minutes. The main responsibilities for the Fairfax County Motor Squad are traffic enforcement, VIP escorts, funeral escorts, traffic control issues involving intersection lights being out, SWAT team call-outs, and lastly the obligatory dog-and-pony shows.

Being one of the most highly visible departments, there is a huge emphasis on keeping the bikes and boots spotless and shiny. This is a skill that I never mastered. Like everything else in my life that I gave too much thought to and/or worried about too excessively, the harder I tried at this the worse I did!

I did manage to successfully complete my training, however. The timing could not have been better since Christmas was only a few weeks away. It was time for the annual "Santa's ride" day when all the motor squads from the surrounding jurisdictions get together and ride throughout northern Virginia collecting toys for the children's hospital and various other area charities.

Although the sight of police motorcycles running with lights and sirens is not uncommon during daily funeral escorts and a "POTUS" (President of the United States) escort, which happens once or twice a month because of our proximity to Washington, D.C., when our police motorcycles are led by a "jolly old elf" riding a Harley Davidson people always stop and take notice! A few area folks complain about Santa screwing up traffic, but the looks on the faces of kids when we pull up makes it all worthwhile! I am always amazed how these hospitalized kids never lose their sense of hope and wonder—no matter what their affliction. As soon as they see Santa they become more powerful than the adults standing around them! It's amazing how such a simple symbol of love and hope has such a profound effect on me as well!

Having officially finished my training, I was able to ride home alone, more comfortable in the saddle. I never imagined that my career would bring me here.

One January morning when the first blast of arctic air hit me, however, I questioned, "What was I thinking when I took this job!" That's right. The Fairfax County Police Motor Squad rides year round! In all fairness we are issued heavy winter gear that includes heated gloves, heated jacket liners and pants, and heated sox. But when the temperature goes below thirty degrees, nothing short of a space suit can save you! I don't care who you are or how cold you think you've been, the fact of the matter is that you don't know what "cold" is until you've ridden a Harley Davidson motorcycle up Virginia I-95 at 65 mph in January at five o'clock in the morning!

On the plus side, your "cool factor" goes way up whenever you pull up at a stop light next to a car full of executives with bewildered looks on their faces that read, "Those cops must be friggin' crazy!"

One of the senior motor guys summed it up best when he said, "You'll never be colder, you'll never be hotter, you'll never be wetter, but you'll never be happier doing anything else!" And he was right!

STILL, I COULDN'T ACCOUNT FOR THE FEELING THAT I DIDN'T BELONG AND THAT I was a fraud. The more I thought about it, the more worried I became. I began to forget assignments, which caused me trouble with my supervisors. Although Jeff was my friend, he was first and foremost my sergeant. So, when he called me into his office one day, I knew that I was in trouble.

"Dude! Is everything okay at home?" he asked right off.

I couldn't answer him.

He reassured me that he and the squad had my back, and that if there was anything that I needed he would help me in any way possible.

LATER THAT NIGHT, JACKIE AND I WERE DISCUSSING MY "ISSUES" WHEN SHE MADE an astute observation.

"You know this is all related to, if not entirely caused by your ADHD, right?"

"ADHD?" I asked.

"You know," she said confidently, "Attention deficit hyperactive disorder."

"Yes, I know what it means," I said. "But how does that apply to me? I was only diagnosed as hyperactive in my childhood."

When I was first diagnosed as hyperactive the condition was just beginning to be understood. The research was just in its infancy. During the thirty-plus years since, there had been numerous breakthroughs in treating the condition, including a new diagnosis.

The symptoms of ADHD are divided into inattentiveness, hyperactivity, and impulsivity. Some children with ADHD primarily have the inattentive type, some the hyperactive-impulsive type, and some the combined type. Those with the inattentive type are less disruptive and are more likely to miss being diagnosed with ADHD.

Growing up, I did not know that I represented the combined type, even though I had most of the symptoms of inattention, hyperactivity, and impulsivity. The signs of all three were there, given my failure to pay close attention to details that led me to make careless mistakes in my schoolwork; my difficulty sustaining attention in tasks and play; my dislike of tasks that required sustained mental effort (such as schoolwork); my channel surfing mind; my being "on the go" as if "driven by a motor"; my impulsive leap into action without thinking about the consequences.

So Jackie began looking for specialists in the Fredericksburg area, and we were fortunate enough to find one near our house.

When I first met Dr. Lee I immediately felt comfortable with him. He had a phenomenal demeanor about him that spoke of a man who knew what he was talking about. Unlike the testing in my childhood, Dr. Lee only gave me a quick questionnaire to fill out. This information, along with the knowledge of my previous history, led him to suggest a different medication. I was somewhat skeptical, but he reassured me that he had several other patients, including police officers, and they had all responded extremely well to Adderall.

"Okay," I thought, "I'll try it!"

At first, things seemed to settle down and get better. Whether it was the placebo effect from knowing that I was being treated, or the actual medication, my "racing thoughts" were beginning to slow down.

I once heard that ADHD is like watching television while continuously changing channels. You see a lot of information, but you can never lock in and absorb any of it! Well, now it seemed that I was absorbing the information.

WORK IMPROVED GREATLY. ALTHOUGH I WOULD STILL GET DOWN ON MYSELF for perceived failures, I'd work myself out of it a lot quicker than I used to. I even started participating in the rodeo competitions.

That summer of 2005 the squad traveled up to Chatham Kent, Ontario, Canada, for The Great Lakes Police Motorcycle Training Seminar! What a phenomenal experience this was for me! I had never traveled outside the United States so I didn't know what to expect, thinking that Canada was exactly the same as the U.S. except that it was a lot cleaner and its citizens a lot more polite! I was right on both counts! The money was different and the government and infrastructure always made references to "the crown." It struck me then that the United States might have ended up similarly had we lost the revolution! Canada is a great country with wonderful people and phenomenal beer!!!

All cops are by nature tightly knit as comrades. Motor cops happen to be even more so, perhaps because of inherent danger. "Only a motorman knows what I go through every day!" is the common belief. The competitions foster a great camaraderie between departments. At this rodeo there were squads from California, Louisiana, Pennsylvania, Maryland, and Michigan just to name a few! And all of us took the time to help one another during the practice runs throughout the week.

Although I was still new at this, I was feeling very relaxed and comfortable. I was clearing the courses cleanly, and my times were improving with each run. Some of the senior guys on my squad started saying that they thought I was sure to win my division. This made me feel great, albeit somewhat jinxed!

The weather had been picture-perfect all week for August in central Canada. We knew that it couldn't last, and it didn't. On game day, Saturday morning, the skies opened up with rain. The competition went forward anyway, since we were motor cops! Still, the conditions were enough to play mind games with me! All those courses that had seemed so easy all week now began to make me feel the way I did on that very first day of

basic motor school, and it showed! I don't think I made it through any of
the courses without knocking over at least a half dozen cones! I was furious at myself. And worse yet, I felt that I had let my squad down. Here I
was, a member of the most highly respected motor squad in the world, and
I looked like some schlep they picked up on the side of the road! My squad,
however, wouldn't hear of it! Noticing my angst, my lieutenant pulled me
aside and put everything into perspective.

"Relax, Dude!" he said, "It's your first real rodeo! I've been doing
these rodeos for fifteen years, and I hit a shit-load of cones myself today!
That's why we call these things "Training" seminars! Besides, none of this
will change the flavor of the LaBatt's Blue we'll be destroying later!"

I laughed when he said this!

As expected, my squad did very well, but the boys from Baton Rouge,
Louisiana, stole the show! They were hard charging competitors, as well
as some of the nicest, most hospitable people I have ever met! They didn't
hang around long, however, since a tropical storm named Katrina was bearing down on the gulf coast states and was expected to become a full force
hurricane by the time it made land-fall. No one could blame them for wanting to get home!

Despite my poor performance I kept repeating to myself what the lieutenant had said, "It's your first rodeo. You'll get better at them!"

Yeah. Easier said than done!

23 SIGNS

What a contradiction! I've always thought of myself as an optimist, but here I was nearing my fortieth birthday as the quintessential pessimist! It seemed that with every success I enjoyed, I also suffered an even greater loss of some kind. As such, I had come to assume that the force that governed my life was out to test me. The *black cloud* feeling was as palpable now as it had been during any other time in my life!

To protect myself, I used reverse psychology on God when working towards a goal! I'd pretend I didn't really want something, or I would say out loud that I was already expecting to fail—in a preemptive attempt to beat the universe in its plan for me to fail! I thought that using this approach would help me ward off worry and frustration. While this reverse psychology helped me cope with my everyday routine failures, I had become a cynic. And cynics can't be surprised, right? Wrong.

Emily started kindergarten in the fall of 2005. I don't know who was more nervous that morning, Emily or me! As soon as she got on the bus, I jumped into my car and followed her bus to school! I know, I'm a worry wart! Yet, how many kids get to say they got a police escort to school on their very first day?

As you can see, I was too preoccupied with the *black cloud* to think very much about my birthday, or to notice that Jackie's organizing skills were in high gear. My parents and Jackie's Aunt Nina and Uncle Tony were coming for what I thought was going to be a quiet dinner with us.

I worked the Saturday of my birthday weekend. When I rode up my street that evening I saw my father standing in the middle of the street.

"Who's Dad standing with?" I thought for half a second, until I realized it was my brother, Rob. As I got closer I saw my entire family, all my nieces and nephews, all my in-laws, and all my friends and neighbors standing in my front yard with all the little kids holding hand-painted signs saying "Happy 40th Birthday!"

At first I stopped short a few hundred yards away in astonished embarrassment. Then I threw on all my lights and siren as I did a U-turn and rode up the block! I quickly turned around and rode back into the crowd of people, who swarmed me. I was reminded of just how lucky and truly blessed I am to have these people in my life! Especially Jackie, who had put so much effort into pulling this together without me finding out!

While being hugged and greeted by everyone, I couldn't help but notice the similarity between this moment and the ending of one of my favorite movies. The only thing missing was a Christmas tree and a copy of *Tom Sawyer*! I could actually picture the words spoken by Clarence Oddbody— "Remember George, no man is a failure who has friends!"

Although I was still somewhat of a guarded cynic, my outlook became much brighter after my birthday. I felt I knew what it was to have 'a good life.'

MY RODEO SKILLS WERE LITTLE BETTER DURING THE COMPETITION HELD IN Alexandria a week after my birthday than they had been in Canada, but I was feeling good and wanted to improve. Seeing some photos taken by a neighbor during my party, I saw that I had put on weight after joining the motor squad full-time.

"Oh man!" I thought. "I've got that motorman pouch going on around my waistline! I need to get back into shape!"

Making that commitment really started to change my life for the better! I began eating healthier the very next day. I decided that from Sunday through Friday I would eat little to no fats, concentrating only on "clean" calories. Saturday would be my "cheat" day.

My food intake actually increased because I was grazing only on fruits, veggies, turkey, and chicken. At night I would drink two huge glasses of skim milk, replacing the package of Oreos that I would normally pack away! This routine showed rapid results! By December I had dropped almost thirty pounds, but more importantly, my body fat percentage had gone from twelve to eight percent!

At this point Jackie says I became obsessed! She was right! I wanted to see just how much body fat I could shave off. I was in better shape now at forty than I had ever been in my entire life! But Christmas would offer the real test of my resilience!

Christmas Eve is always celebrated at our house, and Christmas Day is enjoyed at my in-laws. Both days are dedicated to the type of feasting that only Charles Dickens or Dr. Seuss could imagine!

December 24, 2005, began perfectly. Nat King Cole, Andy Williams, and Johnny Mathis music was playing non-stop. In my "man-cave" I had my DVD player set on repeat so that every two hours or so I could hear Zu-Zu tell her father, "Every time a bell rings, an angel gets its wings." After everyone left for home that night, however, a problem arose.

In our house Santa usually shows up after the girls have gone to bed. Their gifts are neatly placed under the tree in our family room. This night "Santa" realized that he had only three gifts for Emily! He had remembered Sarah's wish list to the letter. In fact her gift-pile looked like a "Babies-R-Us" dump truck had crashed into our family room! No matter how Santa tried to arrange Emily's pile of toys, it was still too small by comparison. As I'm sure every parent knows, there isn't a child who has ever walked this planet who hasn't checked to make sure that they got just as many toys as their siblings! Jackie and I knew Emily would notice, being the sharp kid that she is!

Jackie was extremely upset, and I couldn't blame her. It was well after midnight, and "Santa" had forgotten most of the toys on Emily's wish list! What the hell does a parent do in that situation? Obviously, there were no stores open to help us deal with "Santa's" *faux pas*. Jackie knew that Emily would be heart-broken and think that somehow she had been put on the "naughty list"! That was unacceptable to me!

Something happened that I would never have anticipated in a million years. I kept my cool and thought of a solution! Instead of the usual *black cloud* thoughts shrouding this happy occasion, I remembered that Santa Claus also left presents for our daughters at my in-laws' house! In fact, every year I give them grief for spending way too much money... I mean "Santa" spending too much time and effort at their house! Thankfully, I hoped, this year would be no different.

"Relax, Hon, you know your mother always goes crazy with the girls, right? Well, just call her up, you know she's still up wrapping presents, and tell her what happened. Then I'll ask her if I can come down there now and grab some of them!"

That had the desired effect. Jackie regained her composure and called her Mom.

"Of course! Don't be silly!" her mother said without hesitation and laughed, thinking the situation was pretty funny.

"I'm a terrible mother!" Jackie said, as I was grabbing my keys.

"This is not your fault!" I reassured her.

As I was heading out the door, I kissed her and said, "I'll be back in a little while. I love you! And by the way, Merry Christmas!"

Rocketing southward in my not-so-miniature sleigh with eight not so tiny cylinders, I found myself deep in thought. With no traffic and every radio station playing uninterrupted Christmas music, I found myself very much at peace. I reflected on the night's events, noting how well I was able to cope with it. Indeed, I even thought of a solution rather than having my predictable "Clark Griswold" melt-down!

"Something's different," I thought to myself. "I feel different." It dawned on me how "good" this feeling was! I wondered how long it would last, and if I would react as well the next time a "crisis" came up.

Arriving at my in-laws' house in Palmyra, I was met at the door by my mother-in-law with her usual bright it's-okay-honey-everything's-going-to-be just-fine smile, followed by a genuine giggle!

"And you always yell at me for spoiling my granddaughters!" she said, with an even bigger smile!

This was one of the few times that I was actually glad to be wrong! Being the squared-away grandma that she is, Geri had already stacked up the loot by the front door ready for me to load them on my "sleigh" and head right back home!

"Thanks again, Ma!" I said, hugging her goodnight. "I'll see you in a little while," which was not an exaggeration because it was now 3:30 a.m.!

Not surprisingly, Jackie was still awake when I got home with the gifts. After Jackie skillfully placed them in the pile with the rest of Emily's loot, we stood there for a moment in the light of our massive twelve-foot Christmas tree to do a final inspection. The real scrutiny, however, would come in about an hour's time from our resident "experts".

"This was the worst Christmas, ever," Jackie finally said, matter-of-factly.

"Oh no it wasn't!" I said reassuringly.

WE WOKE UP TO THE DREARIEST CHRISTMAS MORNING ONE COULD IMAGINE, cold and foggy with periods of soaking rain. Sarah woke up with a fever. Oddly enough, I still felt good! The thought "What else could possibly go wrong?" did not enter my head. Almost in answer to my new found sense of well-being, fate set events in motion to challenge it.

Because of Sarah's fever, I decided to stay home with her while Jackie drove with Emily to her mother's for dinner.

"Just make sure you bring me back a ton of left over's and a tray of your mother's cookies and brownies!" I insisted, as they headed out the door.

Sarah was still sleeping, so I decided to start calling my family to wish them all Merry Christmas. About thirty minutes later, while I was on the phone with my brother, John, I heard that annoying tone indicating a call waiting. I personally find this to be one of the most useless mechanisms the phone company has ever come up with! How can anyone carry on a conversation if every five seconds you're saying, "Hold on, I got a call coming in"!

I usually ignore these tones, but for some reason I answered this one. "Hello?" I asked.

"Yeah, Brett?" the voice asked at the other end.

"Yes!" I answered, my voice clearly showing annoyance.

"This is the bridge at dispatch." (The "Bridge" is the command area of our dispatch center, nick-named for its similar appearance to a naval battle ship, or for the USS Enterprise, if you are a Star Trek geek!) "We got a call-out in Great Falls! Are you en route yet?"

"What do you mean a call-out?" I asked. "Why didn't anyone page me?" I said picking up my pager and confirming that it was blank!

"We did. When you didn't call us back, we called you." He replied. "We got a barricade situation up in Great Falls with multiple fatalities. We're calling in all available resources."

"Oh shit!" I thought to myself. "Okay, advise the duty officer that I'm en route," I said, hanging up.

I told John that I had to go and called Jackie on her cell phone to tell her to come home. Thankfully, our neighbor agreed to watch Sarah for me until Jackie's return.

Because of the bad weather, I had driven an unmarked cruiser home. Within minutes I was dressed and headed northbound on I-95. With my lights blazing and siren blaring, I ran code to a call where a grown man decided to shoot and kill his own mother on Christmas day. Then he drove across town to another house and shot three more people!

To turn my thoughts away from the grim event, I listened to an endless stream of Christmas music being played on the radio. When I finally arrived at the crime scene I learned that none of the victims had survived the shooting. Furthermore, the suspect had shot himself when he heard the sirens!

"Whatever motivated him to consider doing such a thing?" I wondered. Had his black cloud become so dark that it had even overpowered the light of Christmas for him? Everyone has experienced the doldrums, especially during the holidays, but how could anyone choose to hurt another person, let alone murder them?

WHEN I ARRIVED HOME LATER THAT CHRISTMAS NIGHT, MY MOTHER-IN-LAW, who had brought us Christmas dinner, was sitting at the kitchen table with Jackie and the girls.

"Merry Christmas, Daddy!" they all said cheerfully. As emotionally exhausting as the day had been, as far as I was concerned the Mormon Tabernacle Choir could not have sung me a better Christmas greeting!

"Just one more reminder of how much I love them!" I thought to myself.

AS 2005 GAVE WAY TO 2006, I FOUND THAT MY POSITIVE EMOTIONS KEPT pace with my physical improvements. Was it just that simple? Was it just because of a physical rush of endorphins, or something else? I couldn't help feeling that something wonderful was coming to me. I was supposed to do something or have something happen to me. I just couldn't put my finger on it. I knew it wasn't that I was supposed to win the lottery or be the motorcycle rodeo champion or anything like that. This was something different. I just didn't know what it was.

I began to notice signs around me that I thought were meant just for me. I'm sure it was no small coincidence that there was a new Superman film about to be released, and it triggered that hopeful little kid in me. Some of the things I noticed from day to day were obvious. On my commute north one morning for instance, something big caught my attention. As you know by now, my normal route to work takes me north on I-95 right past the United States Marine Corp base at Quantico. On this particular morning I was enjoying my new daily ritual of positive feelings and thinking about the endless possibilities of my new-found optimism when something off in the distance caught my eye. The local scenery along the sides of that portion of the interstate is usually a lot of big trees and high-tension power lines. There off in the distance, directly in front of me was a towering glass and steel spire that shot up at a forty-five degree angle from out of the tops of the huge trees on the east side of the interstate. It was a beautiful clear morning, so the sunrise made the structure all the more striking, as if it were made of crystals!

"Man that looks just like the Fortress of Solitude!" I thought to myself. "What the hell are they building?"

I learned later that it was the new U.S. Marine Corp museum. The building was designed to resemble the Marines raising the flag on Iwo Jima.

"Well, I guess it looks like that too."

For the record, I'm not the only one seeing signs. When my family first saw the structure, my little one said, "Look Daddy, there's Superman's house!" So there!

As winter gave way to spring, I started a temporary assignment with the Motor Carrier Safety (MCS) section. This portion of the traffic division does the safety inspections on all commercial trucks and tractor trailers that travel through the county and the interstate highways. I thought that getting my Department of Transportation certification for MCS would broaden my skills as a traffic officer.

Although MCS plays as important a role as any other in law enforcement, it is a thankless, filthy job! When conducting a full inspection, the officer must inspect the entire truck including the underside. Yes, even dump and garbage trucks! As you can imagine, these trucks ooze a lot of fluids that carry a stench that defies description! I didn't really mind it once I was dirty, wearing it as a badge of honor. With time, I began to find my groove with the inspections and had no problem dropping under a truck to do the dirty work.

A favorite route for large dump trucks coming in and out of the southern end of Fairfax County is Lorton, Virginia, a town near the old prison. These particular trucks are the granddaddies of all dump trucks! They can weigh 30,000 to 60,000 pounds and have from three to five axles, the middle of which are called "ponies." When the truck is loaded, these "ponies" are lowered to help disperse the weight more evenly on the roadway. To facilitate easier access to the underside, we usually raise the ponies and have the driver get out of the cab to avoid any accidental deployment of the ponies during the inspection. If someone were under the truck and the wheels dropped, the person would be crushed.

One day my friend, Gibby, and I were out conducting inspections, when we stopped a rolling wreck of a dump truck. The truck had so many safety violations that we removed it immediately from service and instructed the driver to notify the owner and arrange for it to be towed. As I finished up my inspection of the underside of the bed portion of the truck, the owner arrived on the scene, and Gibby informed him of the long list of violations.

From my position under the truck, I couldn't see either Gibby or the owner, so I had no idea what was happening. When Gibby finished explaining what we were doing, he instructed the owner to wait by his Humvee until we were finished with the inspection. Gibby then turned and walked back to the truck. Neither he nor I saw the owner climb into the truck cab.

I've heard that people describe near-death experiences as being very peaceful and warm, with a sense that everything is moving in slow motion so that they have the clarity of mind to realize that "This is it." When I heard the familiar sound of the hissing air that ponies make when they are released, I knew what those people were talking about. As I lay there under that axel and watched it descend on me, I felt remarkably calm. I vividly remember thinking, "So this is how it ends for me." Then, I heard Gibby's voice.

Gibby is a lot like me. Originally from New York, he had also taken the police tests there and moved to Virginia for the better opportunity. Like me, he's a bigger than average Irish guy with a bigger than average temper when people do something stupid. His reaction to my current predicament was far from serene.

"What the @$#*%! are you doin' ??? I've still got a man under the truck. Didn't you hear me tell you to wait by your Humvee!!!" Gibby shouted, as only an Irish cop from New York could.

The axel stopped its descent. Realizing that it was not in fact "my time," I reached up and grabbed the side frame of the truck. In an instant I was on my feet!

"Holy shit!" I said, "That was close!"

Remarkably, I still felt very calm, which I continued to contemplate as I drove home that day. I knew in my heart that there were forces at work in my life that I couldn't comprehend.

"What did all of this mean?" I wondered.

It never occurred to me to blame that *black cloud* for putting me under that truck in the first place. That *black cloud* was the furthest thing from my mind at that moment.

This was a clear sign to me of a change in my life.

You know what they say, "When you least expect it, expect it!"

24 THIS DOESN'T HAPPEN IN FAIRFAX COUNTY

The first weekend in May 2006, Jackie and I took the girls up to my sister Rose's house in Connecticut for my niece Deirdre's first Holy Communion. The girls were excited because they are inseparable from Deirdre whenever they get together! As always, I was looking forward to seeing my family. This was our first visit since Rose's move from Tarrytown, New York, a few years earlier. Rose and her husband, Mark, always worked hard to provide for their children, and it had paid off. Their house is a huge, typically beautiful, center hall colonial on a tree-lined street in Trumble, Connecticut. Like our own neighborhood, it is perfect for raising children.

Nine years earlier, having been unsuccessful at having children of their own, Rose and Mark made the decision to adopt. After doing their research, they went to Russia where they found their son, Christopher. Shortly after they returned home they wanted Christopher to have a little sister, so they went back to Russia and adopted their daughter, Deirdre. I hope that as these two kids grow up they realize just how lucky and blessed they are to have been chosen by Rose and Mark, two of the most caring and loving people that I've ever known!

We arrived at their house late Thursday night, and Rose was the only one still awake. Like our mother, Rose will sacrifice sleep to ensure everything is perfect for a family event. We had a quick visit before everyone crashed for the night. Christopher and Deirdre still had to go to school in the morning, and it was Christopher's birthday. As a birthday surprise for Christopher, Rose had asked me to bring my uniform so we could bring doughnuts to his class for the afternoon celebration.

Christopher and I look a lot alike. And like me, Christopher has a lot of the same issues with school that I had. Rose had mentioned how much she saw me in Christopher whenever the frustrations of school got to him. However, educators today recognize the different ways by which kids can retain information, and so they can set up the classrooms for all children to benefit.

Nothing gets kids' attention in school more than a 6'4" motorcycle cop carrying three dozen doughnuts! The looks on their faces were so bright and happy! Christopher smiled from ear to ear. I was immediately reminded of when I was his age and of those rare times in school when I felt special. "Yup," I thought to myself. "This was definitely worth it!"

Christopher's smile only broadened when I placed my police helmet on his head. This caused every kid in the class to instantly become Christopher's best friend! "Hey Chris, can I try it on?" they all asked, as they clamored their way towards him.

This prompted the teacher to remind them that it was Christopher's birthday, and if they lined up in an orderly fashion, they could look at the helmet. After several minutes of the kids looking at the helmet and asking me questions, the teacher asked the class, "Now isn't there something you'd all like to say to Chris' uncle?"

"Thank you, Officer Brett!" they answered in unison.

"You're welcome!" I told them as I headed out the classroom door.

Rose was smiling as much as Christopher had been, as we walked out of the school. "You don't understand," she said. "He's going to be treated like a rock star after this."

Now, I was the one smiling. Knowing firsthand the frustration Christopher feels on a daily basis at school, I'm happy that now he has a positive experience to associate with this place.

THE REST OF THE WEEKEND WAS JUST AS MUCH FUN. THE ENTIRE FAMILY, including most of our cousins from both the Brett and Sheerin sides, were at the party. Like all great weekends, it went by much too quickly. We were in no rush to get back home, and we certainly didn't want to get stuck in New York city Monday morning rush hour traffic. So, Jackie and I waited until late Monday morning to start heading south.

We took our time, arriving in Viriginia in five hours. Since my office in Fairfax was on our way home, I decided to stop to pick up my bike.

Years ago, my office was an elementary school. Now it is known as Operational Support Bureau (OSB). Like all Fairfax County Police facilities, it is a secure building requiring identification access keys and cipher locks. Motors, the traffic division, SWAT, Explosive Ordinance Disposal (EOD), K-9, and the entire communications/dispatch center are located in our building.

As we drove up, I saw right away that the gate to the secure portion of the lot was open. This isn't uncommon because vehicles are constantly coming and going out of the lot, so I assumed that someone had just left and the gate hadn't closed yet. As we pulled into the lot near the motor garage, I could plainly see that the SWAT weapons truck, EOD trucks, and all of our response trucks were gone. This also was also not unusual because they are all constantly training.

I parked the minivan and invited the girls upstairs, where they could take a bathroom break and see the office. As we walked upstairs, I felt that something wasn't right. With the exception of the two civilian volunteers working in the auxiliary office, no one else was around. Also, something about the way the volunteers were listening intently to the radio traffic noise, which is otherwise so constantly in the background at the station that it is like white noise, seemed odd.

When we walked into the motor office I knew for sure that something was wrong. There were eye glasses left on one of the desks, and there were two separate, full, fresh cups of coffee with steam still coming from them!

I gathered up the girls and walked out of the office. In the hallway we were met by my captain's secretary. "Hey Bill," she said, "What are you doing here? You're missing all of the excitement!"

"What do you mean?" I asked.

"Oh my god, you haven't heard?" she said.

"Haven't heard what???" I asked.

"There's been a shooting out at Sully," she replied.

"Where in Sully?"

"In Sully District Station!" she said, "And two of ours are hit! They don't know if it's a terrorist attack or what, but all government buildings are going into lock down right now!"

That was all I needed to hear. I knew the first thing I needed to do was get my family the hell away from this building as fast as possible! The part that bothered me, however, was that I knew I could not go with them to ensure that they got home safely.

I told Jackie to go straight home, "Don't stop for anything or anyone not wearing a badge!"

As I ushered my family into the rear lot, I saw that the gate was now closed and there were no less than four uniformed officers with M-16's deployed around the rear of the building. Jackie was already nervous, but the sight of those rifles now made her terrified! Luckily, Sarah was too young to know what all the excitement was about, but Emily was much more astute. Six years old, and the daughter of a cop, she knew that a cop holding a rifle in a team sling meant that something was wrong!

"Daddy," she asked. "Why are those policemen holding machine guns?"

"Because, honey," I said lying to her, "They're doing a drill."

Hoping she'd buy that story, I grabbed my equipment from out of the car and kissed them goodbye. Seeing her eyes welling up, I told Jackie, "Don't worry. Everything is going to be fine. I promise." I watched as they drove out of sight before running to the motor garage to change into uniform. With my portable radio now, I began to decipher what was happening.

I recognized the voice of my sergeant, Shawn Maloney. A former Marine, Shawn is a cop's cop. Although not tall in stature, he's a monster in attitude. So much so, his nick-name is "Scrappy." He and the rest of my squad were among the first officers on the scene. I could still hear the chaos in some of the voices over the radio as Scrappy tried to orchestrate resources to respond to the scene. All I could piece together was that two of our officers had been shot with an assault rifle in the rear lot of the Sully District Station. One suspect was dead in the rear lot, but it was unknown if there were multiple suspects, or if there was an orchestrated attack on more than one police facility.

"This kind of shit never happens in Fairfax County!" I thought to myself.

At this point I heard Scrappy call for someone to go back to OSB, grab the cone trailer and get back to Sully to start rerouting traffic patterns. I immediately responded on the radio and advised that I was already at OSB.

I grabbed the only four-wheeled vehicle left—a blacked-out 2004 Ford F-350 super duty diesel dually crew cab—hooked it up to the trailer, and headed west. Only the siren and numerous blue lights hidden throughout its exterior identified this truck as a police vehicle. When all this emergency equipment is turned on, this truck looks like an experimental fighter jet.

Because of the shooting and the media coverage that ensued, traffic was dead-stopped on all major roadways, so I got on I-66 westbound instead. I saw cars falling into two categories: those that move and those that get moved! Most fell into the former that night. Needless to say, I made it to Sully Station.

The weather seemed to mirror the day's events. What started out as a dreary, gray day had turned into a steady down-pour. After deploying all the necessary cones to divert the traffic away from the scene, my captain called us all together on the street corner for a quick roll call/debrief. There in the pouring rain, with the state police and the FBI/HRT helicopters still hovering in the area, we were briefed on what had happened.

Earlier in the afternoon, Sully patrol units were dispatched to an attempted car-jacking in the vicinity of the shopping center near the Sully station. While en route to that call, patrol units were notified that the same suspect had just succeeded in the car-jacking of a small white work van. While this was going on, senior MPO Mike Garbarino had changed out to go home early to go on a trip with his family. While shutting down his cruiser computer, he noticed a small white work van pull into the secure lot next to the gas pumps approximately fifty feet away from him. This was not unusual because the van looked like ones used by the county's facilities department. By the time MPO Garbarino realized the mistake, it was too late.

The suspect was an eighteen-year-old local kid who stood 6'3" tall and weighed well over 250 lbs. Before today, he had never really been in any trouble. Like most kids his age, he was addicted to his computer and spent little time doing anything else. Unfortunately, he had parents who were little involved in his life since they were caught up with their own priorities. Add to this that his father irresponsibly kept an extensive gun collection unsecured in the house—including several assault rifles and various semi-automatic pistols. Maybe it was the over-exposure to the violent video games he played day-in-and-day-out, or perhaps it was the seemingly popular opinion by some people on the internet to demonize law enforcement. Whatever the cause, on this particular day, this young man decided it would be a good idea to take his father's gun collection and go kill police officers.

As the first several shots were fired into MPO Garbarino's cruiser, Detective Vicki Armel had been just fifty yards away getting into her own cruiser. She heard the initial car-jacking calls while in her office and was heading out to assist the patrol units in looking for the suspect. When she heard the shots coming from the direction of the gas pumps, she caught sight of the suspect who now was looking at her. She managed to get several rounds off from her 9mm service pistol, but they were no match for the heavy rifle rounds now being fired at her. She never had a chance. Detective Vicki Armel died next to her cruiser.

Although he was mortally wounded in the first salvo, MPO Garbarino managed to call for help on the radio. He advised responding units of the suspect's location, and even warned them not to come into the rear lot for fear of them getting hit! Several officers inside the station attempted to reach MPO Garbarino but were pinned down by the heavy rounds from the suspect's rifle.

Unbeknownst to the suspect, Officer Rick Marshal was already in the rear lot. Having worked the midnight shift, he had been in court that morning and was in his car catching up on sleep when he heard the shooting.

At first he thought it was the SWAT team doing a practical exercise, but he soon realized that this was a real shooter. As he got out of his car, he used the other vehicles to conceal himself while getting a better advantage on the suspect. Armed only with his 9mm duty weapon and a single magazine, Officer Marshal engaged the suspect and emptied his weapon on him. Although several rounds had found their mark, the suspect was not down for long. Out of ammunition and out of options, Officer Marshal made a tactical retreat to the side door of the station and inside to safety. Unbelievably, the suspect got back on his feet and continued looking for targets coming from the station. He never thought to check the fence-line behind him. Good.

Having just finished an off-duty overtime assignment, PFC Andy Jeffries was in his personal vehicle on his way home. With his portable radio turned on, he heard MPO Garbarino's first call for help. Off duty and in civilian clothes, he was only a few blocks away from the scene and could be there in seconds, except that he was on Route 50 in a car without police lights and sirens. For those not familiar with the area, Route 50 is an eight-lane main thoroughfare, just one quarter mile south of Dulles airport, with heavy traffic moving routinely at fifty miles an hour!

Incredibly, PFC Jeffries got out of his car and was able to stop the on-coming traffic using only his badge and portable radio! He then jumped back into his jeep and sped to the scene. He advised dispatch of his response and gave his description to avoid being mistaken for another shooter. Driving up the street out of sight of the shooter, PFC Jeffries met K-9 operator, PFC Dave Michaels. Hearing MPO Garbarino's desperate calls for help through the sustained gunfire, they decided to move in through the tree line behind the station and attempt to flank the suspect since they still could not see him. As they got to the fence line, they could see that the suspect was fixated on the station's rear doors and was oblivious of their presence.

Utilizing their cover and concealment, they decided to separate to improve their line of fire. At that very moment the suspect began firing again. A former Marine who had recently served in two combat tours, PFC Jeffries engaged the suspect from more than thirty-yards away using only his 9mm service pistol. At that moment, PFC Michaels had also reached his desired firing point. Aside from his .45 caliber semi-automatic service weapon and his four-legged partner, PFC Michaels also carries an M-4 carbine assault rifle with high powered scope. In less than two seconds their combined salvo finally ended the siege.

Both MPO Garbarino and Detective Armel were air-lifted from the scene, but sadly, Detective Armel was pronounced dead at the hospital. MPO Garbarino succumbed to his injuries a few days later.

Once again, I'm baffled by what people do. What was this kid thinking about when he stole that van and drove up to the Sully station? What was he thinking when he saw MPO Garbarino in his cruiser? Did it even occur to him that this man might have two beautiful daughters and a loving wife who were waiting for him to get home? Would it have mattered?

As my captain finished briefing us, my cell-phone started ringing. I saw my home number on the display knowing that Jackie and the girls had made it home.

"Hey! You made it home okay?"

"Yeah," Jackie said, quietly.

"How are the girls?" I asked, knowing Emily was going to have some questions for me.

"They're fine. Sarah's sleeping, but Emily won't turn off the TV. I took the side roads home. I figured the traffic was going to be insane because of what was going on, and I was right." She continued, "The whole way home, every government building we passed had numerous SWAT guys around them! Emily was very quiet for the entire ride but stared at every cop she saw. As soon as we got home, we turned on the TV. Every station was covering the shooting, and of course, there you are with your squad closing off the streets, and Emily sees more cops with machine guns! I tried to change the channel, but she begged me to let her watch for you!"

"Shit," I said out loud.

"She said something else that almost made me cry." Jackie continued, "After flipping through the channels and seeing you several times, she got the gist of what was going on. She finally asked me, "Mommy, is Daddy gonna be okay?"

"Yes, honey, Daddy is going to be just fine," I told her. "Why don't you say a prayer and ask God to watch over and protect Daddy?"

"But I don't know how," Emily said.

"It's easy. Just talk to God like you'd talk to anyone you love, and ask him." Jackie said Emily hesitated for a moment, then said out loud, "Dear God, please protect my Daddy and make sure he comes home safe... I promise I'll be good from now on."

As tears came to my eyes I could hear the emotion in Jackie's voice. After a few quiet moments, I asked if anyone from my family had heard what happened.

"Are you kidding?" Jackie said. "Who hasn't called? Not only both of our families but most of your friends and a bunch of your cousins have been calling non-stop!"

I had forgotten that such an event would more than likely make the national news.

"Okay," I said, "Let me get back to work. You try to get some sleep."

"When will you be home?" Jackie asked.

"Don't bother waiting up," I said mostly because I really didn't know when, or even if I'd get off. With that, we hung up.

Some of the guys had seen me starting to well up and asked if I was okay. After I told them what Emily had said, my buddy, Chuck, said, "That kid gets ice cream and cookies for dinner for the rest of her life!" That one made me smile.

I couldn't help wondering, however, what prayers the Armel or Garbarino children might be saying tonight.

THE FOLLOWING TWO WEEKS SEEMED TO BE ONE LONG SHIFT. NO ONE WAS getting much rest. For a few hours each night we'd go home to catch a nap, take a shower, and head right back into work.

The one bright spot in all of this was the unbelievable outpouring of support from the general public. Not only the citizens in and around Sully District Station, but folks that I'd run into down in Fredericksburg would stop me and offer their condolences! It was a gentle reminder of how decent people really can be to one another in times of crisis. This was so apparent on the days of both funerals.

Police funerals are always an awesome sight. Detective Armel's and MPO Garbarino's would be no exception. Held a little over a week apart, their funerals drew thousands of officers from all over the country! Having participated in police funeral escorts in other jurisdictions, I was not surprised at the number of officers who participated. What surprised me was the reaction of the citizens as we rode by.

These processions are several miles long, and for obvious reasons the entire route is closed to traffic. On this occasion people who were driving in the opposite direction, who weren't even being delayed, took it upon themselves to move to the side and stop their cars as a sign of their respect. Thousands of citizens stood with their hands over their hearts as we passed by. In the face of this, I struggled to maintain my composure. I finally became overwhelmed when we passed an entire family on westbound I-66. They had ridden an ATV (All Terrain Vehicle) to the middle of a field about a quarter mile away. Standing on top of the ATV, they saluted while holding an American flag! I found myself feeling as I had that morning at the World Trade Center. Although this was a profoundly sad occasion, I couldn't help feeling a surge of pride.

"This is why we take this job!" I thought to myself. "To protect people like these!"

"They're a great people Kal-El. They wish to be. They merely lack the light to show them the way. It is for this reason above all— their capacity for good, that I have sent them you, my only son."
(From *Superman*, the movie).

Riding home after MPO Garbarino's funeral, I once again found myself deep in thought. My euphoric feeling from several weeks earlier was now gone, but I wasn't consumed with black cloud thoughts. What the family out in the field demonstrated helped to keep me in a calm and balanced flow.

Then, as I arrived home, I saw my neighbor Gary mowing my lawn! Having been so busy the last couple of weeks, my yard work definitely had been neglected. Knowing how hectic things were at work, Gary took it upon himself to make sure I had one less thing to worry about.

I am so blessed to be surrounded by such people!

25 For The Last Time

Spring gave way to summer, and work was going great. Jackie and the girls were healthy and happy. Physically, I was in the best shape of my life. My six-pack abs had become an eight-pack, which I never thought I could achieve in my lifetime! My physical well-being was again filling me with optimism, and *Superman Returns* with Brandon Routh in the lead role was soon to be released! I felt as if I were twelve again!

In July my squad was invited to compete in the first annual Palmetto Police Motorcycle Skills Competition in Charleston, South Carolina. My boss wanted to make a good showing and decided to send ten officers to compete. Although I had been practicing the cone courses and had shown improvement, I still knew my skills were mediocre compared to the rest of my squad. Because a lot of the better riders were too busy with family obligations to make the trip, I was delighted to be chosen to go. I was feeling invulnerable! Also, the week following the rodeo I would be taking Jackie and the girls up to Long Island for a ten-day vacation!

"This is going to be a great summer!"

Having never traveled further south than Richmond, this was a new experience for me. Like me, my lieutenant could find humor in almost any situation, so when he heard I had never been "south of the border" he started laughing and teasing me.

We were taking several of our support trucks and trailers for the bikes, as well as various pieces of equipment. As we headed south on I-95, he kept getting on the radio with the rest of the guys in the convoy, "Hey, did you guys know Billy's never been south of the border before?"

I couldn't understand what the significance of this tease was until I saw the first billboard.

Every five miles we would pass a sign reading, "Jose says make sure you visit us at South Of The Border!"

"Apparently, I'm the only human being living south of the Mason Dixon line that has not been to South of the Border," I said. When we finally passed the place, I knew why. South Of The Border can only be described as the cheesiest cliché of a tourist trap one could possibly imagine. Its one striking landmark was a huge sombrero ride that could be seen for miles away! Although the place looked abandoned for years, the guys assured me that South of the Border had always looked that way!

"Well, we may as well stop and check it out!" I insisted. The lieutenant just laughed and said, "Maybe on the way home, Billy." Of course that would be the source of endless material for the rest of the trip to Charleston.

As soon as we arrived in Charleston, I could see the southern charm of this historic seaside city. The hospitality of the people of Charleston was everything and more than one could expect!

We were treated to a private tour of the museum that housed the wreck of the H. L. Hunley, the first combat submarine in naval history to see action. Its only mission during the American Civil War was scored a success, but unfortunately the sub sank in Charleston Harbor on its way back from the mission, claiming the lives of all seven crewmen. The Hunley was right in front of me now in a massive tank of water to prevent its decay. Very cool!

The rest of our time was dedicated to practicing the cone courses, the usual array of twin five-course scenarios: one for precision, and one for a timed, speed run. The rodeo was to be held in the parking lot of the Charleston Sports arena, a brand new facility with a perfectly flat parking lot that made it ideal for a police motorcycle skills competition! I needed all the advantages of such a facility!

Although the weather was extremely hot, it was clear and dry, so everyone could push their bikes to their limits.

I could feel a difference in myself from the very first moment that I started to practice. I didn't feel any apprehension at all! I felt completely at ease, and I gained more and more confidence with each practice run.

MPO's Pat Hurley and Brian Peterson are arguably the best motorcycle riders on the planet, and they routinely win any competition they enter, so when they tell me something, I listen!

"I don't know what you've been doing," Pat said, "but you've been riding so smoothly this week."

"You are so far ahead of where you should be right now," Brian added. "We just wanted to tell you we're proud of your effort. If you stay this smooth, you're definitely going to place in the competition tomorrow!"

I can't tell you how good this made me feel! But I didn't dwell on it. Normally, I'd focus on the fact that "The Big Boys" were watching me now, so I'd better not screw up! This time, I was simply thrilled at what they said, stayed relaxed, thanked them for their confidence, and assured them that I'd give my best effort. I had no idea how difficult that would be!

The next morning we all got up in the pre-dawn hours and rode over to the competition. As is the normal routine with rodeos, all riders get together for a meeting where the rules are discussed and the courses given a final walk-through. After some words of encouragement from the Charleston Sheriff and local police chiefs, the competition began. I was surprised at how relaxed I still felt, considering it was game day. As you know by now, even as a kid, no matter how much I prepared for something I would inevitably get those game day jitters that would lead to my eventual failure. That wasn't happening today! My *black cloud* was nowhere in sight, and as far as I was feeling, it didn't even exist anymore.

As it turned out, my *black cloud* hadn't disappeared. It had followed me to Charleston and was in hiding waiting to ambush me!

I did my precision run... clean! "Perfect so far," I thought.

Then I lined up for the speed run. As I pulled my bike up to the starting line, I vividly remember repeating in my head the mantra Pat had taught us in basic school. "Smooth is fast, smooth is fast..." I didn't notice, however, that my heart rate was increasing. The judge at the starting gate said, "Okay it's on you. When your foot comes off the ground, the clock starts."

"Okay," I thought, "here we go!"

As I increased the throttle and released the clutch, the bike leapt off the starting line. In an instant I was in the gate of the first course! I had underestimated the power and speed of my bike and had to jump on my rear brake to keep from hitting the first few cones in the gate. It was too late. My speed was too high. Hitting the brake so hard caused my rear wheel to lock, sliding me right into the side of an entrance and crushing six cones as I did so.

Time seemed to stop. I was furious! When I realized my mistake, I had no choice but to stop, walk the bike backwards, re-enter the cone course and continue my speed run. I went through the rest of the courses as though I had never seen them before. I could feel myself trying to rip the handle bars off as I fought the bike with each turn. Somehow, I managed to finally cross the finish line but not before hitting several cones in all five courses!

As I pulled out of the course, I parked the bike next to my squad trailer. I needed every ounce of self control I could muster to keep from kicking my bike over and smashing it with my helmet! I can remember my friends trying to approach me but the look on my face must have persuaded them that "now's not the best time for a pep-talk!"

I walked away and kept walking. I lost track of time as I continued to ponder the fact that there were obviously forces at work in my life that were beyond my control. "How could this possibly happen?" I kept thinking. "Why does this continue to happen to me?" After forty-plus years of trying, I was consigned to a life of under-achievement. I knew that no matter what I did, where I went, or how hard I might try, that *black cloud* would be waiting to destroy any plans of success I might dare to have! Not understanding why haunted me.

On the ride home the guys tried to cheer me up. I tried to keep up a positive outward appearance, but all I could think about was the "how and why."

BACK HOME, JACKIE TOLD ME TO GIVE UP THE RODEOS FOR A WHILE BECAUSE they were obviously causing a problem for me. I tried to explain that it went a lot deeper than just the rodeos. This was something a whole lot bigger. We both agreed then that I should speak to a specialist, but the earliest appointment I could get would be at the end of August.

During the following week in Long Island, my family noticed that I was totally preoccupied. Fearing that it might lead to depression, my mother made an appointment for me with her therapist and begged me to go see her. I reluctantly agreed. I figured I needed a sports psychologist or something, but that it wouldn't hurt to go talk to my mother's doctor.

Although the doctor was a very nice person and easy to talk to, she was unable to tell me anything I didn't already know. She was good at dealing with the emotions that were caused by some of these events, but she didn't shed any light on their cause. There was no logical explanation for a lifetime of underachievement. The questions still remained: How? Why?

Despite my preoccupation our vacation was a good one. We went to the beach a lot and got to visit with all my friends and cousins. All in all, that aspect of my life was indestructible. Back home in Fredericksburg, the rest of the summer just rolled on with little improvement in my outlook. Then, at the end of August I met someone who would change the course of my life!

Linda Minor, CSW, was a referral by my doctor, who told me that Linda was excellent at dealing with the issues specific to ADHD. Meeting with Linda, I gave her the "Reader's Digest" version of Billy Brett.

"You're one of the most intense people I've met in a really long time," she told me.

"Me?" I asked.

I've always thought of myself as a happy-go-lucky kind of guy! People have often told me that they see me this way as well, so how does this lady see such an intense individual? The reason I was sitting there now was because of my crappy outlook of late, and that's the person she's now meeting for the first time!

"I guess that's not who you really are though, is it?" she asked. "A lifetime of perceived failure can lay pretty heavy on one's outlook, if left unchecked." She continued, "I want you to read a few books I think might help you. They are called *Driven To Distraction* and *Delivered From Distraction*, a series of books written by two Harvard professors who are specialists in the field of ADHD. I think you might see yourself in their books."

"Okay." I thought that this couldn't hurt. Besides, at this point in my life I was so desperate to find answers, I'd try just about anything!

So convinced was I that there was some kind of negative force overshadowing my life, that not only did I purchase the books on ADHD, I also bought several books on spirituality and the powers of positive thinking. I was going to uncover this negative entity and force it into the light once and for all!

I only allowed myself to be cautiously optimistic with this research material. So I tried to maintain an even calm as I started with the first of the books by the Harvard professors. Calm vanished after only reading a few pages.

"HOLY SHIT!" I thought. "Could these guys have somehow been studying me?" I felt like Jim Carey in *The Truman Show*! My heart rate increased as I kept reading about all these other people who were EXACTLY LIKE ME, including Dr. Ned Hallowell, co-author with Dr. John Ratey of the friggin' books! I couldn't read fast enough! I whipped through the first book in a day and a half! I was now officially obsessed! Like the robot in the film *Short Circuit* after being struck by lightning and becoming self aware, I needed "More Input!"

I read three more books in rapid succession. For the first time in my life I felt that I was finally starting to really understand my life's experiences. I had to call my parents.

"Hey, Sweet William!" my father said in his usual upbeat manner, "What's going on?"

Those would be the last coherent words he would be able to speak for the rest of that phone call. I wanted him to know how much I loved him, and how much I appreciated what he and my mother had done for me throughout my life despite my unusual "gifts." After I finished, his end of the phone was silent for a moment. Then, all he could manage to say was "Call your mother!"

"Okay!" I said. "I love you," then we hung up.

My mother's reaction was similar, though she was not surprised. A mother of six children is able to pick up on all the subtle signals given off by her children. She said, "It was because of your issues that I worried about you the most, Billy. That's why your sisters always teased me for calling you 'My Heart Child'!"

My mother and I spoke for awhile before hanging up. "Now," I thought. "Time to get back to work!"

I can honestly say that I had never felt the powerful emotion that I felt in the following weeks now that I understood "how" my life's experiences were the way they were. But the "why" was still missing.

Some pieces of the ADHD puzzle were still unsolved. I felt as if I had discovered a door to a room in my house that I had never known about!

This room contained all sorts of equipment and technology that I couldn't have imagined existed! The problem was, however, that I didn't have the owner's manual!

To me then the "standard" wiring for the human brain was like a brand new Rubick's Cube—a perfect square with each side made up of nine individual squares of uniform color that is at rest and orderly. My brain is that same cube but it never comes to rest in an orderly way since it is constantly in a state of flux. I was always trying to get the red squares away from the green squares, and the green squares away from the yellow squares, etc.

This "flux" kept me distracted. Even now, as I immersed myself in finding the answers, I became what the experts called "hyper-focused." I knew this term well! It's not always a bad thing. It's one of the reasons I was able to do so well at the academy! But more often than not, I would tend to hyper-focus on the negative aspects of my life, thus causing somewhat minor problems to become catastrophes!

While I was distracted with my new-found zeal for research, I had no clue that my *black cloud* was planning an all out attack on everything I had worked so hard for!

Financially we barely managed. Usually we would "Borrow from Peter to pay Paul." Not only was this poor financial planning, it had a nasty tendency of causing even bigger problems! I had become accustomed to seeing the "Final Notice" letters in the mail, but when we began to fall behind with the mortgage, I knew that we were in serious trouble!

Once again, I found myself losing interest in everything. Resigned with this doomed outlook to the fact that this negative entity was never going to let me succeed, I dropped all my work in researching my issues.

During the next several months I was able to work overtime to bolster the household funds, but we were still forced to borrow money from our families on several occasions to save the house. The ship was sinking.

Any doubts that I may have had that the *black cloud* was an entity which thrived on my misery consolidated one afternoon while I tried to get my mind off my problems.

I had a fairly decent day, when I decided to practice the cone courses. I had three flawless runs in a row and was feeling good when I went for a fourth. Like the three before it, this run was smooth and quick. However, as I was exiting the final gate of the final course I had nothing but clear asphalt in front of me when my front wheel slid out and I went down—hard! My left knee was torn open, and my boots were scuffed badly. But when I went down, my right hand had come off the throttle and had caught the stainless steel post of the rear view mirror. The post split in between the ring and pinky finger while inertia pushed my arm forward. I thought I had broken my hand! Alone in the parking lot, I had to pick up my bike and limp it back into the garage.

I told my boss right away what had happened, but didn't tell him how much I hurt. He didn't buy my story that I did not hurt and made me check out my hand. The doctor said what I already knew, that I'd have to be off the motorcycle for a few weeks until my hand healed. That meant light duty, which meant no overtime. No overtime meant that I was screwed! This was the final financial torpedo! We were done, and there was nothing more that I could do to save the house. I was consumed with the absolute despair of failing as a husband, and worse yet, failing as a father to my two daughters! They didn't deserve to lose the only home they'd ever known because their father wasn't smart enough to make better financial decisions!

Even at work I couldn't conceal my feelings. My usual bright outward persona was, in my mind, gone forever. After a few weeks, everyone stopped asking "What's wrong, Bill?"

Let me be clear on this point. Although I was in a very dark place, I never ever thought of harming myself! But I understood the despair that goes through one's mind when feeling that there is nothing left to live for. Although I knew I would always have my family to live for and keep me going, I began to better understand how others, not so fortunate as myself, might become overwhelmed and do something foolish.

One evening while Jackie and I were in our bedroom watching television, the topic of the law of attraction came up and Jackie asked me if I was familiar with it. I thought I remembered that it had something to do with one of Albert Einstein's theories, "like attracts like," or something like that. With that, Jackie handed me a book with quotes from dozens of historical figures as well as contemporary motivational coaches, all citing this universal law.

Having already heard something about this book and its theories, I knew it wouldn't tell me anything I didn't already know. The problem,

For The Last Time 209

I theorized, was that I was the antithesis of the theory! In fact, the more I read what was said in this book, the angrier I became! It just reinforced what I knew to be true... I was the only exception to this universal law! I knew that no matter how positive I had been throughout my life, no matter how hard I worked towards something, I would ultimately fail. I was the lightning rod for negativity in this universe!

As though on cue, my theory became reality. Jackie and I had run out of financial options and were facing foreclosure. I was left with no other choice but to clean out my retirement fund to the tune of over fifteen thousand dollars to save the house. Even as I did so, I knew that this was just a temporary solution. It was just a matter of time before we would lose the house.

I couldn't stop thinking how cheated I felt. This law of attraction was a crock of shit!!! How many times had I been told "If you really want something in life you have to stay positive and never give up!" And how many times after failing I'd still eventually get up and keep trying only to fail again? There were no logical explanations for this constant onslaught of negative occurrences in my life. How could I spend a lifetime demonstrating effective prowess at certain tasks only to fall short at them when it really counted?

Although nonsectarian, I have a firm belief in God and begin each day by giving thanks for all the many blessings in my life. I also ask for guidance, which is why the current financial crisis was all the more puzzling! My daily prayer was reduced to asking simply, "Why?"

My negativity became an avalanche. The majority of my days were spent in a haze of emotional conflict with only momentary conscious effort with my daily tasks.

One day I was assigned to assist the power company with a temporary road closure while they ran new overhead lines. I took control of the intersection and began directing traffic away from the obvious work zone with its road cones and "DETOUR" signs. Also, anyone seeing me should have known that the road was closed. On auto-pilot directing all the vehicles away from the crew, I saw a car ignore my direction and attempt to drive over the median and through the cone pattern. I blew my whistle as loudly as I could and waived the driver to stop. An elderly man wearing a baseball cap that identified him as a military veteran simply looked at me and waived me off. Pointing to the closure, he indicated that he was going to go through regardless of what I thought! I persisted and yelled for him to stop. As I approached his open window, I could feel my anger building. I reasoned that this was an elderly veteran and that he was probably just confused. Those thoughts quickly evaporated when this harmless little old man started F-bombing up one side and down the other! "I don't care what you said! I want to go that way!"

Here I was in full uniform with my motor boots, leather jacket, and motor- cycle helmet, with my badge of authority prominently displayed on my chest, and this old fart was cussing me out! I felt stunned and angry.

I don't know how or why I was able to stay in control, but I remained composed and asked for his license and registration to which, thankfully, he complied. As I walked back to my bike, I knew this was not just some con-fused old man pissed at me for making him late for his "early bird special." This was something else—another test of some kind. There was no other logical explanation for it. I pride myself on my ability to get along with anyone, and I never give anyone a reason to go off on me the way this guy just did! As I scratched out a warning ticket, I knew in my heart that some-thing was coming. All of this had to be leading towards something terrible, but I didn't know what! As I walked back and handed him the warning, he drove off without so much as a single word. "Wow!" I thought, "That was sort of anti-climactic!"

I can't even remember what, if anything, I did for the rest of that day, so consumed was I with the fact that all of the collective negativity of the entire universe had descended on me. I couldn't shake the thought that if that old man had just run me over that all my troubles, as well as my family's, would finally be solved.

This would be the part in the story that reads, "Hey Dickhead, watch out what you wish for!"

It's a perplexing condition, this ADHD. When I hyper-focus on some-thing, whether it's good or bad, I'll lose touch with time and place. I was so consumed with self pity that afternoon that I hadn't noticed that I was now only about two miles from home. I also hadn't noticed that I was on a particular stretch of roadway that shrinks from two lanes to one, where every afternoon during rush hour everyone jockeys for lane position as if they're in the Daytona 500! What I did notice were the brake lights of the car that had just cut me off.

"Fuck Me!"

My training, however, kicked in without a conscious thought. I managed to drop two gears, lock the handlebars hard to the left and dip the bike, thus avoiding a rear-end impact! Although I succeeded in missing the car's rear end, the weight and speed of the bike was too much for the front end of the bike to handle and the front tire lost traction on the pavement. Down I went.

I remember trying my best to stay with the bike, but the friction from my body caused the bike to pull away from me, and it sort of shook me off, as if to say, "Get off me!" I can vividly remember seeing the license plate of the pickup truck that was traveling directly behind me and marveled at how close I was to it as I rolled over and over and over. Thankfully, it was driven by a U.S. Marine Corp aviator who had the wherewithal to stop before squishing me into motorman road-kill!

When I stopped rolling, I jumped up and checked my boots. I know, I know. "Stoooopid!" But they were brand new, and I had just taken them out of the box that morning! I then looked down the road and saw that the car that had caused this whole mess had stopped about a hundred yards away. I angrily gestured for it to pull over to the side of the road. With that, I watched as its brake lights released and the car drove out of sight. Since I was in no condition to chase the car down, my wrecked bike now blocking the entire roadway and bleeding all its fluids, the driver got away. Witnesses behind me, however, got a good description of the vehicle.

Having used up the remainder of my adrenaline dump, I decided to sit down on the curb and have a little nap. Luckily for me, the two Devil-dog Marines were kind enough to stop and pick up my bike for me. When one of them saw me trying to lie down, he shouted at me as only a Marine can, "Sir, you need to sit up!" Worried that I might have a concussion, he instructed the other motorists who had also stopped to assist, not to let me lie down under any circumstances!

An ambulance soon arrived and the Emergency Medical Techs (EMT) started checking me over. As they checked my vitals, I noticed that my left knee was bleeding through my torn breeches, yet I hadn't felt this happen. I then noticed that one of the EMT's had a pair of scissors in his hands, and that he was reaching for my left boot.

"No way, Doc!" I shouted. "I didn't just survive a motorcycle wreck with my brand new $800 boots relatively undamaged just to have you cut them off of me!"

"Okay," he said. "Suit yourself."

Placing me on a rigid backboard, they secured me with what felt like fourteen rolls of duct tape! I was then put on the gurney and secured in the back of the ambulance. Before pulling away, the fire chief was kind enough to secure my equipment and notify my supervisors of the wreck.

"Is there anyone else you want me to call?" he asked.

Before I could answer, I heard the familiar voice of one of my neighborhood friends. "Hey Bill, you want me to go by the house and let Jackie know what happened?"

"Yes, please," I said. Better to hear it from a friend in person than from a stranger's voice over the phone, I thought.

As we pulled away, all I could do was focus on the ceiling of the ambulance. I thought how oddly soothing the white noise of the diesel engine was. The paramedics had offered me pain killers, but I wasn't feeling any pain. In fact, I was amazed at how good I was feeling! This surreal sense of peace and calm had totally replaced the sense of chaos and self-pity that I was feeling just a few minutes earlier. At that moment I realized that I had been so totally focused on getting run over that I was run over!!!

I thought of how sad my daughters were going to be when they heard that I had been in a wreck. Suddenly, I remembered the line from the film, *It's a Wonderful Life*: "Strange, isn't it? Each man's life touches so many other lives. When he isn't around, he leaves an awful hole, doesn't he?"

The anger I was feeling turned to determination. I promised myself that the guy who was riding that motorcycle before the wreck was left there on the asphalt! My family deserved better!

I was still aware of all my troubles, both financial and personal, but the feeling of hopelessness was completely gone! I was okay, and everything was going to be okay! "Holy shit!" I thought to myself, "Maybe those motivational coaches were on to something!" I knew I needed to get back to my research, and quick! But first, I needed to get off this gurney!

Jackie arrived at the emergency room of Mary Washington Hospital shortly after we did, and although she had a look of concern, her demeanor was one of confidence. Thankfully, none of my injuries were serious. A few bumps and bruises and a torn pair of breeches were a small price to pay for a desperately needed "wake up call"!

As we waited for my paperwork, the Virginia State Trooper who was dispatched to work the wreck arrived to get my statement. After confirming that my story matched the witnesses, he was satisfied that the driver of the car was at fault for the wreck. Although all the witnesses gave the same description of the offending vehicle, the license plate did not show up when the trooper ran it through his computer. A brief search of the surrounding neighborhoods also met with negative results. "It was as though that car just disappeared off the face of the earth!" the trooper told me. In my heart I believed that he was right!

When we left the hospital, Jackie was quiet at first. I asked her if she was scared when Ed, our neighbor, told her what had happened to me.

"I was nervous at first," she said. "But then as I was driving to the hospital I felt an odd sense of calm—like I knew you were going to be fine."

Over the previous months Jackie was not only worried about our financial problems, but also that I was internalizing them as well. So, for her to be feeling the same "odd sense of calm" at the same time I started feeling it, reaffirmed that forces outside my control were at work here. I told Jackie about my earlier encounter with the old man before the accident.

"This wreck was no coincidence," I said. "I was so miserable that I kept wishing that old man would just run me over. I figured that you and the girls would be cared for and that the insurance check would help pay off the house. Everyone's problem would be solved. That was my only thought the entire ride home until boom, I almost got my wish!"

Jackie was understandably quiet for a moment, then asked, "And how do you feel now?"

"Damn lucky!" I reassured her. "I have no doubt in my mind that all of this was meant to drive me towards something, something that would finally explain the "why" in my life."

My rekindled determination was amplified tenfold the moment we pulled into the driveway and we were met by Emily and Sarah. Being so young, all Sarah wanted to know was if I had any boo-boos. Emily was un-characteristically quiet, but the tears in her eyes spoke volumes.

"I'm fine, sweetheart." I reassured her.

"You're an asshole, Billy!!!" I thought to myself. Like my Uncle Bob said to me all those years ago after I had wrecked my friend's Camaro, "What do you think, Billy? Is this enough? Is this enough heartache you want to cause the people who love you the most?" It was indeed.

I knew in my heart that I was better than events of life had led me to believe. Now it was time to prove it. After putting the girls to bed, I started reading the book about the laws of attraction again. Now, I understood the truth of what these teachers and philosophers were saying. The dots were beginning to come together. Jackie had long since fallen asleep. Not wanting to wake her, I kissed her gently on the cheek and whispered, "I love you."

After turning out the light, I stared into the darkness for a moment as though I were looking into the face of the *black cloud*.

"You will never beat me!" I finally said out loud, "You've rained on my life for the last time!"

26 IRRESISTIBLE FORCE

In the days following my wreck, I felt a drive that I never dreamed was possible! I was reading on the law of attraction and several books by authors such as Tony Robbins, Eckhart Tolle, and Jack Canfield. I finally began to see the connection between all of these theories and my own issues. There were connections not just to my ADHD, but to how my emotional reactions influenced future events, and how my expected failure of an event worked to make it happen!

With all that had happened in the last few weeks, I wanted to speak to Linda. I needed some feedback, and with her experience, I knew she could help me navigate these waters! As soon as I walked into her office, she told me that she could see a difference in me. The intensity was still there, but it was more purposeful, more focused. I then brought her up to speed on what I had been experiencing and the connections that I had finally made. As I continued to speak I couldn't help but notice a slight grin on her face.

"What?" I finally asked her.

"It's wonderful to see the transformation in my clients as soon as they begin to harness all of that energy!" she said. "What you really need to do is write all of this down." The suggestion hit a chord with me. I needed a record of all my life events and thought processes surrounding them!

More lights were coming on in my mind now, and I couldn't research fast enough! The whole picture of my existence was finally coming into focus. The beautiful irony is that all those years of struggling against the tide were all self-induced!

As a child I could always use my imagination to escape from the perceived harshness of reality. In that respect, my ADHD gave me a universal view of the world free from any one school of thought. As I grew to adulthood, I pulled away from consciously using my imagination. So when my powerful imagination went unchecked for all those years, it tended to arch like a broken power line. I had also mistakenly thought that I had outgrown my hyperactivity. I understood now that the difference between the "standard" mind and the ADHD mind is that with the ADHD mind everything tends to be heightened.

While reading one day, I came across a quote by Albert Einstein that stopped me dead in my tracks. "Imagination is everything. It is the preview of life's coming attractions."

This was another of now frequent "Holy Shit" moments! Of all people who could have told me what I'd been experiencing, it turned out to be Albert-friggin-Einstein! All of these teachers, authors, and motivational speakers echoed one another. None of them were "selling salvation." Rather, they all knew that everyone had the ability to forge their own future and to save themselves from anything life had to throw at them.

All too often I had locked in on the negative events in my life and hadn't even considered that I had been the one calling most of it, if not all of it, into being! I'd been looking outside for the answers, when all I ever needed was within me! Having spent a lifetime of trying to be "normal" and failing at every turn, I felt like a total loser. I hadn't taken into account that everything good and bad happens for a reason.

I began to see the means to respond positively and puposefully to life, even when it is tragic.

My squad and I had just finished a funeral escort and had stopped for lunch at a big, fancy Italian restaurant in Tyson's Corner. I had gotten up to go to the rest room when I noticed one of the waiters staring at me. It wasn't the type of glare that I might get from a "former client," but a look of recognition that put me at ease. He appeared to be a Hispanic man in his early thirties, and like the rest of the staff of this restaurant, he was well groomed. When I came out of the rest room and walked back to my table, he approached me.

"Excuse me, Officer Brett?" he said.

"Yes, sir." I answered cautiously.

"You probably don't remember me, but you came to my house a couple years ago when my wife and I were having problems. We had been fighting over our baby and things almost got out of hand until you showed up." He continued, "You separated us and spoke to us like no other police officer ever had. Not only were you respectful to us, but your kindness and perspective reminded us that our priorities should be on our baby and not with our individual needs." Their infant baby had been ill for some time, and the stress was causing strife between the two. I had vaguely remembered the incident and asked how things turned out.

"Sadly, we lost our baby to the illness," he said. Seeing the look on my face, he continued, "But that's not why I stopped you. I just wanted to thank you for what you did. It was because of you that my wife and I got counseling and we were able to work things out."

Taken aback, I offered him my sincere condolences and wished him all the best. This man explained the reason for my involvement in his family's life, and although they suffered a heart-breaking loss, he saw our meeting as a positive experience.

At the time of this encounter, I could not see its full significance for me. Now I am starting to make sense of it. Today, one of the things I know about myself is that I am good at talking to people. With zero effort or conscious thought, I can gain common ground with anyone and find a solution to almost any conflict.

ON THE ONE YEAR ANNIVERSARY OF 9/11 MY FRIENDS AND I TRAVELLED TO NEW York City for the ceremony at the World Trade Center. (I will never refer to it as "Ground Zero.") I remember standing on Church Street before the ceremony and being transfixed as I looked into the hole where the trade towers had once stood. Lost in my thoughts, I caught the movement of several uniforms to my right, which caused me to turn and see what was going on. As I looked at the police officers and fire fighters from various jurisdictions, they all spun around and, coming to attention, rendered honors to someone behind us. I turned to look and immediately saw several hundred "Bobbies" from the London Metropolitan Police Department walking in perfect formation proudly carrying in front of them the American Flag and the "Union Jack"!

Without a word, we all followed suit and rendered honors to our brothers and sisters from across the pond! As the ceremony began, we found ourselves intermingled with the Brits, rapidly becoming fast friends! As we all looked on, it was as though this hallowed ground acknowledged the event. A wind kicked up a two-hundred-foot vortex of dust and dirt. As quickly as it had formed, the column of dust was gone without a trace, just like the buildings that had once occupied the space.

When the ceremony ended, we decided to head over to O'Hara's Pub for a beer. O'Hara's is located directly behind the FDNY 10 House on Liberty Street, opposite where the south tower once stood. The last time we saw this place a year earlier it had been covered by a foot of ash and dust. We were happy to see that it had been totally rebuilt and was packed with cops and firemen! Although numerous jurisdictions from all over the world were there, you would think we were all long-lost-cousins at the funeral for our mutual grandfather.

I made my way to the bar to order a first round and bumped into a few of the Brits we had just met at the ceremony. Before we could utter a word, they handed over several beers and offered a toast for the lost souls.

One of the Bobbies was a fireplug of a man named Steve. His nick-name was Stumpy. Although short in stature, his quick wit and disarming smile were huge. He and I hit it off immediately. It wasn't long before the topic of conversation turned to where we were and what we experienced one year earlier. After listening to my story, I could see that Stumpy was obviously emotional, as his eyes began to fill with tears. I told him how moved I was to see how many Brits had come a year ago to assist with the rescue and recovery effort, and now for the anniversary ceremony!

Fighting back the tears, Stumpy said, "You Americans don't realize how important you are to the rest of us, and how profoundly this attack affects the rest of the world." He continued, "For this country to suffer a loss on such a scale is beyond belief!"

No strangers to terrorism themselves, the United Kingdom had their share of recent attacks, but nothing that compared with this. As we spoke, Stumpy told me of his own terrible loss at the hands of terrorist extremists. His father had been killed while defusing an IRA bomb back in the early 1980's. I was struck at the lack of bitterness in his voice. Heartbroken to be sure, he said, "Bullies are bullies, no matter what their beliefs are! They need to be confronted and dealt with wherever they are!"

I must admit, I was awestruck by Stumpy's outlook. He never lost sight of the mission to protect people first, while putting his personal feelings aside. After a long night of commiserating, we exchanged addresses and Stumpy informed me that I absolutely had to come to the UK for Christmas! "We spend the entire day playing rugby and drinking beer!" he proclaimed proudly!

"Yeah," I said, "That'll go over big, considering I just spent our ninth wedding anniversary here with a bunch of drunk cops and firemen!"

A COUPLE OF WEEKS LATER WHEN I GOT HOME FROM WORK JACKIE SAID A PACKage had arrived from the UK. As soon as I opened it, I saw that it was from Stumpy. He had sent me an official Scotland Yard T-shirt and other assorted British goodies. But the most touching gift was the birthday card, "Billy, here's to remembering the date for the happy occasion it was meant to be! Happy Birthday and Happy Anniversary! All the best, Steve H."

In the years since, Stumpy has never forgotten my birthday!

I can only make sense of The World Trade Center attack as a place where I lost one of my best friends in Fred, but I found a new one in Steve!

FOR THE FIRST TIME IN MY LIFE, I'M FEELING AN INNER PEACE THAT I HAVE NEVER known. As I'm discovering the amazing amount of time and energy I wasted on worrying, I noticed that I'm not the only one! Indeed, it seems that while I've been distracted with my own illogical worries, the entire planet has become consumed with self-doubt and fear. Everywhere I look, I see people panicking about the future. "We're killing our planet!" "We've destroyed our economy!" "The swine flu will kill us all!" "A Mexican culture that hasn't existed for over 6000 years predicted that the world will end on December 21, 2012!" Etcetera.

I know now that there's nothing that's been done that can't be undone short of the loss of someone's life. Have we as a species become so arrogant as to think that, not only can we single-handedly destroy the planet, but we can predict the future so precisely as to know the actual date in which it will happen?

Eckhart Tolle said it best, "All forms of fear—worry, unease, anxiety, stress, and tension—are caused by too much future and not enough presence." He continued, "A great deal of what people say, think, or do is actually motivated by fear..."

The problem is and will continue to be that we prefer to be scared. In fact, we'll pay through the nose to get scared! Why was The Exorcist one of the top box office grossing horror movies of all time? Why does the media continue to lead off all the nightly news telecasts with the most horrific or depressing news stories that they can find? Because they know we're going to eat it up!

When I was a little kid, I remember my sisters had a poster on their bedroom wall that went something like, "Worry never fixed a dent, worry never paid the rent, worry never made a cent... So, why worry?"

If you need something to be afraid of, go jump your neighbor's fence—you know, the one protecting you from the 160 pound Rottweiler in his backyard— and kick over the dog's food dish. I guarantee you'll never be as scared again! As for the news media, turn off the TV! The only news relevant to you is the traffic and the weather. Everything else is just bullshit meant to scare you!

The late, great George Burns used to say, "Every morning when I wake up, I immediately skip the entire newspaper and go straight for the Obituaries. If my name's not listed, I get up and have breakfast." That man was a genius!

It all makes sense to me now. I understand the "how" and the "why." I know that I'll always have these ADHD issues. In a sense, my life really is a never-ending battle. But as I said earlier, my views of this world are nothing like the "standard" views. Being in the constant "flow," my ADHD gives me a new vantage point on life every day!

SO WHAT DOES ALL THIS MEAN? WHEN I STARTED THIS ADVENTURE, I WAS hoping to find all the answers. I found a lot of them, but no one ever finds all the answers. What fun would that be? What adventures could I embark on if I had found all the answers? From this effort, at least my little girls will know who I really am and why I think I was put here.

Maybe some of you have seen yourself in my story. If so, I hope you can come away with answers to some of your questions, too. I hope that you have the courage to challenge yourself to look even further for the answers you have yet to find. One thing's for certain, no one is going to save you! There is only one person in this entire universe that can do that, and that's you!

So what are you waiting for? Get outside and expose yourself to that yellow sun!!! Show the world and yourself just how "Super" you really are!

At the very least, I hope this might help some other little boy who at this very moment is staring out the window of his classroom and wondering why he feels so out of place, and why his teacher has to say to him, "Billy! Get your head out of the clouds, and pay attention!"

"Don't worry kiddo, you'll find the answers. And it will all be worth it!"

Epilogue

It's another picture perfect morning in Fredericksburg, and our hero is in his driveway preparing his motorcycle for another day of crime-fighting. As he does so, he hears his daughters as they run out the front door to the corner of their street to await the school bus. To see their beautiful faces, and to hear the sweet sound of their laughter as they tease each other and play with their friends, never ceases to amaze our hero. As he looks on, he feels a warm sensation on the right side of his face, and he turns to see one of the most magnificent sunrises in recent memory. He closes his eyes and absorbs the energy he feels immersed in. "No wonder they chose this as the ultimate source of his powers!" he thinks to himself. Too caught up in the moment, our hero doesn't notice his five-year-old daughter walking up on him. Curious as any healthy little girl would be, she wonders why her daddy is smiling at the sun. "What are you smiling at, Daddy?"

Embarrassed that his little girl was able to sneak up on a "seasoned super-hero" such as himself, he tells her, "I'm smiling because I'm the lucki-est guy in the universe! I'm the one and only guy that gets to be yours and sissy's daddy!"

"You're silly, Daddy!" she replies as she tries unsuccessfully to break his hug. After laying a big smack-a-roo on her, he finally releases her and she runs to hop on the bus that has just arrived. Our hero then jumps on his motorcycle and pulls up to the corner where his beautiful wife is chatting with some of the other neighborhood moms. As he rolls to a stop, she walks towards him expecting the usual, "Have a good day, Hon, I'll talk to you later," peck on the cheek. Instead, he grabs her off guard and lays a passionate kiss on her lips—the kind that made them fall in love in the first place! This causes the neighbors to make the obligatory

"WOOOOOOOOO" cheer. As our hero finally releases his now blushing wife, his says simply, "I love you," and rides out of sight.

Trying to compose herself, she is asked by one of her neighbors, "So what is it like to be married to Superman?

Always quick on her feet, without hesitation she replies, "Oh, you know, the usual. Speeding bullets, tall buildings in a single bound, super-villains. It's a never-ending battle."

As our hero is making his way northbound on I-95, he checks the left lane, then the right lane. As he checks again, it's as if he actually heard the words spoken by his wife.

He smiles as he accelerates. "Up, up and away!"

"OK. Book came yesterday, opened it just to "glance" and that was it! HOOKED. 5 hours later... done! Great read, tears, giggles and some very valuable insights into the grown-up world of ADHD. A treasure of a book and a powerful message to us all on the power of controlling our own thinking! Thank you, Billy, for sharing this heartfelt story! Congratulations Superman!"—*Jojo*

♦

"Billy Brett is a talented writer and storyteller, allowing the reader to experience life through his eyes. Good and bad, up and down, Billy brings you along for a very interesting ride. If you have ADHD or love someone who does, this book may help answer some questions. I loved this book, I read it in one sitting because I couldn't put it down. I eagerly await his second." —*Mary O.*

♦

"William Brett does a wonderful job at giving you a clear voice into his thoughts and actions in this quick read. The 222 page real life description of a regular man with super-human powers is laugh-out-loud funny and very relatable. It doesn't matter if you are 20 or 80 years old, William Brett will make you see life and the world from his eyes.

Being a teacher, I have not had the chance to read such an honest, gut-wrenching account of someone living with ADHD.

This book gives funny anecdotes, tales and one-liners that will keep you turning page after page and not wanting to put the book down. From police officer to author, Mr. Brett does a marvelous job at executing his thoughts, feelings and emotions onto the pages and keeps his readers wanting more and more. This is Mr. Brett's first published book, and hopefully for his readers, not the last!

Go ahead, buy it—just don't blame me when you are beach side laughing so loudly that people are staring at you... I warned you!"—*Capitalgirl*

♦

"I think I can sum up this book in one word—AMAZING!!!!

I have a son with ADHD and my wife and I have read many of the medical books on what the "experts" say to expect, how to deal with certain situations, blah, blah, blah... .

NONE and I mean NONE of the books we read gave us a REAL WORLD PERSPECTIVE the way "Billy's never-ending Battle" did. As I read through the various phases of Billy's life, I could easily imagine that I was reading about my son. A perfect example is when Billy explains why he lied for no reason when in school. My wife and I seem to have a never-ending struggle with my son lying, and while reading Billy's book, the simple truth was right there in front of us—he is attempting to divert attention from the fact that he doesn't know the answer and feels inadequate.

One word of warning though—if you have a child with ADHD, read this book in private because your eyes will swell with tears (numerous times) as Billy sheds light on the "what" and "why" of your child's struggle at every turn in the road. I am incredibly grateful to Jor-El and Lara for sending Billy (AKA Kal-El/Superman) into our lives—he truly is a superhero. [The last sentence will become clear after you read the book]"—*Kevsil*

CPSIA information can be obtained at www.ICGtesting.com
261139BV00004B/1/P

9 780971 780699